ROOKWOOD POTTERY
Jeffrey B. Snyder

Schiffer Publishing Ltd®

4880 Lower Valley Road, Atglen, PA 19310 USA

Dedication

To Olive, my grandmother
To Jim and Mary Alice, my parents

Library of Congress Cataloging-in-Publication

Snyder, Jeffrey B.
  Rookwood pottery / Jeffrey B. Snyder.
    p. cm.
  ISBN 0-7643-2277-X (hardcover)
1. Rookwood pottery—Catalogs. 2. Art pottery, American—
Ohio—Cincinnati—19th century—Catalogs. 3. Art pottery,
American—Ohio—Cincinnati—20th century—Catalogs. 4.
Rookwood Pottery Company—History. I. Title.

NK4340.R7S69 2006
738.3'09771'78075—dc22

                                                    2005020135

Designed by John P. Cheek
Cover design by Bruce Waters
Type set in University Roman Bd BT/Souvenir Lt BT

ISBN: 0-7643-2277-X
Printed in China

Published by Schiffer Publishing Ltd.
4880 Lower Valley Road
Atglen, PA 19310
Phone: (610) 593-1777; Fax: (610) 593-2002
E-mail: Info@schifferbooks.com

For the largest selection of fine reference books on this
and related subjects, please visit our web site at
www.schifferbooks.com
We are always looking for people to write books on new
and related subjects. If you have an idea for a book
please contact us at the above address.

This book may be purchased from the publisher.
Include $3.95 for shipping.
Please try your bookstore first.
You may write for a free catalog.

In Europe, Schiffer books are distributed by
Bushwood Books
6 Marksbury Ave.
Kew Gardens
Surrey TW9 4JF England
Phone: 44 (0) 20 8392-8585;
Fax: 44 (0) 20 8392-9876
E-mail: info@bushwoodbooks.co.uk
Free postage in the U.K., Europe; air mail at cost.

Contents

Acknowledgments

While writing and photographing this book, I was supported and assisted by a number of generous, knowledgeable individuals who not only added significantly to the book, but also made the job far more interesting and enjoyable. These people took time from their busy schedules to work with me in amassing the images and details presented in this book. I want to thank them all. Special thanks to: the Cincinnati Art Galleries, LLC and Riley Humler; David Rago Auctions and Denise Rago-Wallace; Clarence Meyer; Seekers Antiques; Bob Shores and Dale Jones; W & D Antiques; the friendly, hardworking staff members from Sha-Dor/Pappabello who provided me access to the Northern Virginia Antiques Show and Sale in Arlington, Virginia (a marvelous annual event); the historians at the Smithsonian Institution and the Cincinnati Art Museum, Rachel V. Markowitz of the Philadelphia Museum of Art; the archivists at the Library of Congress; and those who prefer to remain anonymous.

I also wish to thank the talented staff at Schiffer Publishing for making this book a work of art. You know who you are! Thanks for everything.

Special thanks to my family, who stand beside me through thick and thin, making it all worthwhile.

Finally, a heartfelt thank you to readers everywhere.

Introduction

These are pleasant times and places, when women give their leisure and means to the founding of an artistic industry. Mrs. Maria Longworth Nichols, by this use of time and money, practically opens a path in which unlimited work for women may eventually be found.

— Mrs. Aaron F. Perry, May 1881

Figure 2. Light Standard glaze ewer, decorated by Anna Marie Valentien in 1893. The decoration features large, detailed poppy flowers. Marks include the flames mark, shape 387 D, an impressed W for white clay, an incised L for Light Standard glaze, and the incised initials of the decorator. 12" h. *Courtesy of Mark Mussio, Cincinnati Art Galleries, LLC.*

Figure 1. During the waning decades of the nineteenth century, Rookwood would produce art pottery of such beauty that the firm would be forever associated with their early, hand-painted, artist-signed work. Standard glaze flat-sided jug decorated by Sadie Markland in 1898, depicting an ear of corn and husk. This jug had been sent to the Gorham Manufacturing Company of Providence, Rhode Island, where delicate silver overlay depicting grapes amid vines was applied, as well as a stopper with chain. Marks to the silver include the Gorham hallmark, the designation R 2538, and the notation 999/1000 fine. Marks to the jug's base include the Rookwood conjoined logo with flames (referred to hereafter as the "flames mark" ... even when only a single flame is present) (*see Manufacturer's Marks subheading*), which incorporates the date, shape 794, and the incised initials of the decorator. 7.25" h. *Courtesy of Mark Mussio, Cincinnati Art Galleries, LLC.*

Rookwood Pottery was established by Maria Longworth Nichols, a woman of means with a passion for Japanese design, in a converted Cincinnati schoolhouse in 1880. Mrs. Nichols's mission statement was simplicity itself, "While my principal objective is my own gratification, I hope to make the Pottery pay expenses." (Owens 1992, 11) Despite a modest goal and humble surroundings, during the waning decades of the nineteenth century Rookwood would produce art pottery of such beauty that the firm would be forever associated with their early, hand-painted, artist-signed work. By 1893, the influential ceramics scholar and future curator and director of the Philadelphia Museum of Art, Edwin AtLee Barber, extolled the company's virtues in print in his book *The Pottery and Porcelain of the United States.* Management of a ceramics firm receiving praise in *Pottery and Porcelain* knew they had arrived. In an age when many ceramists in the United States were struggling to both free themselves from the long shadows cast by their more experienced brethren in England, Europe, and Asia, and to create a distinctive American style all their own, Barber had this to say of Rookwood, "It is safe to assert that no ceramic establishment which has existed in the United States has come nearer fulfilling the requirements of a distinctly American institution than the Rookwood Pottery of Cincinnati, Ohio." Further, Barber added, "Today its exquisite ceramic creations may be found in almost every home of culture and refinement and in every prominent Art Museum in the land..." (Raabe 2003)

Rookwood Pottery, known familiarly as "the Pottery," quickly established and maintained a reputation as a producer of expensive, one-of-a-kind, luxurious, hand-decorated art pottery sold to influential up-and-coming middle class and wealthy society women of urban America through prestigious china and jewelry stores. The Pottery would continually experiment with new glazes, decorations, and ceramic bodies that kept the firm on the leading edge of pottery development. Over the years, Rookwood hired many talented artists who used vases, plaques, and bowls as canvases upon which to paint delicate works of art reflecting the fascinations, passions, and dreams of a rapidly changing society, all protected beneath the delicate, glassy veneer of glaze.

Once the nineteenth century slipped into the twentieth, Rookwood added commercial, mass-produced, and significantly less expensive artware to the company's product line to meet both company expenses and a changing nation's desire for simplified, lower-cost ceramics. Rookwood would remain in business through two world wars, economic depression, and several changes in ownership until 1967 when the company finally ceased operations far from its original home.

Figure 3. Over the years, Rookwood hired many talented artists who used vases, plaques, and bowls as canvases upon which to paint delicate works of art reflecting the fascinations, passions, and dreams of a rapidly changing society, all protected beneath the delicate, glassy veneer of glaze. Scenic Vellum plaque by Elizabeth F. McDermott, titled *Winter Twilight*, 1919, with a snowy landscape at dusk. It is mounted in the original frame provided by Rookwood Pottery. Base marks: flames mark and artist's signature. Plaque: 9" x 11". *Courtesy of David Rago Auctions.*

Figure 4. While exploring the many forms, decorations, and glazes, pay particular attention to the hand decorated wares. Take special notice of the many floral motifs. The flowers are often represented with an attention to detail worthy of a botany text. Rookwood's clientele loved these floral designs. Standard glaze vase decorated in 1892 in a water lily motif by Kataro Shirayamadani. Base marks: flames mark, shape number 664B, an incised W, and incised artist's signature. 11" h. *Courtesy of Bob Shores and Dale Jones.*

Captured here is a sampling of the vast array of decorative ceramics produced over the decades from the 1880s to the 1960s by Rookwood Pottery. While exploring the many forms, decorations, and glazes, pay particular attention to the hand decorated wares. Take special notice of the many floral motifs. The flowers are often represented with an attention to detail worthy of a botany text. Rookwood's clientele loved these floral designs, in fact they insisted on them, much to the exasperation of Maria Longworth Nichols. Mrs. Nichols preferred decoration of a more exotic sort, as described by Mrs. Aaron F. Perry in an 1881 article in *Harper's New Monthly Magazine*. Describing ceramics produced and decorated by Maria Nichols herself, Perry wrote, "A majority of the large pieces [vases measuring thirty to thirty-two inches high] of Mrs. Nichols are Japanese grotesque in design, with the inevitable dragon coiled about the neck of the vase, or at its base, varied with gods, wise men, the sacred mountain, storks, owls, monsters of the air and water, bamboo, etc. decorated in high relief, underglaze color, incised design, and an overglaze enrichment of gold." Regardless of the passions of Rookwood's founder, the customers wanted flowers and flowers they received!

What's In A Name?

Before venturing into the history and production of Rookwood Pottery, it will be useful to define certain terms and art movements that will be referred to throughout the book.

Art Pottery and Artware

Rookwood is regarded by many as having been the leading ceramics manufactory in the American art pottery movement. Art pottery in America first appeared in the 1870s, driven by Victorian women's passion for china decoration and taking inspiration from the Arts and Crafts Movement's desire to create handcrafted beauty to counter the increasingly mechanized lifestyle of an industrialized age. Well-educated Victorian women, including Maria Longworth Nichols, took up pottery decoration with enthusiasm to fill their free time, helping to push the early development of art pottery forward. In fact, Mrs. Nichols initially felt her company would be an ideal place for women to gather and pursue their passionate pottery-decorating hobby.

Art pottery is decorative ware that has the appearance of being handmade (the degree to which it was made by hand varied from one pottery firm to another—in fact, Rookwood Pottery began with wheel turned, handmade ceramic bodies in the 1880s but chose mold formed, mass-produced bodies in increasing numbers during the 1890s for uniformity and economy) and features hand decoration including images from nature, soft glaze color transitions, and a Japanese design sensibility. (Japanese influence on American design stemmed from the 1876 Philadelphia Centennial Exhibition where Japanese wares were first displayed to large audiences in the United States.) Art pottery is also frequently signed by the artist who decorated the piece.

Figure 6. Rookwood artware 1928 "production" vase decorated with molded flowers around the rim, the stems extending down the length of the body. An artware item is referred to amongst Rookwood fanciers as either a "production" or "commercial" item. We will follow that trend here. Base marks: flames mark, shape 2090. 4.5" h. *Courtesy of Clarence Meyer.*

Artware developed over time from art pottery. Artware ceramics are mass-produced, using molds to form the bodies; they are decorated with striking glazes and limited hand decoration (if any). Artware developed out of the potter's need to reduce production costs, increase output to meet demand, and expand the clientele by producing decorative wares at lower costs available to a broader range of consumers. The mass production techniques employed reduced the overall number of skilled artists required to make a given piece of pottery, thereby both reducing the cost and the production time.

Also at work as time passed, and economic and social conditions changed, was a demand for ceramics more compatible with a simplified lifestyle. The nineteenth century ideals of handcrafted workmanship espoused by art movements and embodied in art pottery were replaced by twentieth century necessity. The more economical, mass-produced artwares were what the twentieth century public increasingly sought to accompany their changing lifestyle. Elegant Queen Anne homes were giving way to simple bungalows, formal dinners were replaced with outdoor barbeques and serve yourself buffets, and elaborate art pottery was being replaced with simple, yet stylish artware. When referring to Rookwood's artwares, many describe them as "commercial" ware or "production" pieces.

In the trade journal *Ceramic Industry,* Glen Lukens spoke to the difference between art pottery and artware very bluntly from his perspective in August 1945. Of art pottery, he said,

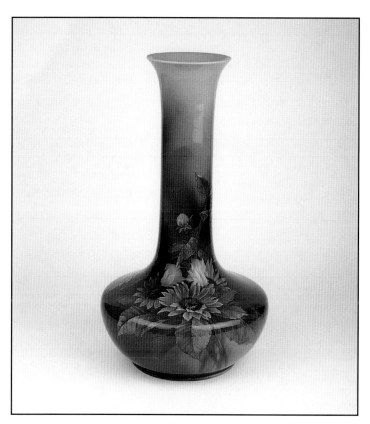

Figure 5. Standard glaze art pottery vase decorated with sunflowers painted in 1890 by Matthew A. Daly. Base marks: flames mark, shape number 463 A, incised W, and incised monogram of artist. 22" h. *Courtesy of Bob Shores and Dale Jones.*

…art potters discouraged distribution in prewar days by the outrageous prices they asked. They had the notion that they possessed a little more of the divine essence than other people and held inflexible ideas about altering their designs an iota, even though the change would help sales. They were geared only to limited production, not too reliably on schedule. And they were unable to comprehend the pressure for volume that made the production of the small pottery of puny consequence to harassed sales representatives and buyers.

While Lukens may have been overly harsh, some of Rookwood's practices lend credence to his complaint. During the 1890s, when demand for Rookwood wares exceeded supply, the company would short-change their smaller retailers in favor of their larger retail outlets, ensuring their largest stores remained well stocked while smaller venues were left wanting.

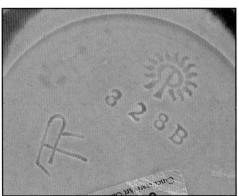

Figure 7. Standard glaze cylindrical tankard shaped art pottery piece with a single handle gracefully wrapping around one side. This item was decorated by Frederick D. H. Rothenbusch in 1897, featuring a grapes on branch motif with grape leaves on the back. Base marks: flames mark, 328B, and impressed artist's mark. 6" h. *Courtesy of Bob Shores and Dale Jones.*

In 1904, Rookwood Pottery produced a mail-order catalog entitled *The Rookwood Book*. This catalog stressed the unique nature of each art pottery piece produced. So unique were these items that the company warned that the decorative wares illustrated on its pages may or may not still be available when the customer placed an order. Prices for these unique items were listed in ranges as well (prices varied for a number of reasons, including the size of the pot, the complexity of the decoration, and the fame of the decorator), instead of a single price. All of this was likely a bit off-putting to potential customers.

Speaking in favor of artware manufacturing techniques, Lukens admonished,

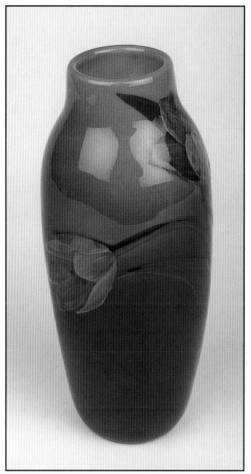

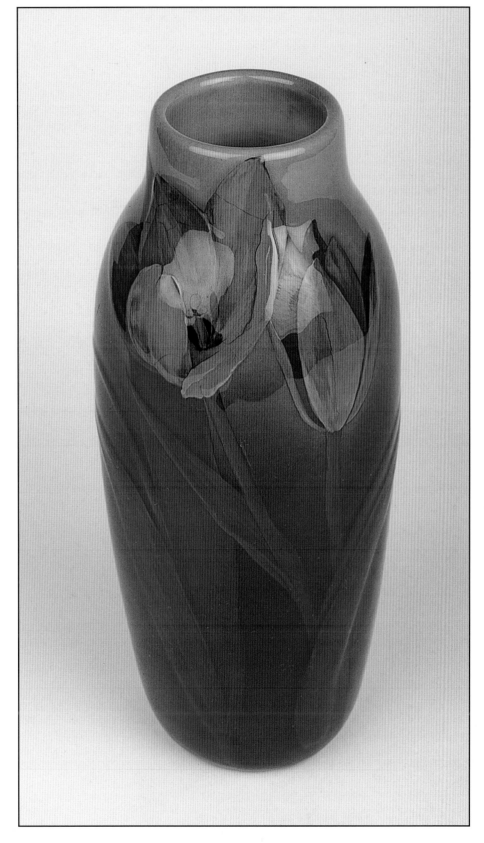

Figure 8. Prices for Rookwood's unique art pottery wares were listed in ranges (prices varied for a number of reasons, including the size of the pot, the complexity of the decoration, and the fame of the decorator), instead of a single price. Standard glaze vase with embossed and painted tulips, decorated in 1904 by Elizabeth N. Lincoln. Base marks: flames mark, date, shape number 932 D, and incised artist's initials. 8.5" h. *Courtesy of Bob Shores and Dale Jones.*

Remembering that he [the potter] is a businessman, as well as an artist and technician, he must study production costs against the day when prices will have to be shaved to meet competition. He needs smoother, steadier, more controllable methods of production as a means to surer output and alleviating delivery disappointments. ... he must study the market so as to be able to understand buyers' problems and work with them on common ground.

When studying Rookwood ceramics, one observes the gradual transition from hand decorated, artist signed, art pottery production of the late nineteenth and early twentieth centuries to ever-increasing use of the mass production techniques of artware.

Earthenware and Porcelain

By 1880, river, canal, and rail transportation was well established in the United States. Rookwood Pottery was able to avail itself of raw materials from many regions in the country and to send forth its finished products to urban centers across the nation. Rookwood's management sought out clays from their native Ohio, from neighboring Indiana, Kentucky, and Tennessee, and from farther afield in Alabama. These clays came in a variety of colors, including cream, ginger, yellow, sage green, gray, and dark red. This wide range of clay bodies in many colors offered the company a great deal of flexibility in decoration. From varied clays, the company produced both earthenware and porcelain bodies.

Earthenware bodies are fired at kiln temperatures ranging from 1462 to 2012 degrees Fahrenheit and are porous. Without a coating of glaze to cover them, earthenware bodies will absorb water. Earthenwares are also not translucent—light will not pass through them—and are coated with lead or alkaline glazes, both for protection and decoration.

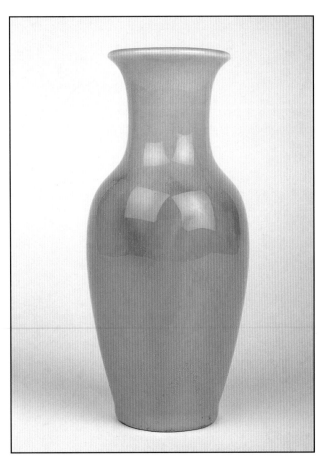

Figure 9. Artware ceramics are mass-produced, using molds to form the bodies; they are decorated with striking glazes and limited hand decoration (if any). Artware 1932 "production" vase with a narrow neck and colorful glazes, including yellow at the rim and neck shading to turquoise below. Base marks: flames mark, 6308 C. 7" h. *Courtesy of Bob Shores and Dale Jones.*

Figure 10. Standard glaze earthenware vase decorated with lotus flowers, buds, and leaves amidst sweeping waves by Albert Valentien in 1888 and set off with Mahogany glaze. Base marks: flames mark, shape 392, impressed R for red clay, incised artist's initials, and incised D for dark yellow Standard glaze, which combines with the red clay to constitute the Mahogany glaze. 25.25" h. *Courtesy of Mark Mussio, Cincinnati Art Galleries, LLC.*

Porcelains are much harder, with translucent bodies produced from a mixture of kaolin (a fine-grained clay), feldspar, quartz, and water. Porcelains are fired at high kiln temperatures, roughly 2552 degrees Fahrenheit or above. The high firing heat fuses the clay to form vitrified (glass-like, waterproof) bodies. While glazing is not required to make the porcelain body impervious to water, porcelains are often glazed for decorative purposes. In 1915, for Rookwood's thirty-fifth anniversary, the company added Soft Porcelain to the mix.

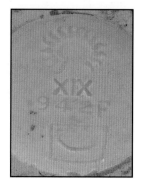

Slip Decoration

Rookwood Pottery used colored slips to create both their background colors (used to cover the ceramic body and act as an underlying color for the primary decoration adorning the piece) and their decorative motifs (ranging from the aforementioned floral decorations, fauna, sea life, and birds to elaborate portraits of Native Americans). Slip itself is a mixture of potter's clay and water, having a creamy, near-liquid consistency. The color of the slip was altered with the use of mineral oxides, creating a broad color palette from which the artist could work.

Decorators painting in slip had to be talented artists, confident in their work, as slip painting required the artist to work quickly. The decorator also had to be sure of his or her color palette as the colors of the slips changed once they were fired in the kiln. Despite the challenges, the process and end results were reminiscent of oil paintings, lending credibility to Rookwood's claim that each hand-painted decoration was a unique work of art.

Figure 11. Porcelain vase decorated in 1919 by Arthur Conant. The decoration includes two bunches of flowers and berries connected by garlands. Base marks: flames mark, date, shape number 942F, and incised artist's monogram. 3.75" h. *Courtesy of Bob Shores and Dale Jones.*

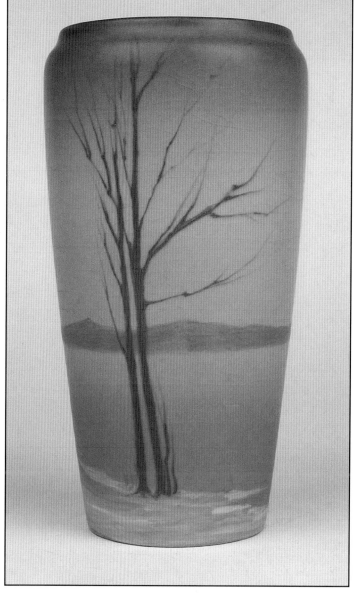

Figure 12. Decorators painting in slip had to be talented artists, confident in their work, as slip painting required the artist to work quickly. The decorator also had to be sure of his or her color palette as the colors of the slips changed once they were fired in the kiln. Despite the challenges, the process and end result were reminiscent of oil paintings, lending credibility to Rookwood's claim that each hand-painted decoration was a unique work of art. Scenic Vellum vase decorated by Elizabeth McDermott, 1917, with a snowy landscape, lonely trees, and distant mountains. Base marks: flames mark, date, 1369, and artist's initials. *Courtesy of Seekers Antiques.*

Glazes and Glaze Lines

Protecting both the clay body and the slip-painted decoration of a Rookwood vessel is a glaze coat. Generally speaking, glaze is a thin coating of glass that is applied to the body of a ceramic vessel. Glaze is produced by heating the ingredients of glass, grinding down the resultant glass into a fine powder, and then dusting or spraying an unfired or fired ceramic body (if unfired, the body is called "green;" when fired, it is referred to as "bisque," or "biscuit") with glaze or dipping that body into a suspension of glaze powder and water. Once glaze is applied, it is fired in a kiln to melt and evenly spread the glaze across the body.

Various mixes of metallic oxides in the glaze will create different glaze colors. Glazes may be either translucent or opaque. For Rookwood's art pottery, various colored, translucent glazes were used to enhance the colors of the decorations they coated. For the company's later artware, the glaze coat became a major decorative feature. Over the years, Rookwood chemists experimented with a wide variety of glaze treatments to create many distinct product lines.

When a specific glaze color, ceramic body type, and decoration were used together on a variety of vessel forms, a "glaze line" was created. Rookwood Pottery marketed their wares by glaze lines. Among the best known of Rookwood's glaze lines today are Ivory/Cameo, Dull Finish, Standard, Tiger Eye, Goldstone, Sea Green, Iris, Aerial Blue, Mat Glaze, and Vellum. Provided here is a brief thumbnail sketch of each of these popular glaze lines. For a more detailed description of these lines and others, see Anita J. Ellis's book *Rookwood Pottery: The Glaze Lines.*

Produced from 1884 to 1892, the Ivory/Cameo glaze line employed a translucent, colorless, gloss glaze over slip-painted decorations comprised of petite white flowers over ground colors in varying hues of brown, pink, or pale blue. Frequently, these ground colors fade away to white. Cameo adorned useful wares, including tea and coffee sets, tablewares, plant holders, and vases.

From 1884 to c. 1900, Rookwood Pottery produced the Dull Finish glaze line, featuring a translucent, colorless smear glaze. A smear glaze is applied so thinly as to give the object the appearance of lacking glaze altogether and creates a dull finish completely devoid of glossy sheen. This dull, smear glaze overlies slip-painted decoration predominantly featuring floral motifs, with some fauna added for variety, all accented with lighter tints of blues, pinks, and whites. Quite frequently, Dull Finish glaze line objects were further adorned with overglaze gilt decorations for added luster.

Figure 14. Dull Finish ewer decorated by Albert R. Valentien in 1887. The decoration features white flowers over a pink background, with accents of fired on gold. Base marks: flames mark, shape 262, incised S for Smear Glaze, W7 for a type of white clay, and incised artist's initials. 12" h. *Courtesy of Mark Mussio, Cincinnati Art Galleries, LLC.*

Figure 13. Cameo Glaze creamer by Sallie Toohey in 1889, featuring encircling white apple blossoms. Base marks: flames mark, shape 330, an impressed W for white clay, an incised W for clear glaze, and the decorator's incised monogram. 2.75". *Courtesy of Mark Mussio, Cincinnati Art Galleries, LLC.*

From 1884 to roughly 1909, Rookwood produced Standard, featuring a translucent, yellow-tinted, gloss glaze overcoat protecting and complementing slip-painted flora and/or fauna decoration applied over darker toned ground colors in brown, green, or yellow. Prior to 1890, the clay body was most often yellow; after 1890, the clay body could be various colors, most often white, but also including ginger, sage green, red, and on rare occasions a dark green color achieved by introducing color into the clay itself. When the Standard glaze is applied over a red body, the line is referred to as "Mahogany," an offshoot of Standard. At times, Standard was also decorated with electro-plated gold or silver adornments.

The ground colors and yellow-tinted glossy glaze are all very Victorian. Victorians were quite fond of colors that reflected the natural world, including browns, yellows, greens, olives, and gray tones. They painted their houses with these colors and incorporated them in their interior decoration as well.

Tiger Eye and Goldstone were both produced from 1884 to c. 1900 and both were "happy accidents." Tiger Eye consists of a crystalline glaze that gives the appearance of gold foil glinting beneath its glossy surface. This striking glaze treatment usually adorns ceramics featuring incised, relief, or slip-painted flora or fauna. The ceramic body beneath Tiger Eye is most frequently red and is considered to be a spin off of the Mahogany glaze line. Tiger Eye was a temperamental glaze that could never be recreated with any degree of reliability.

Figure 15. Standard glaze chocolate pot with decoration composed and painted by Caroline Steinle, featuring orange and brown nasturtium, 1899. Base marks: flames mark, shape 772, and the artist's initials. 9" x 6.25". *Courtesy of David Rago Auctions.*

Figure 16. Rare Tiger Eye pitcher painted by Albert R. Valentien in 1886, featuring a butterfly above a blooming branch in slip relief. (This item was from the Cincinnati Art Museum collection [almost 2300 pieces of Rookwood pottery dating back to 1880 had been on extended loan to the museum during the early twentieth century. This loan was recalled in 1942 and the pieces sold at auction as Rookwood Pottery changed management.], probable trial marks). Base marks: stamped ROOKWOOD, 1886, R, 263, artist's initials A.R.V., X, C. An X on the base indicates this piece of pottery was imperfect and therefore a "second." The imperfection was apparently a glazed-over chip to the rim. 10.5" x 4.75". *Courtesy of David Rago Auctions.*

Goldstone was a glossy, aventurine glaze with a yellow tint that gave the appearance of numerous gold flecks caught deep beneath the glossy surface. Overglazed with Goldstone were incised or slip-painted floral or faunal motifs. Fish have often been found flashing among those golden flecks. As with Tiger Eye, the ceramic body color beneath the glaze was red.

From 1893 to roughly 1904, Rookwood produced the Sea Green glaze line, featuring a translucent, glossy, green-tinted glaze. This glaze most often covered marine life decorations, particularly fish or waterfowl. Occasionally, the ever-popular floral motifs were applied to this line as well. Sea Green was most often found adorning a white clay body.

Figure 18. Rare and important Sea Green tyg (a drinking mug, large in size, most frequently having two to four handles, although as many as eleven evenly spaced handles adorn some tygs) by Kataro Shirayamadani with electroplated silver mounts on the rim and handle tops, produced in 1900. Shirayamadani's decoration includes two owls perched in a pine bough with a large full moon behind them. The metal mounts were decorated with three dimensional acorns and oak leaves. Base marks: flames mark, shape number 659 B, and incised artist's cipher. 7.75" h. *Courtesy of Mark Mussio, Cincinnati Art Galleries, LLC.*

Figure 17. Goldstone vase. Base marks: ROOKWOOD in block letters, the date 1885, shape S 513, and R for red clay. 8.5" h. *Courtesy of Mark Mussio, Cincinnati Art Galleries, LLC.*

Figure 19. Sea Green vase painted in the squeeze bag technique by Artus Van Briggle with brown leaves on a celadon ground, 1897. Base marks: flames mark, shape, 735D, artist's initials, G, X. The second mark was applied for glaze inconsistency around the base. 6.75" x 4". *Courtesy of David Rago Auctions.*

The Iris glaze line was produced from 1893 to roughly 1912, featuring a translucent, glossy, crystal clear glaze over slip-painted floral decorations (with animal life appearing on rare occasions). The background colors gradually shaded from dark to light. White clay bodies usually received the Iris glaze, although green and blue-gray ceramics were infrequently employed.

The short-lived Aerial Blue glaze line was available from 1894 to 1895. The glaze was glossy, translucent, and colorless. Beneath the glaze were slip-painted floral or faunal motifs in shades of white on a delicate, sky-blue ground. Among the subjects decorating this line were rural and Dutch landscapes, ships at sea, animals, and portraits. The ceramic body is most often blue, although white bodies were also used. At times the ground color was slip-painted; however, most often the blue ground is the color of the clay body beneath the glaze.

A variety of Mat Glaze lines were used from 1898 to c. 1915, including Conventional Mat, Incised Mat, Modeled Mat, Painted Mat, and Painted Mat Inlay. With the exception of Vellum, to be discussed separately below, these were opaque glazes, primarily in a single, solid color although at times in several colors. These glazes were applied to vessels featuring carved, incised, or painted decorations. The earthenware body color was often light buff to white.

Figure 21. Rare Conventional Mat glaze vase decorated in 1902 by Kataro Shirayamadani, featuring a dragon among windswept clouds. Base marks: flames mark, date, shape number 907 C, and the incised artist's cipher. 14" h. *Courtesy of Mark Mussio, Cincinnati Art Galleries, LLC.*

Figure 20. Iris glaze bulbous vase painted by Constance Baker with lavender and purple pansies, 1902. Base marks: flames mark, date, shape 921, artist's initials. 6" h. *Courtesy of David Rago Auctions.*

Figure 22. Incised Mat vase. Base marks: flames mark, date, 1358C. 10.5" h. *Courtesy of Seekers Antiques.*

Figure 23. Modeled Mat tyg shaped and decorated by Kataro Shirayamadani in 1901. Base marks: flames mark, date, shape 830 E, and the artist's incised signature. 4.75" h. *Courtesy of Mark Mussio, Cincinnati Art Galleries, LLC.*

Figure 24. Painted Mat cylindrical vase decorated by Olga Geneva Reed with branches of berries and leaves in red on a purple ground, 1908. Base marks: flames mark, date, shape 1124E, and the artist's initials. 6.75" x 3". *Courtesy of David Rago Auctions.*

Vellum was employed by Rookwood from 1904 to 1948, featuring a mat, semi-translucent, slightly hazy glaze coat over slip-painted or carved decorations including land- or seascapes, flora, or fauna. The ceramic body beneath the glaze was white.

Figure 25. Vellum vase decorated in 1923 by Katherine Jones with blue bachelors' buttons on a blue-green ground. Base marks: flames mark, date, shape 295E, and the artist's initials. 7.5" x 3". *Courtesy of David Rago Auctions.*

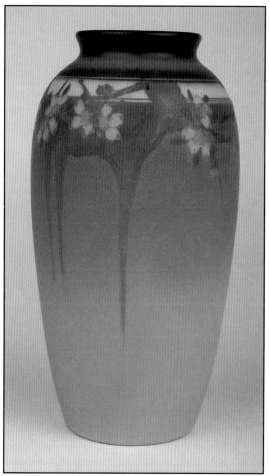

Figure 26. Vellum vase decorated by Elizabeth Neave Lincoln with a floral motif encircling the base. *Courtesy of Seekers Antiques.*

Figure 27. Vellum vase decorated by Edward Timothy Hurley in 1948, with flowers and boughs on the upper shoulder over a blue and white ground. A white ring accents the shoulder. Base marks: flames mark, date, shape 922 D, and the artist's incised initials. 7.25" h. *Courtesy of Seekers Antiques.*

Figure 28. Scenic Vellum plaque decorated by Edward Diers, who worked at Rookwood Pottery from 1896 to 1931. The plaque is entitled *Birch Trees*, displaying birch trees along a stream and a country lane among a mountainous background, all under a pink-to-blue sky. The plaque is signed with the artist's initials in the lower right hand corner while the back is marked with the Rookwood logo. A small paper label is attached to the frame, providing the title and the artist's name. 8.5" x 12". *Courtesy of Mark Mussio, Cincinnati Art Galleries, LLC.*

Manufacturer's Marks

Commonly, art potteries marked the bases or undersides of their products with manufacturer's marks. Such marks identified the company that produced the ware and, from 1887 to 1967, Rookwood's conjoined "RP" monogram mark consistently dated the ware. Manufacturer's marks are convenient for identification and were changed over time if a company survived for a considerable period. These changes in manufacturer's marks help identify the wares of different periods of production.

Manufacturer's marks were useful to the company as they identified their product for consumers. As America became an increasingly mobile society, people relocating across the country sought out the familiar wherever they went. It was reassuring to find familiar names in strange places. Once consumers associated a particular manufacturer's name or product's name with quality and reliability, they tended to stick with that name brand. It behooved Rookwood to mark their wares.

Among the company's earliest marks were two incised or painted marks applied by the decorator. The first featured the company name "Rookwood Pottery" and often included the date. This was the company's most common early mark. The second incised or painted mark was comprised of the following initials "R.P.C.O.M.L.N.", which stood for "Rookwood Pottery, Cincinnati, Ohio, Maria Longworth Nichols."

From 1880 to 1882, the company used an impressed or raised relief anchor. At times an impressed date and/or incised decorator's mark accompanied the anchor.

From 1881 to 1882, Rookwood used an impressed oval mark. Written within the oval was "Rookwood Pottery 207 Eastern Ave. 1882 Cincinnati O".

Figure 29. Extremely rare Rookwood stamp and mold used for marking the wares prior to firing. Left: A plaster mold for the impressed anchor mark used from 1880 to 1882. 1.25" in diameter. Right: A bisque fired white clay stamp for the rare Eastern Avenue location used briefly from 1881 to 1882. These rare items were owned by Albert Valentien. *Courtesy of Mark Mussio, Cincinnati Art Galleries, LLC.*

Two banner marks were also employed on rare occasions from 1880 to 1882. These were raised relief marks reading "Rookwood Pottery Cin. O." The mark also appeared without the Ohio state abbreviation.

Famous for his paintings of Native Americans, Henry F. Farny took time to create a rectangular Rookwood mark featuring a bottle kiln in the center of the rectangle. The rectangle is bracketed on either side with a rook on a branch. Each bird peers intently inward toward the kiln. This was the company's only printed mark. It was placed under the glaze.

In 1883, the company flirted with an impressed bottle kiln mark, at times associated with the "Rookwood" name and an impressed year date.

From 1882 to 1886, the firm used a simple, impressed "Rookwood" mark, most often accompanied by the year. The date changed with each passing year until June of 1886, when the firm's famous conjoined "RP" logo mark was first employed.

In June 1886, the impressed, conjoined "RP" mark began to appear on virtually every piece of Rookwood produced, and would continue to do so until the company's final days in 1967.

In 1887, the conjoined mark was first accompanied by a single flame, impressed above the logo. This flame represented the year. Every year after that, another flame was added to the mark until, by 1900, virtually the entire logo was surrounded in flame. From 1901 onward, a Roman numeral was added below this logo with its fourteen flames. The Roman numeral changed with each passing year from "I" on up.

In 1962, after Rookwood had moved to Starkville, Mississippi, the famous logo was copyrighted. From 1962 to 1967 an impressed ® registration mark accompanied the logo.

Figure 30. Conjoined Rookwood RP mark with flames, dating the mark to 1897. *Courtesy of Seekers Antiques.*

From roughly 1920 to 1960, the name and location of the pottery manufactory were impressed upon Rookwood objects.

Rookwood moved to Starkville, Mississippi, in 1960. At that point, until the company's closure in 1967, the firm used an impressed "Rookwood Pottery Starkville Miss." mark on larger wares. On smaller pieces there was not enough room for such an expansive mark.

Accompanying the manufacturer's marks at times were: anniversary marks celebrating the firm's fiftieth, sixtieth, and seventieth anniversaries; shape numbers (referring to body shapes) ranging from 1 to 7301; letters referring to the size of a particular item ranging from A (the largest) to F (the smallest) (for a size larger than A or smaller than F, a XX mark was employed); a letter designation indicating the type of clay body used (G for ginger, R for red, W for white ... and from

Figure 31. From 1901 onward, a Roman numeral was added below this mark with its fourteen flames. Here are the 1901 and 1902 marks. *Courtesy of Bob Shores and Dale Jones.*

1915 to c. 1925 P for porcelain); letter designations for different glazes; and potter and artist/decorator signatures or marks. There is much information to be gleaned from the base of a Rookwood pot.

Influential Art Movements

The Arts and Crafts Movement was a reaction to nineteenth century industrialization. As the Industrial Revolution swept through Western society, families attracted by new job opportunities moved from rural to urban communities, radically changing their daily lives and routines. Husbands and wives who had once worked side by side on the land were separated, he going off to work in the factory or office and she left to tend to the home or to take up job opportunities that were slowly opening to women. Families were distanced from the land. Many, living in crowded, dirty cities and working in poor conditions for low wages, looked back wistfully to an earlier, simpler, agrarian age. Industrialization brought with it a wide range of low quality, mass-produced wares as well. Those seeking to explain the low product quality observed that without any single person following a product from beginning to end in the modern factory, no individual took pride in the end result. Without concern for the finished product, the results were shoddy.

The Arts and Crafts Movement originated in England and by the latter decades of the nineteenth century spread to the United States, where adherents were inspired by the teachings and examples of William Morris and John Ruskin. The ideal of the movement was to allow individual artists the opportunity to create wares in the decorative arts that were beautifully handcrafted products from nature. Such products were to be both useful objects and works of art produced from high quality, natural materials. The decorative motifs taken from nature reflect that desire for a closeness with the natural world that was largely lost in the urban setting. As members of a social movement, Arts and Crafts practitioners sought to improve working conditions, free artists to be creative, and bring affordable quality art to all peoples. It was also hoped that the presence of art would elevate social values.

The Arts and Crafts Movement would remain influential in the United States into the first quarter of the twentieth century. In ceramic production, the Arts and Crafts ideal of hand forming natural materials into beautiful, useful products led to art pottery. Art pottery was characterized by Japanese design sensibilities, recognizable images of the natural world, and soft color transitions. In Cincinnati, Ohio, two influential women would lead the way regionally in the art pottery movement, Mary Louise McLaughlin and Maria Longworth Nichols. Mary L. McLaughlin was the first in the Midwest to develop a technique for underglaze slip-painted decoration using colored slips, a technique she referred to as "Cincinnati Limoges" or "Cincinnati faience." She also founded the Cincinnati Women's Pottery Club as a haven for women passionate about handcrafted ceramics and china painting. These were considered therapeutic pursuits consistent with the ideals of the Arts and Crafts Movement.

Figure 32. Mary Louise McLaughlin made this set of four decorated porcelain salad plates with floral decoration during 1888 and 1890. Three plates are decorated with shamrock decoration with gold and platinum slip and one has red poppies with gold vines. All four are done on Haviland & Company blanks (blanks are undecorated ceramics), whose work Mary McLaughlin much admired. Three plates are signed "M.L. McLaughlin Cinti. 1890" in red slip and the other plate is marked "LMcL 1888" in red slip. 7.25" in diameter. *Courtesy of Mark Mussio, Cincinnati Art Galleries, LLC.*

Figure 33. Losanti porcelain vase by Mary Louise McLaughlin, produced circa 1903, with three dimensional oak leaves done in both gloss and mat glazes. The leaves are in a glossy cream slip with mat green accents. The rest of the surface is mostly mat blue and mat white glaze with glossy blue patches appearing underneath the mat. Base marks: Losanti logo in blue slip along with McLaughlin's incised monogram, the numbers "1111" (indicating the date to be 1903), and "207." 7" h. *Courtesy of Mark Mussio, Cincinnati Art Galleries, LLC.*

Figure 34. Very rare "Chinese lantern" with crab decoration created in 1882 by Maria Longworth Nichols. There are crabs and leaves on both sides along with fired on gold and a black collar and foot. An attachment point is cast into the top for hanging. Marks on the top of the piece: "ROOKWOOD" in block letters, the date, and incised artist's initials. *Courtesy of Mark Mussio, Cincinnati Art Galleries, LLC.*

Figure 35. Early organically-shaped pitcher almost certainly painted by Maria L. Nichols in the Limoges style, with spiders in a web amidst bamboo plants. This unusual piece was produced at Rookwood Pottery in 1883. Base marks: stamped ROOKWOOD 1883. 8" x 7.5". *Courtesy of David Rago Auctions.*

Figure 36. Early Limoges style vase, most likely "Cincinnati Limoges," from around 1878, decorated with dogwood flowers and a small bird in flight. Unmarked. 14.75" h. This is reminiscent of early Wheatley, early McLaughlin, *and* early Pottery Club with its yellow Ohio clay and clear Limoges underglaze decorative style. *Courtesy of Mark Mussio, Cincinnati Art Galleries, LLC.*

Maria Longworth Nichols initially founded Rookwood more intent on producing fine art than profit. She too looked to engage talented women in this decorative art. Laura Fry, working for Rookwood in 1883, created a process to apply colored slip ground colors using an atomizer that created striking color shadings, blending one color softly into another. Rookwood was one of many potteries that picked up on the Arts and Crafts philosophy, producing beautiful art pottery in a studio atmosphere rather than a factory's production line. While the nineteenth century wares were generally not intended to be affordable to all peoples (as would be the case with much of the materials produced by this movement in the end, despite the idealistic goal of art for everyone), there was hope among consumers that Rookwood's ceramic art in the home would indeed elevate the morals of family members exposed to it.

While the Arts and Crafts Movement rebelled against industrialization and the lowering of social values in Victorian Society, Art Nouveau (1890-1914) railed against the Victorian penchant for designing objects steeped in the antiquarian's historicism (pulling designs and motifs from the ancients and applying them to new wares). Gardens, both the large public and small private varieties, were extremely popular in this period. Nature was viewed with a romantic eye. Art Nouveau designers took to those gardens and to the natural world beyond for their inspiration. The results were decorative wares taking their forms from nature rather than history. Straight-lined precision symmetry was replaced with asymmetrical, sinuous, botanical … and even faunal … forms. Divorced from the designs of the past, Art Nouveau was considered truly modern.

The Art Nouveau Movement also recognized the stressful nature of the urban lifestyle. It was believed that a room decorated in the Art Nouveau style would offer a restful space, providing the peace of nature to all who resided there. Therefore, the home or public space adorned in Art Nouveau style would be therapeutic to the frazzled nerves of modern humanity.

Despite its purported therapeutic qualities, Rookwood's management was leery of "the new art." American critics such as Irene Sargent and Josephine Locke were railing against Art Nouveau. It broke with historical tradition, they said; it lacks structure and is chaotic, they said. Frankly, its sinuous lines, lush organic forms, and shapely nudes were feared to be all too erotic for Rookwood's clientele. With the exception of a limited number of pieces created by a few decorators trained in Paris, Rookwood largely skirted the Art Nouveau movement.

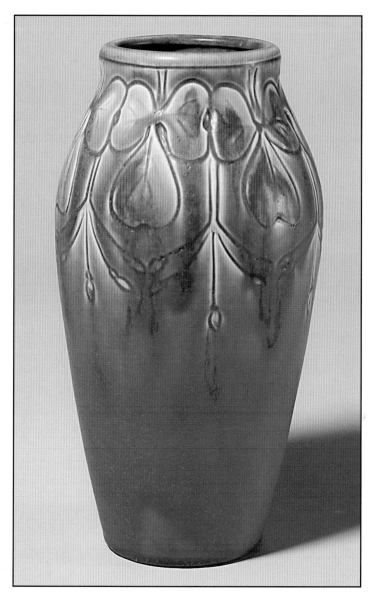

Figure 37. Arts & Crafts style Carved Mat vase decorated in 1905 by Rose Fechheimer, featuring bleeding hearts encircling the shoulder. Base marks: flames mark, date, shape number 925 C, and the incised artist's monogram. 9.25" h. *Courtesy of Mark Mussio, Cincinnati Art Galleries, LLC.*

Figure 38. Art Nouveau decorations by Anna Marie Valentien, 1905, adorn an early Vellum vase, with yellow nasturtiums, green leaves, and stems. Base marks: flames mark, date, shape 905, impressed V, incised V for Vellum, and the artist's incised initials. 10.5" h. *Courtesy of Mark Mussio, Cincinnati Art Galleries, LLC.*

Art Deco was the style most influential between 1925 and the beginning of World War II. Geometric forms and lavish decorative techniques were the early hallmarks of Art Deco. It was at the 1925 Paris Exposition (the Exposition des Arts Décoratifs et Industriels Modernes) that the public was made aware of Art Deco. Exhibitions of this sort had long been used both to show the public the best of modern design and to give international competitors a chance to compare products and glean new trends. It became clear in Paris that the organic Art Nouveau lines were being replaced with the geometric, streamlined forms and rich decoration of Art Deco.

Figure 40. Jewel Porcelain coupe-shaped vase painted by Lorinda Epply with Art Deco pink and yellow blossoms on an ivory ground, 1931. Base marks: flames mark, date, shape 2254E, and artist's initials. 4.5" x 5.5". *Courtesy of David Rago Auctions.*

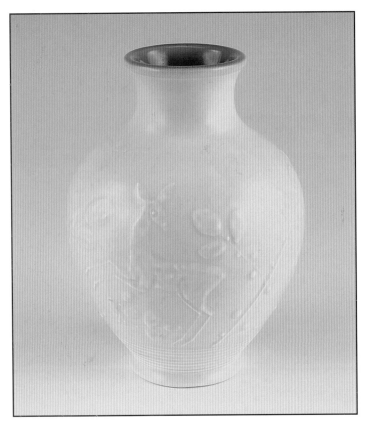

Figure 39. Production Art Deco baluster vase embossed with deer and honesty branches under Mat Ivory glaze, 1928. Base marks: flames mark. 7.75" h. *Courtesy of David Rago Auctions.*

By the late 1930s, Art Deco was being replaced by a style that has come to be known as "mid-century modern." The forms were considered organic, free-form, and futuristic. They used the plasticity of clay to great advantage, creating soft, rounded shapes and curling rims. The lines were smooth and decoration was kept to a minimum. The movement was seen as an attempt to create a truly American style, one completely devoid of elements derived from overseas. Competition from foreign potters was on the rise, with low cost ceramics arriving in ever-greater numbers on American shores. This movement attempted to stem the tide, providing homegrown, imaginative, distinctive wares to tempt American consumers away from cheap foreign pottery.

Art Deco style would reach its height of popularity and influence in 1935. In America, the Depression brought Art Deco styling to new forms. Many Americans found themselves cash-strapped and in no mood to purchase expensive luxuries in a lavish, new streamlined style. As a result, Art Deco motifs were incorporated into simple, durable, mass-produced, vividly glazed, and inexpensive ceramics. Frederick Hürten Rhead's description of his interpretation of Art Deco ware sums up the American Art Deco style well, "… an easy going informal series of articles, smart enough to fit in any house and obvious enough to furnish spots of emphasis …" (Rhead 1937)

The simplified, streamlined forms of Art Deco reflected the streamlining of society as well. The Victorians' fondness for elaborate social strictures and formal behavior was abandoned in favor of a more relaxed lifestyle requiring fewer accoutrements. In part, this was society bowing to necessity, as the Depression era of the 1930s limited consumers' buying power and made the formal dinner parties and lavish interiors of their Victorian grandparents an impossibility.

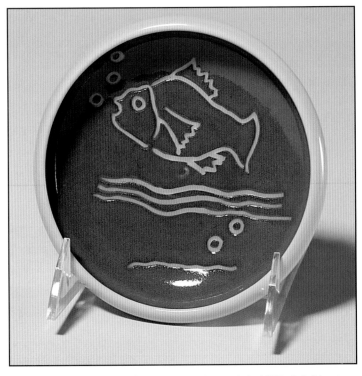

Figure 41. Shallow bowl decorated with a stylish 1950s fish blowing bubbles. The design was incised by John Wareham in 1952. Base marks: flames mark, date, and artist's incised initials. 1" deep x 5" in diameter, *Courtesy of Mark Mussio, Cincinnati Art Galleries, LLC.*

"Retail Agents" and Purchasers of Rookwood

"The demand for decorated wares is constantly increasing, and during the past year the advance made in meeting the wants of the public has been greater than any previous year." (*The Manufacturer and Builder* 1880, 75)

Figure 42. Dull Finish potpourri jar decorated in 1886 by Matthew Daly, decorated with a chickadee flying among tall grasses. The jar was accented with fired on gold and features a reversible lid. Base marks: ROOKWOOD in block letters, the date, shape 277, and the artist's initials. 7.75" h. *Courtesy of Mark Mussio, Cincinnati Art Galleries, LLC.*

Among the famous and influential who owned Rookwood ceramics were Samuel Clemens, Thomas Nast, and President and Mrs. Woodrow Wilson. The presidential couple had received their Rookwood in a way no doubt common among recipients, as wedding presents. Samuel Clemens, the venerable Mark Twain, is said to have purchased his during a tour of the Rookwood facilities in Cincinnati.

Most of Rookwood's customers purchased their artful pottery through "retail agents." In the nineteenth and early twentieth centuries, Rookwood's management sought out prestigious retailers to carry their wares. Only one such agent per city was allowed, initially either a china dealer or a jewelry shop. Among the sophisticated shops carrying Rookwood were Davis Collamore and Company of New York City, Briggs & Company of Chicago, and George Shreve and Company of San Francisco.

Throughout the late nineteenth century, Rookwood remained aloof to the allures of department stores' shelves. The firm felt department stores did not cater to the best sort of consumers, the "top drawer" trade. By the twentieth century, with the palatial twelve-story Marshall Fields department store rising to fame in Chicago, Rookwood's managers changed their minds. Now Rookwood ceramics could also be found in large department stores catering to people of means, stores that discouraged patronage by those with modest incomes with their sumptuous appearance alone. Department stores of sophistication seen as promoting a "genteel lifestyle" were now of interest to Rookwood.

Rookwood Pottery also placed advertisements in magazines targeted to the middle and upper class markets, including *Century, Country Life in America, Harper's New Monthly, House Beautiful*, and *Ladies Home Journal*. Prior to the introduction of artware, the Pottery emphasized that their wares were individual works of art, signed and unique, the equal of any statuary or painting. Rookwood aimed their advertisements directly at the women who were charged with decorating the home in the late Victorian era, women who were avidly reading magazines and books on appropriate home decoration that were thriving during that period.

The Victorian middle and upper class women seeking to fill sizable homes with wares designed to lend an air of civility, success, and proper moral attitude had a lot of territory to cover. Advice books of the day stated that there was no more harmonious place for attractive, decorative ceramics than in the bedroom. The lady's private boudoir and gentleman's library, where each conducted their business, would also welcome artful Rookwood.

Figure 43. Diminutive perfume jug, circa 1882, decorated with leaves and branches against a background of clouds in the Limoges style. Base marks: an impressed "Y" and unclear incised initials of the decorator, which appear to be a conjoined CM. 3.5" h. *Courtesy of Mark Mussio, Cincinnati Art Galleries, LLC.*

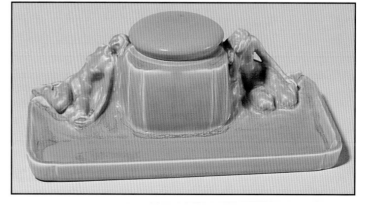

Figure 44. Rare Mat glaze inkwell and pen tray designed by Louise Abel (working for Rookwood from 1919 to 1932). It features two nudes, one on either side of the well, and comes with an inner cup and lid. Base marks: company logo, date, shape number 2929. 3" x 9.5". *Courtesy of Mark Mussio, Cincinnati Art Galleries, LLC.*

In public spaces, ladies would seek out Rookwood for the drawing room or parlor. Elegant Rookwood vases, in shapes reminiscent of classical Greek, Japanese, or Chinese forms or more contemporary European forms, adorned with depictions of the natural world, would be at home on the mantle next to elegant oil paintings, in the whatnot case, atop the built-in bookcases, nestled in recessed alcoves, or prominently displayed on polished tabletops.

By the Victorian era, the woodland regions around developed areas in the United States were now "tamed," devoid of large predators and indigenous peoples. Victorians felt free to view the relatively safe natural world around them with a romantic eye, rather than as the potential threat to life and limb it had once been for their forebears. The Industrial Revolution also provided Victorians with greater access to the world at large than ever before. Explorers returned from around the globe with stories of exotic locales, flora, and fauna. All this led to a fascination with nature, a fascination well represented in Rookwood's decoration. Elaborate gardens and large porches were constructed. Massive public parks and arboreta were seen as refuges from the crowded, bustling urban life and beneficial to all. Private gardens were viewed as the epitome of good taste. Porches invited residents to enjoy the natural world without leaving the comforts of hearth and home behind. The porches were considered extensions of the home's interior and, as such, were suitably decorated.

Figure 45. Standard glaze vase decorated by Lenore Asbury with what appear to be delicate persimmon flowers amidst leaves and branches. Base marks: flames mark, shape 387 C, and the artist's incised initials. 10.25" h. *Courtesy of Mark Mussio, Cincinnati Art Galleries, LLC.*

Figure 46. Standard glaze urn decorated by Sturgis Laurence with a portrait of a young man in classical Greek style, 1897. Base marks: flames mark, shape 827, and the artist's initials. 10.75" x 6.25". *Courtesy of David Rago Auctions.*

As a further expression of this passion for nature, Victorians constructed elaborate hothouses and indoor conservatories. Nature was ushered into the Victorian home. Rookwood Pottery produced some impressive jardinieres and garden urns to meet the needs of their nature-loving clientele.

Whether found in elegant conservatories, on porches, or in the garden, decorative flowers and plants around the house were considered evidence of cultural refinement. If the jardinieres and urns were beautiful objects, so much the better.

Figure 47. Standard glaze jardiniere decorated in 1889 by Kataro Shirayamadani, adorned with orange flowers, leaves, and branches on a green-to-orange-to-green background. The decoration encompasses the jardiniere. Base marks: flames mark, shape 300 B, a G for green clay, an incised L for Light Standard glaze, and the artist's incised Japanese signature. 10.5" h. *Courtesy of Mark Mussio, Cincinnati Art Galleries, LLC.*

Figure 48. Large two-handled garden urn with crackled sky blue glaze dripping over the unglazed ground. This urn features a factory-drilled base hole to release water. Base marks: stamped "RP" mark. 26.5" x 15". *Courtesy of David Rago Auctions.*

Passionate About Flower

Rookwood's management turned to their retail agents for information concerning the desires of their customers. The company took seriously the intelligence they received. As mentioned once before, they learned that their customers were completely enamored with flowers. Women were avidly reading gardening books and magazines for advice on decorating their own gardens, porches, and conservatories. Those ladies who preferred to keep their hands out of the soil turned to drawing botanical prints.

Special meanings were ascribed to different blossoms, while flowers generally were seen as morally uplifting. A hopeful homemaker might place flowering plants prominently around the home in the belief that she could elevate the morals of those she lived with. These ladies passionately sought Rookwood art pottery decorated in myriad floral motifs to further surround themselves and their loved ones with the flowers that so fascinated them.

To meet the never-ending demand for diverse floral motifs, Rookwood's grounds were planted with a wide variety of flowers for reference, the fields beyond the Pottery were scoured, and botany texts and magazines from the company's own design library were studied. As the years went by, Rookwood produced a phenomenal number of floral decorations, including those displayed here.

Maria L. Nichols spoke of this situation herself in 1889:

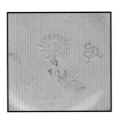

I would only wish to say in extenuation of the excess of floral decoration, which is not at all what I like best, that the agents demand it and we have to try in a measure to bend to popular taste by making things that sell. The Pottery would otherwise be far too expensive a luxury. (Owens 1992, 179)

Figure 50. Iris glaze vase adorned with daffodils arranged in Art Nouveau manner, painted in 1906 by Sara Sax. The background color shades from cream to yellow to slate to cobalt. Base marks: flames mark, date, shape number 904CC, incised W for White (iris) glaze, and impressed artist's monogram. 9.5" h. *Courtesy of Bob Shores and Dale Jones.*

Figure 49. Small Standard glaze vase with flaring shoulder and narrow neck, decorated by Howard Altman, 1902, featuring hand painted flowers on stems. Base marks: flames mark, date, shape 679, and the artist's incised initials. 6.25" h. *Courtesy of Bob Shores and Dale Jones.*

Men were not entirely overlooked by Rookwood. Ale sets, whiskey jugs, and humidors were produced. Decorating these wares were a variety of impressive portraits and images of various game animals and dogs more in tune with manly tastes. These items would have been at home in the Victorian Billiard-room or Smoking-room.

Cigars were symbols of manly status and success for Victorians. After a formal meal, while ladies retired to the drawing room for tea or coffee and conversation, the men drank port and smoked cigars. Victorian etiquette declared a gentleman must never smoke in front of a lady. Hence, the Smoking-room was a man's territory where he was free to indulge in a cigar without offending the ladies. Rookwood humidors were produced to house those cigars in appropriate style.

Figure 51. Men were not entirely overlooked by Rookwood. Standard glaze humidor painted by Adeliza Drake Sehon, featuring the portrait of *Chief Whiteman -Kiowa-*, 1901. Base marks: flames mark, date, 813, the artist's initials, and the title *Chief Whiteman -Kiowa-*. 5.75" x 5.75". *Courtesy of David Rago Auctions.*

Figure 52. A pilgrim flask decorated by Edward Pope Cranch (decorating for Rookwood in an imaginative style all his own from 1880 to 1892), with incised decoration consisting of a large horned owl perched on a branch on one side and an agitated ape screaming at a seated wolf on the other. Below the ape is a bird apparently falling earthward. Base marks: ROOKWOOD in block letters, date, shape number 85, G for ginger clay, and the artist's last name, "Cranch," in block letters. 6.5" h. *Courtesy of Mark Mussio, Cincinnati Art Galleries, LLC.*

While Rookwood was producing art pottery in the late nineteenth and early twentieth centuries, the firm tried at times to reach more rural communities and less affluent folk, people the company believed to have lesser means but cultivated tastes nonetheless. In the 1880s, Rookwood would sell less-than-perfect ceramics in small towns, rural communities, Women's Exchanges, and vacation spots for significantly lower prices than their wares that were free of flaws and imperfections. This practice was dropped in the 1890s.

Figure 54. *The Rookwood Book*, a catalog produced by Rookwood Pottery in 1904 to advertise the company's wares. This volume contains thirty-four pages of color and black and white photos of ceramics and price listings. 7" x 5.5". *Courtesy of Mark Mussio, Cincinnati Art Galleries, LLC.*

Figure 53. While this vase was made far later than the period currently under discussion, it is an example of a company "second," a less-than-perfect item, as indicated by a wheel-ground X on the base of the vase. In the 1880s, Rookwood would sell less-than-perfect ceramics in small towns, rural communities, Women's Exchanges, and vacation spots for significantly lower prices than their wares that were free of flaws and imperfections. This second is a Red high glaze vase, with drips of blue, red, and tan at the rim. Base marks: flames mark, date, shape 6197F, and the wheel-ground X. The second mark was probably applied for either a pinhead sized grinding chip or, possibly, an area where the drip was not entirely uniform. 5" h. *Courtesy of Mark Mussio, Cincinnati Art Galleries,*

By the 1890s, mail-order catalog sales were growing rapidly. Catalogs were seen as an easy way to reach those rural communities where stores were few and far between. Rookwood Pottery produced their catalog in 1904, *The Rookwood Book.* However, Rookwood's wares proved too expensive for most people living in rural or working-class communities.

At the turn of the twentieth century, the deep colors and highly reflective glazes of Rookwood's very popular Standard glaze line would no longer hold fascination for consumers. Critics and consumers alike turned away from these elegant, detailed wares. Following Gustav Stickley's lead, and reading his periodical *The Craftsman*, the public began to seek simpler forms, cleaner lines, less vibrant colors, simplified stylized designs, and less conspicuous mat glazes.

Figure 55. Back, left to right: The 1904 paperbound *The Rookwood Book* catalogue with color photographs of different lines; a c. 1915 pamphlet; and a 1930 pamphlet with a woodblock print on the cover. Front: a 1908 postcard with a view of Rookwood's Mount Eden factory site. *Courtesy of David Rago Auctions.*

As the first decades of the twentieth century rolled by, Rookwood Pottery was forced to turn increasingly away from hand-decorated, artist-signed art pottery forms to more economical artwares featuring colorful glazes and molded bodies (with molded or incised decoration) in shapes reflecting the art trends of the passing decades. The tastes and needs of their consumers were changing with the times.

Figure 56. As the first decades of the twentieth century rolled by, Rookwood Pottery was forced to turn increasingly away from hand-decorated, artist-signed art pottery forms to more economical artwares. This artware vase was produced in 1910 with hand-incised decoration around the shoulder. In time, this form of decoration would be replaced with decorations included in the structure of the mold and transferred to the ceramic body during the molding process. 6.25" h. *Courtesy of Bob Shores and Dale Jones.*

During the 1920s, America recovered from the effects of World War I, finding new and exciting diversions, entertainments, machinery, and nightclubs to pursue. Radios sold by the millions and brought the world home. Henry Ford made it possible to move out en masse into that world, once listeners' radio shows were finished. Prior to World War I, the automobile was unattainable by most. After the war, Ford's assembly line approach to auto manufacturing produced cars nearly everyone could afford. This new-found mobility would move people out of cities to newly established suburbs in droves, send them traveling back to town for shopping; movies featuring Charlie Chaplin, Buster Keaton, and Tom Mix; and to speakeasies.

During the Prohibition era from 1919 until the early 1930s, speakeasies attracted large crowds for music, dance, and illegal beer, gin, and whiskey. These were the "Roaring Twenties," and consumers were looking for artful ceramics that reflected the bright and exciting times they were living in.

However, factories in the "Roaring Twenties" had been producing goods in great volume, yet paying workers too little to make them good consumers. Farmers who had needed loans to keep up with record demands for crops during World War I were faced with declining needs for their produce in the 1920s and discovered they could not easily pay their debts. An extended drought in the American Midwest worsened their problems. Further, during the giddy years of the 1920s, many speculated in the New York stock market, seeking a quick and easy road to riches. By 1929, the economy slowed, the stock market crashed, and economic depression hit the nation hard. By 1932, twelve million Americans would be out of work. Thousands would lose their homes; millions would seek out charities for basic necessities.

Consumers were finding life difficult at best in the 1930s and pared back their expectations. An article in the trade journal *Ceramic Industry* dated May 1935 summed up the needs and desires of consumers during the Depression years.

Figure 57. With so much to do and so many different items available for purchase during the Roaring Twenties, consumers were looking for stylish objects at economical prices, such as this small artware (production) vase with a very white body. This piece now has molded flower decoration around the rim, rather than incised as was seen in the 1910 vase. This vase is marked with shape number 2111 and dates from 1922. 6.25" h. *Courtesy of Bob Shores and Dale Jones.*

Figure 58. Glaze Effect vase, dating from 1932, shows a gunmetal glaze dripped over a Coromandel glaze. Base marks: flames mark, date, shape 6326, and a wheel-ground X (indicating this item was an imperfect "second"), probably for two glazed-over chips on the base. 6.5" h. *Courtesy of Mark Mussio, Cincinnati Art Galleries, LLC.*

The article stated that the depressed economy created a "drab atmosphere" that housewives sought to relieve with bright and cheerful color schemes for the home, including lively art pottery and artware for inspiration in soft pastel shades that would emulate the drapes and furniture home decorators were promoting.

Figure 59. Unusual, lively yellow tinted high glaze porcelain vase decorated with green flowers having blue centers and long leafy stems, all done with slip trailing by Elizabeth Barrett in 1935. Base marks: flames mark, date, shape number 904 D, and the artist's monogram in green slip. *Courtesy of Mark Mussio, Cincinnati Art Galleries, LLC.*

Figure 61. Vase thrown and decorated by Ruben Earl Menzel in 1952, adorned with morning glories and butterflies around the vase under a green-tinted high glaze. Base marks: flames mark, date, an S for Special shape, the artist's "whorl" and his incised initials as a decorator. Menzel was both a master potter who "threw" clay and a decorator at the Pottery. 7" h. *Courtesy of Mark Mussio, Cincinnati Art Galleries, LLC.*

Having weathered the Depression, Rookwood Pottery would continue to produce a range of artwares, including decorative wares, bookends, figurines, and paperweights, designed to keep up with the public tastes of the times right on through the 1940s, 1950s, and into the 1960s.

Figure 62. Porcelain vase carved with a Greek key pattern under a glossy brown glaze by Ruben E. Menzel, dated 1961. Base marks: flames mark, date, and the artist's initials. 6" x 4". *Courtesy of David Rago Auctions.*

Figure 60. Interesting vase painted by Margaret Helen McDonald in 1942, featuring white poppies with reddish brown centers and brown and green leaves and stems in a watercolor-style on a high glaze green to yellow ground. Base marks: flames mark, date, shape 1126C, and the artist's initials painted in green slip. 9.25" h. *Courtesy of Mark Mussio, Cincinnati Art Galleries, LLC.*

Chapter One

Rookwood Pottery
of the Nineteenth Century

The State of the Industry in 1880

When Maria Longworth Nichols opened Rookwood Pottery in 1880, there were eight hundred potteries manufacturing a wide assortment of ceramics across the United States. Collectively, these firms employed thousands of artists and laborers. Many of these ceramists had worked previously for well-known British potteries in England's Staffordshire potting district. In Cincinnati alone in that year, there were roughly thirty active firms. It is also safe to say that the vast majority of these operations were owned by men.

Figure 63. Early 1882 pitcher, incised with the initials C.B.F. (ostensibly for the pot's owner), decorated with a lion, goats, and a bison in black on an ivory ground. Base marks: "ROOKWOOD 1882" and the initials "FCE." 8" x 5". *Courtesy of David Rago Auctions.*

Additionally, most pottery manufactories in Cincinnati were producing wares entirely unlike Nichols's art pottery. Most of the city's potteries were making practical, no-non-

sense molded utilitarian wares ranging from bowls, basins, and spittoons, to bottles, mugs, and tea or coffee pots. Since colonial days, consumers had turned to Britain for their refined, quality ceramics, especially to the wares of Staffordshire. The British government had discouraged all competition and left potters in the colonies with little to make except simple, useful pots best suited for the kitchen or the barn. In fact, even in the nineteenth century, American consumers were biased against the homegrown talent, many still firmly believing the best products came from Staffordshire.

The 1876 Philadelphia Centennial Exhibition, a gathering of talented manufacturers from the United States and abroad exhibiting their best wares to the general public, had been considered by ceramists in the United States as their first big chance to change that belief. Thwarting the opinion that American wares were inferior by nature was one of the many challenges to face a fledgling Rookwood Pottery.

In an article in *Harper's New Monthly Magazine* from 1881, the author, F.E. Fryatt, asserted that by 1877 British ceramists were truly concerned about the state of American pottery manufacturing. According to Fryatt, the powerful potteries of Staffordshire were on the verge of losing their long, historical grip on the American market to American potters. While no doubt somewhat biased in this cause, Fryatt asserted, "A ... prominent potter declared [at a meeting of a British board of arbitration in Hanley, England] that the States not only have all the requisite materials, but they are superior to those used in Staffordshire; that as for the quality of their wares, he wished he could make as good ..." Further, Fryatt reported, "Other speakers, referring to the superiority of American wares, confessed they experienced great difficulty in retaining their trade in that quarter, prophesying that 'at the present rate of progress in the United States, in ten years English crockery would find no market there at all'." (Fryatt 1881, 357-370) While this reporting proved a bit optimistic on the author's part, potteries in the United States had indeed made significant inroads into the once nearly exclusive British trade in quality ceramics. Certainly, by 1887, Rookwood was establishing a strong name for itself as a studio creating fine art pottery.

Indeed, one of the major obstacles facing potters in the United States in decades past and during the colonial period was lack of easy and reliable access to the ready supply of raw materials available to them. By 1880, well-established river, canal, and rail systems had eliminated this particular barrier to quality ceramics production. Ohio alone had abundant supplies of clay and natural gas ready to be utilized by those who could reach them. In 1880, Ohio was poised on the brink of the birth of a lively art pottery industry, a state soon to be the home of significant art potteries producing wares sold in shops across the nation and purchased as wedding gifts and presents for special occasions. Such art pottery objects would go far to dispel the entrenched myth that Americans could not create quality ceramics.

Also by 1880, employment opportunities for women were expanding. Modern inventions, including prepared foods and sewing machines, were freeing women's time for pursuits outside the home. Their influence on the art pottery market as decorators would be at least as significant as their influence on that market as consumers. Rookwood Pottery would have its share of women decorators who rose to the status of much respected, widely recognized professional artists.

Methods of Manufacture in 1880

Before proceeding with the history of Rookwood Pottery in its earliest decades, it will be useful to review manufacturing techniques employed by nineteenth century ceramists at the time Maria L. Nichols was establishing her pottery, in order to gain an appreciation of the many operations involved in successfully producing pottery in the 1880s. F.E. Fryatt reported in detail on the process in an 1881 article, "Pottery in the United States." Here are the highlights from that article.

The tour begins in the mill-room, where quartz and feldspar are crushed to a fine powder beneath the weight of large, rotating iron cylinders. The room is filled with noise and cracking stone. After several steps, the crushed stone is ready to be added to clay for strength.

Meanwhile, in the slip room, clay, quartz, feldspar, and water swirl in large, half-filled wooden cisterns to create the slip that will be used to form ceramic bodies or, when appropriately tinted, to decorate their surfaces. The slip is filtered down through silk to remove impurities. Once properly filtered, to form clay slabs rather than liquid slip, the slip is dried with heat or pressure, removing excess water and leaving a doughy clay mass behind.

From there, clay moves to a large room where "wedgers" and "throwers" wait with boys or girls to assist them. Wedgers cut and pound the clay, removing air from the mass in preparation for throwing or molding. Throwers attending potter's wheels take the prepared clay, throw it on the wheel, and form hollowware items (vases, pitchers, bottles, jars, bowls, and all other circular forms) by hand. By 1880, the American invention of the steam driven wheel had increased the productivity of the thrower. During the 1880s, this wheel work would be central to Rookwood's operation.

Molded wares could also be produced on the wheel when a uniform shape was desired. A plaster mold was secured into a metal top known as a "jigger-head." As an example, to produce a cup, a clay lump was thrown into the cup-shaped recess in the mold and the wheel was set in motion. As the mold revolved, gentle pressure from a sure hand conformed the clay to the mold's walls, quickly creating both the interior and exterior form of the cup. Removed

from the mold, the cup was taken to the storeroom to set up to a leather hard consistency.

A single thrower and his assistant could produce fifty or sixty dozen such cups a day. In an improvement on this method, a piece of steel cut to the shape of the cup's interior came to replace the thrower's hand when forming the cup's interior and increased production by that thrower to one hundred dozen cups daily.

In the same room, plates were formed using a mold in the shape of the plate's interior. Clay was placed over the mold, trimmed to the mold's edge, and spun on the wheel. As it spun, a "profile" tool cut to the shape of the plate's exterior profile was gently applied to the turning clay, smoothing its surface to the appropriate shape.

In the mold room, slabs of clay were pressed into the two halves of a plaster mold. Once the clay fit snugly into all the contours of both halves of the mold, the two halves were joined. Excess clay compressed through the joint was trimmed away and the plaster rapidly absorbed the clay's excess moisture. As the clay dried, it shrank and was easily removed from the mold when the time came. (In later years, liquid slip would be applied to plaster molds. Liquid slip filled the molds and was allowed to set for a predetermined length of time. As it set, the clay closest to the plaster mold walls would dry first. The longer the slip was allowed to set up in the mold, the thicker those clay walls would become. When enough time had elapsed, the excess liquid slip was drained from the mold's center and what remained was the clay vessel conformed to the shape of the mold.) Once removed from the molds, damp cloths were used to remove seam lines and handles were attached. Then the "green" wares were moved to drying racks to await kiln firing.

Young men carried boards and trays filled with ware to the kiln rooms for firing. In the kiln room, groups of men carefully arranged the ware in various "saggars," protective clay boxes that kept the wares from direct contact with the kiln's flames, fumes, and smoke. Once filled, the saggars were stacked in tall columns within the fifty-foot high interior of the kiln. Small spaces were left between the columns to allow heat to flow evenly.

Once the kiln was filled, or "charged," and the crevices in the saggars sealed with fire clay, the kiln's large iron door was closed and sealed with clay and fires were lit in the surrounding furnaces. Great care was required in the firing to ensure the clay bodies fully contracted during the firing process. If they did not, the fired bodies would shrink further later on as water remaining within the improperly fired clay slowly dissipated. The hard glaze coat overlying such a shrinking body could not contract with it and would crack. These cracks in the glaze coat formed a web of spidery lines known as "crazing." During kiln firing, several men would remain with the kiln throughout the night to keep feeding the fires to maintain a steady heat.

Once the firing was complete and the kiln cooled, many hours later (the article reported fifty hours were required for the firing and forty for cooling), young men with ladders reentered the kilns and removed the saggars, passing those closest to the kiln ceiling down to other men waiting to carry them away. Removed from the saggars, the fired "biscuit" was carried away by boys and girls to the decorating department.

Artists awaited in the decorating department, men and women who would apply painted, printed, enameled, or banded decorations to the fired wares. Of hand-painted decoration, the author stated, "And here are some flowers very gracefully and freely painted by hand. One can say little, however, about coloring, for tints shown at the present stage are in no way indicative of what they will be after they pass the ordeal of the enamel kiln." (Fryatt 1881, 368)

Once decorated, a glaze coating was applied as previously described in the Introduction, and the decorated ware was fired again at a lower temperature to melt the glaze to the body of the ware. Of the finished product, Fryatt would say, "Here come two or three trays loaded with completed wares ... [they are] wonderfully well defined, considering the intense heat in which not less than half the pieces are destroyed." (Fryatt 1881, 369)

That was the state of the ceramics industry when Maria Nichols fired her first kiln in the winter of 1880.

Figure 64. Perfume jug decorated in the Limoges style by an unknown artist in 1884. The jug is decorated with a swallow flying above Oriental-style foliage against a deep blue sky. Fired-on gold accents the piece. Base marks: ROOKWOOD in block letters, the date, shape 61, and an impressed G for ginger clay. 4.75" h. *Courtesy of Mark Mussio, Cincinnati Art Galleries, LLC.*

Rookwood Pottery in the 1880s

Maria Longworth Nichols's Background

Maria Longworth was born in Cincinnati, Ohio, on March 20, 1849. Maria's father, John Longworth, was a wealthy man, the inheritor of his father's (Nicholas Longworth's) fortune, which had been made in real estate. John Longworth expanded the family's land holdings, was considered an eminent citizen of Cincinnati, and was a patron of the fine arts.

Maria Longworth married Colonel George Ward Nichols in the late 1860s at the age of nineteen. The Colonel was a respected Civil War veteran and would become the president and general manager of Cincinnati's College of Music. Together the couple had two children, Joseph Longworth and Margaret Rives.

Maria L. Nichols began her exploration of china painting in 1873.

Before Opening Rookwood

Women with a passion for china decoration spurred on America's early ceramics art movement. Writing in *The New England Magazine*, Edwin AtLee Barber traced the movement's origins, "After the war [American Civil War], when travel was again resumed, American women who visited Europe found that painting on china was a fashionable diversion ..." Seeking instruction in the art of china decoration, these women turned to Edward Lycett, an émigré from England who had worked for the British pottery firm Copeland & Garrett before setting up shop in association with other artists with a decorating kiln on Green Street in New York City in 1861. In Barber's estimation, Lycett's shop was the "... only place where painting of the finer kind was being done as a regular business ..." in the United States and he drew a prestigious list of pupils from among the wealthy, prominent ladies of the day. Barber states, "Some of these students afterwards became prominent as artists, and among Mr. Lycett's pupils have been daughters of many eminent public men, including two presidents of the United States, and a large number of women who later achieved distinction as leaders in ceramic associations in various parts of the country." (Barber 1895, 40)

Mr. Lycett even had a passing association with Maria Longworth Nichols and her first husband, George W. Nichols. Maria Nichols sent a number of her early decorating experiments to Lycett's Green Street kilns for firing. Her husband accompanied the wares to the kilns, observing the process, taking copious notes, and drawing the various steps in kiln firing. The information George Nichols gathered, he later published in his book, *Pottery and How it is Made*.

Two years after beginning her study of ceramic decoration in earnest in 1873, Maria L. Nichols would be associated with the activities of the Women's Centennial Executive Committee of Cincinnati. The purpose of the committee was to ensure that china painting produced by women would be on display at the 1876 Philadelphia Centennial Exhibition, a world's fair coupled with the nation's Centennial celebration. This committee was one of many women's committees across the nation holding art exhibitions, bazaars, concerts, and tea balls to raise funds for the forthcoming Exhibition. Despite hard economic times, these determined women raised over $100,000. Their efforts were two-fold, to see women's accomplishments had a place at the Centennial and to ensure that the works of foreign nations were well represented for the edification of what they felt was a somewhat provincial American public. These ladies were so effective at obtaining foreign exhibitors that they lost their own exhibition space in the Main Building on the Centennial fairgrounds. Undaunted, the Women's Centennial Executive Committee built their own pavilion on the fairgrounds. Within the Women's Pavilion, the first of its kind at any world's fair, roughly six hundred exhibits displayed women's contributions to many fields ranging from the arts to science.

In May 1875, the Cincinnati branch of the Women's Centennial Executive Committee held an "International Entertainment" as a fund raiser. The Centennial Committee invited local women prominent in china painting to decorate wares provided and fired by the Committee. Among the ladies whose decorated wares were displayed were:

Mrs. Maria L. Nichols, Miss M.L. McLaughlin, Mrs. S.S. Fisher, Miss Clara Fletcher, Mrs. L.B. Harrison, Mrs. William Hinkle, Mrs. E.G. Leonard, Miss Lincoln, Mrs. A.B. Merriam, Mrs. Richard Mitchell, Miss Clara Newton, Miss Rauchfuss, and Miss Schooley (Perry 1881, 834)

The hand-painted china displayed at the 1875 International Entertainment was sold after the exhibition at auction. During the auction, thirty-five cups and saucers were sold. The highest bid placed on a single decorated cup and saucer was twenty-five dollars. The auction raised a total of $385 for the Centennial Exhibition. Aside from the fund-raising aspect of the International Entertainment, Mrs. Aaron Perry, writing in 1881, would see deeper significance and portents in the wares displayed in Cincinnati, "...the exhibit in 1875 was a suggestion of suitable work for women, and also of a future of commercial importance for Cincinnati as a center of activity in pottery work." (Perry 1881, 844)

At least two women from that list were present in Philadelphia for the Centennial Exhibition. During Maria L. Nichols's trip to Philadelphia in 1876, she was inspired by the Japanese exhibit, finding their decorating techniques and motifs captivating. So enamored with Japanese decoration was Nichols that she briefly entertained the idea of moving a Japanese pottery works, complete with workers, to Cincinnati. Mary Louise McLaughlin was entranced by the display of the French Haviland Limoges. She would spend the years 1877-1878 and significant sums of money experimenting with underglaze decoration techniques comparable to those of Limoges. Once perfected, McLaughlin's technique was dubbed "Cincinnati Limoges." Based on her work, Mary L. McLaughlin wrote *China Painting: A Practical Manual for the Use of Amateurs in the Decoration of Hard Porcelain*. Given the fascination of the day with china painting, the book sold 23,000 copies.

In the spring of 1879, McLaughlin established the Cincinnati Pottery Club. She invited a number of women pas-

sionate in china decoration to join and share in her underglaze decorating technique. The Pottery Club took up residence in a room in the Frederick Dallas pottery works. Frederick Dallas employees, Joseph Bailey, Senior, and his son Joseph, Junior, had assisted Mary McLaughlin with many tips of the trade during her years of experimentation with underglaze decoration.

In the May 1881 *Harper's New Monthly Magazine* article, "Decorative Pottery of Cincinnati," the women involved in the art pottery movement were described,

Interest in this part of the country is not confined to Cincinnati, but to some extent pervades the towns and cities of Ohio generally. Ladies from Dayton, Hillsborough, and more distant points come here for lessons, send to the potteries for clay and "biscuit" ware, and return their decorated work for firing and glazing. Decorated work is sent here to be fired from New York, Iowa, Kentucky, Michigan, Minnesota, and Indiana. The number of amateurs in the city alone whose work is fired at the pottery of F. Dallas is more than two hundred, and of this large number all but two are women.

It is curious to see the wide range of age and conditions of life embraced in the ranks of the decorators of pottery: young girls twelve to fifteen years of age find a few hours a week from their school engagements to devote to over or underglaze work, or the modeling of clay; and from this up, through all the less certain ages, till the grandmother stands confessed in cap and spectacles, no time of life is exempt from the fascinating contagion. Women who need to add to their income, and the representatives of the largest fortunes, are among the most industrious workers; and it is pleasant to know that numbers of these self-taught women receive a handsome sum annually from orders for work, from sales, and from lessons to pupils. (Perry 1881, 842-3)

The club membership, established with twelve active and three honorary membership positions, included:

Miss Mary Louise McLaughlin, president; Miss Clara C. Newton, secretary; Miss Alice B. Holabird, treasurer; Mrs. E.G. Leonard; Mrs. Charles Kebler; Mrs. George Dominick; Mrs. Walter Field; Miss Florence Carlisle; Miss Agnes Pitman; Miss Fannie M. Banks; Mrs. Andrew B. Merriam; one vacancy; honorary members: Mrs. M.V. Keenan; Miss Laura Fry; Miss Elizabeth Nourse. (Perry 1881, 836)

Conspicuous in her absence was Maria Longworth Nichols. Some say Nichols was snubbed by McLaughlin as a rival; others state Nichols's invitation to the Pottery

Club was lost. Under the circumstances, the recording of "one vacancy" in the list above is interesting. That vacancy would remain unfilled for the eleven years of the Pottery Club's existence. Regardless, Nichols also established herself, along with Mrs. William Dodd, in another room in Frederick Dallas's pottery works. Consequently, by late 1879, the Dallas works constructed two new kilns, one for firing ceramics with underglaze decoration and the other for overglaze decorations. The cost for the kilns was borne by McLaughlin and Nichols. Writing of the work of Dodd and Nichols, Perry states, "[they] practice every style of work on 'green' and 'biscuit' ware, from incised design as delicate as the spider's web, to Cincinnati faience, and relief work in clay so bold that one is tempted to reach forth her hand and take the bird from the bough." Speaking of Nichols's ceramics and abilities, Perry added, "...for her talents enable her to throw off work with uncommon rapidity. Among her pieces, during the last year, has been a succession of vases, each some thirty inches high. The body is of Rockingham in some cases, in others a mixture of Rockingham and white pastes, giving a soft buff color in some pieces, in others a rich cream. ... Other pieces by Mrs. Nichols are in fine-grained red clays of Ohio, decorated in incised and relief work, and an illumination of dead gold; surface finish with semi-glaze; also in a mixture of blue and yellow clays, producing charming tints of sage green, blue-gray, etc." (Perry 1881, 837)

That brings the story up to 1880.

Of Small Beginnings and Rapid Ascents

John Longworth purchased a Cincinnati schoolhouse beside the Ohio River for his daughter Maria in 1880 to be used as her first pottery works. Maria Nichols named the establishment Rookwood in tribute to her family's estate of the same name. Ever helpful, Joseph Bailey, Sr., from Frederick Dallas's pottery works, assisted in the purchase of equipment and materials for the operation. He also arranged for an outlet to sell the new Rookwood Pottery wares. Rookwood Pottery was ready for operation in September 1880 and fired their first kiln on Thanksgiving Day 1880.

The first wares from the kiln included utilitarian wares, art pottery, undecorated wares, and amateur work. In the tradition of other pottery works, Rookwood supplied undecorated shapes to amateur decorators and then fired their decorated wares.

With the death of Frederick Dallas in June 1881, and the closure of his pottery works, which had helped so many amateur ceramics decorators, Joseph Bailey, Sr., joined Rookwood. He brought with him a deep understanding of pottery manufacture that Maria L. Nichols lacked and was instrumental to the early success of the company.

Many fledgling pottery companies of the nineteenth century began with the production of practical, utilitarian ceramics useful around the house. During the company's first two years, Rookwood produced simple, sturdy gray or cream stoneware tableware in recognizable English forms decorated in transfer prints with motifs from Japanese books. This was a far cry from the original works of art Nichols foresaw her company producing and was a short-lived endeavor.

In September 1881, Maria Nichols hired her first full-time, trained decorator, the nineteen-year-old Albert Robert Valentien. Valentien was a native of Cincinnati and had attended the University of Cincinnati's School of Design (later to become the Cincinnati Art Academy), beginning when he was thirteen.

Of his time with Rookwood, Valentien would later write, "I was the first regularly employed decorator ... and served in the capacity of chief decorator for the period of twenty-four years during which time I originated and developed many of the chief effects which have made that institution famous throughout the world." (Kamerling 1978, p. 2, par. 4)

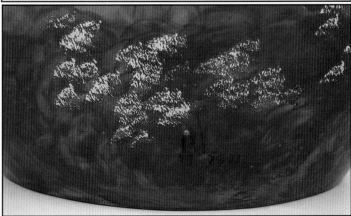

Figure 65. In September 1881, Maria Nichols hired her first full-time, trained decorator, the nineteen-year-old Albert Robert Valentien. Two years later, Valentien decorated this monumental floor vase in 1883. It is adorned with birds perched amidst branches of cherry blossoms in pink, green, and brown against a gold, green, and beige ground. Base marks: impressed Rookwood 1883, 243. The artist's initials and date are found on the side. 23.5" h. x 11" d. *Courtesy of Bob Shores and Dale Jones.*

Figure 67. Early basket-shaped sugar bowl and creamer with pierced rims painted in the Limoges style by Nicholas Joseph Hirschfeld, who worked for Rookwood from 1882-1883. These pieces are adorned with bats in flight and an owl on a branch. This is a very rare set. Base marks: incised artist's initials. Sugar bowl: 5" x 4.5". *Courtesy of David Rago Auctions.*

Figure 66. Rookwood's foremost painter of flora, Albert Valentien, produced a detailed rendition of the leaves and fruit of Ohio's state tree, the Buckeye, in Standard glaze. Base marks: Rookwood logo, the date, shape number 537 C, W for white clay, an incised L for light Standard glaze, and the incised initials of the artist. 14.5" h. *Courtesy of Mark Mussio, Cincinnati Art Galleries, LLC.*

Over the course of the next two years, Nichols hired another seven decorators, including Laura Fry who, in 1883, would develop the technique for applying colored slips using an atomizer as discussed in the Introduction. All seven had received some instruction from Cincinnati's School of Design. As all of these decorators were essentially well-educated amateurs, and all were contending with both limitations on kiln space and raw materials, the early end results were primitive and experimental. Nichols imposed no decorative dictates on these talented artists and there was much experimentation with decorative styles, clays, colors, and glazes. However, from the beginning the design emphasis was on surface decoration.

Figure 68. Another example of an early Rookwood plate decorated in the Japanese style in 1882 with an artful branch of flowers. The second item, to the left, is a Standard glaze footed covered jar decorated by Mary Perkins with branches of holly in 1896. Plate: 7.75" in diameter; covered jar: 4" in diameter; *Courtesy of David Rago Auctions.*

The decorators would receive specific ceramic bodies and were challenged to create surface decorations to fit the forms. The bodies themselves remained relatively simple in form; even the early wheel thrown bodies were rarely altered to change their shape after they were thrown. Following the trend of the Victorian age, Rookwood decorators and throwers turned toward the classics for designs and forms. European and Asian body shapes were used. Decorative motifs from Japan, England, France, and Germany were employed, taken from every handy source including photos and sketches.

During the 1880s, Rookwood decorators also made use of gold and platinum gilt. This gilt served two purposes, to impart a certain impression of luxury to the wares and to hide defects in the pots.

As Joseph Bailey, Sr., was hired to provide the deep knowledge of pottery manufacture Nichols lacked, her friend William Watts Taylor, hired in June of 1883, provided the knowledge of business management Nichols needed. Discovering an amazing paucity of record keeping, Taylor quickly established a Shape Record Book to record, for the first time, the shapes and decorations the company utilized. Included in this reference were the source for a shape design employed, its method of manufacture (thrown, jiggered, cast, pressed, or molded), the method of decoration as well as the decoration itself, dimensions, size, shape, and number of pieces sold, at what time, and to whom. It is worth noting that in 1883 when the Shape Record Book was established, quite a bit of the pottery produced was not thrown by hand. While this defied the purer ideals of the Arts and Crafts Movement, the mold formed vessels saved time and money and provided a more uniform canvas for the real art, the hand-painted decoration. The Shape Record Books remain an invaluable source of information on the Pottery.

Figure 70. Early Limoges style pillow vase decorated by Albert Humphries in 1882, decorated with a scene of a quail hiding in some tall grasses with billowy white clouds in the sky. Four curved feet support the vase. Base marks: Rookwood in block letters, the date, an impressed anchor mark, and the incised artist's initials. 8" h. *Courtesy of Mark Mussio, Cincinnati Art Galleries, LLC.*

Figure 71. Limoges style pilgrim flask decorated by Maria Longworth Nichols, circa 1882. It is distinctively decorated with red flowers, gold crescent moons, and smiling suns. Base marks: shape number 85, a W for white clay, and the artist's initials. *Courtesy of Mark Mussio, Cincinnati Art Galleries, LLC.*

Figure 69. Rare and early Limoges style six-sided vase (shape 23) signed by both Albert Valentien and Albert Humphreys in 1882. The decoration consists of sprigs of evergreen, clouds, a single dragonfly and four small children playing on the ground. Base mark: "Rookwood 1882" in block letters along with the impressed anchor mark and the incised initials of both Valentien and Humphreys. 7" h. Very few Rookwood pieces benefit from the collaborative efforts of two talented artists. *Courtesy of Mark Mussio, Cincinnati Art Galleries, LLC.*

Figure 72. Limoges style bowl decorated with detailed bamboo and a single butterfly by Albert Valentien in 1882. Clouds dot the sky behind the bamboo and fired on gold is used to enhance the exterior. Base marks: Rookwood in block letters, the date, shape number 121, G for ginger clay, and the incised artist's initials. 4" h. x 9" in diameter. *Courtesy of Mark Mussio, Cincinnati Art Galleries, LLC.*

Figure 73. Early carved ewer, decorated with stylized flowers and designs by Harriet Wenderoth in 1882 and covered in a green high glaze. Base marks: ROOKWOOD in block letters, the date, shape number 101, an S for sage green clay, and the artist's incised initials. 11.5" h. *Courtesy of Mark Mussio, Cincinnati Art Galleries, LLC.*

By 1884, Taylor had taken another significant step in company organization. Taylor divided the company's output into three glaze lines, Ivory/Cameo, Dull Finish, and Standard. The products created in Rookwood's early years either fit into one of these three lines or were quickly dropped. Of the three lines, Standard was held in highest esteem as the most artistic. Within that Standard glaze line would develop Mahogany, and the future award winning Tiger Eye and Goldstone lines.

With the company's records in order and glaze lines organized, Taylor turned his attentions to establishing Rookwood's reputation as a producer of one-of-a-kind works of art.

Figure 74. Cameo covered butter dish painted by Artus Van Briggle in 1887. This butter dish is decorated with white roses on a blue and pink ground. It is complete, including a pierced interior tray for the butter. This is a rare piece. Base marks: flames mark, the shape number 892W, the artist's initials, and "77." 3.5" x 5". *Courtesy of David Rago Auctions.*

Figure 75. Dull Finish perfume jug decorated with brown daisies and accented with fired on gold. Incised into the surface of the vase is the inscription "P.B. Moulton, CCC, Oct. 13th 1883," indicating that this was a souvenir from an activity sponsored by the Cincinnati Commercial Club. Base marks: ROOKWOOD in block letters, the date, shape number 61, the letter "c," and a kiln mark. 4" h. *Courtesy of Mark Mussio, Cincinnati Art Galleries, LLC.*

Figure 76. Standard glaze jar (with a missing lid) decorated in 1888 by Amelia Sprague. It is decorated with stylized flowers on a two-colored background. Base marks: flames mark, shape number 399, an impressed W for white clay, an incised L for Light Standard glaze, and the artist's incised initials. 4.5" h. *Courtesy of Mark Mussio, Cincinnati Art Galleries, LLC.*

Of Amateurs, Schools, and the Pottery Club

In the early years, Maria Nichols established the Rookwood Pottery School to help support the Pottery and cultivate new decorators for the company. She charged a childhood friend, Clara Newton, and a Rookwood decorator, Laura Fry, with teaching the students. The school charged each student three dollars a week tuition or one dollar an hour for private lessons. The school drew students from as far off as Chicago and Pittsburgh.

In another early development, when Rookwood added extra space to the facility, the Cincinnati Pottery Club rented a portion of it and moved in. Between the Pottery Club and the amateurs' work, all using undecorated vessels identified as Rookwood product, confusion developed over who had decorated what. For a company attempting to establish an identifiable name and reputation, this quickly became an unwanted distraction.

Ever concerned with organization and the company's reputation, William Watts Taylor grew disturbed about the disruptive presence of the school's amateur students and the Pottery Club. He came to see Mary Louise McLaughlin as a potential rival to Maria L. Nichols and her work in art pottery. Pointing out that the students of the school were not becoming decorators at Rookwood and were merely a financial drain on the company, Taylor recommended the school be closed and the Pottery Club evicted. In 1885, Taylor's recommendations were implemented and amateurs were removed from Rookwood Pottery.

Figure 77. Large perfume jug from 1882 decorated by Katharine de Golter, a member of the Cincinnati Pottery Club, in mat chocolate brown with incised, gold decoration of leaves, berries, and stems, some inside a circle or a square, and additional decoration of an esoteric symbol and the letter "B." Base marks: ROOKWOOD in block letters, the 1882 date, an R for red clay, and the artist's incised initials. 9" h. *Courtesy of Mark Mussio, Cincinnati Art Galleries, LLC.*

Figure 78. Large Limoges style Chinese lantern vase decorated with birds in flight, birds perched on a snow covered bush, and berry laden branches, in 1882 by either Maria Longworth Nichols or Clara Belle Fletcher, a member of the Pottery Club. This piece created the confusion of attribution that William Taylor sought to avoid. The vase is marked Rookwood in block letters on the base, along with the date and with a small paper label which reads "Miss Fletcher." This vase is decorated in Maria Nichols' style, especially in the berry-laden branch, the snow covered bush, and the black collar and foot; however, there is that label, which suggests Clara Belle Fletcher may have decorated this piece in Nichols' style. Who actually decorated this piece may never be known. *Courtesy of Mark Mussio, Cincinnati Art Galleries, LLC.*

By the mid-1880s, with Ivory/Cameo, Dull Finish, Standard, Tiger Eye, and Goldstone glaze lines on the market, Rookwood Pottery was establishing itself as a producer of luxury art pottery. They were setting a standard others would follow in years to come.

Most of the company's early decorators did not remain long with the firm. All but Albert Valentien and Laura Fry were gone by 1884. Fry herself would not remain much longer. To fill the voids, William Taylor hired Anna Marie Bookprinter, Matthew Andrew Daly, and William Purcell McDonald in 1884. All of these decorators would become very well known for their work. Anna Marie Bookprinter, another Cincinnati native, had been educated in art at McMichen University's School of Design. Beginning work in October 1884, she would marry Albert Valentien on June 1, 1887. In this, she and Albert set a trend, with more romances and marriages among the staff to come.

In 1885, Maria L. Nichols was widowed. In 1886, she married Bellamy Storer, Jr., a Cincinnati lawyer and politician. With her second marriage, Maria changed her name last name to Storer and gradually shifted her attentions from pottery production to her new husband's political career.

Figure 79. Early Standard glaze pitcher cast in 1887 and decorated by Anna Marie Bookprinter with Oriental-style cherry blossoms and branches. Base marks: flames mark, shape number 220, an impressed W7 for a type of white clay, and the artist's signature. 6" h. *Courtesy of Mark Mussio, Cincinnati Art Galleries, LLC.*

Figure 80. Small Standard glaze jardiniere decorated by Matthew Daly in 1887 in apple blossoms. Base marks: flames mark, shape number 131, impressed R for red clay, incised D for Dark Standard glaze, and the artist's initials. 5" h. *Courtesy of Mark Mussio, Cincinnati Art Galleries, LLC.*

In May of 1887, the Pottery, always enamored with Japanese motifs, hired native Japanese design talent. Born in Tokyo, Kataro Shirayamadani was a skilled porcelain painter who had been working in Boston for the Fujiyama import retail and decorating shop when Rookwood hired him. In 1886, Maria Nichols had met Shirayamadani at the Thirteenth Cincinnati Industrial Exposition, where he had been part of a Japanese contingent sent by his government to build interest in trade between the nations. Shirayamadani's work was different from most other decorators of the day. He preferred to cover the entire surface of a vessel with his designs, rather than confining them mostly to the front of an object as was common practice. By October 1887, examples of Shirayamadani's artistry were on display with other Rookwood wares at the Piedmont Exposition in Atlanta. In 1889, Shirayamadani's work would earn Rookwood a gold medal at the Exposition Universelle in Paris, greatly adding to the company's reputation. With the exception of a return to Japan from 1911 to 1921, Shirayamadani would remain with Rookwood until his death in 1948.

Figure 81. In May of 1887, the Pottery, enamored with Japanese motifs, hired native Japanese design talent, Kataro Shirayamadani. Tall Light Standard glaze vase painted by Kataro Shirayamadani with orange berries and green leaves, 1889. Base marks: flames mark, shape number 486A, the artist's Japanese signature, and L. 13.25" x 6.5". *Courtesy of David Rago Auctions.*

By the late 1880s, the standard method of decoration at Rookwood was set with slip painting. The method, first developed by Mary Louise McLaughlin and refined by Rookwood, was to be used to great effect. Seemingly endless slip-painted floral motifs decorating Rookwood wares received much praise and were eagerly sought. Other slip-painted subjects included animals, birds, fish, humans, and geometric designs.

To garner national, and international, attention, Taylor had Rookwood wares competing in regional, national, and international exhibitions, gave pieces to museums for display, and provided interviews for professional writers working with established publications.

International exhibitions (such as the previously mentioned Philadelphia Centennial Exhibition) were world's fairs where smart manufacturers went to check on their competition, learn about new decorative motifs and technological changes from around the globe, and compete for judged awards that would increase their standing with both their colleagues and the general public. Additionally, nowhere else during the nineteenth century could a manufacturer expect to have his or her wares so broadly viewed by such a large portion of the consuming public at one time. At the Philadelphia Centennial Exhibition, the trade journal *The Manufacturer and Builder* reported that monthly attendance ranged from around 70,000 to 140,000 people per day. (1876, 244) Many manufacturers took these exhibitions so seriously they created special traveling stock of their best wares to send from one exhibition to the next. Other exhibitors sold their wares at the end of an exhibition to turn a tidy

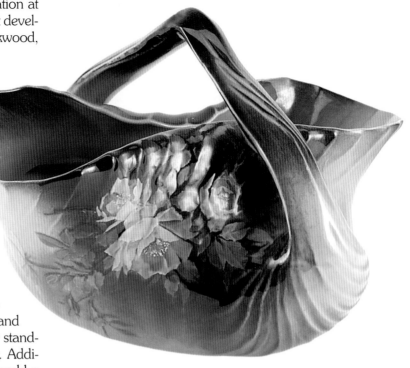

Figure 82. By the late 1880s, the standard method of decoration at Rookwood was set with slip painting. Light Standard glaze folded and fluted basket painted by Albert R. Valentien with striking slip painted yellow roses, 1889. Base mark: flames mark. 8" x 12.5". *Courtesy of David Rago Auctions.*

profit before departure. William Taylor made sure Rookwood Pottery had a presence at these affairs.

In 1887, Rookwood would receive special mention at the Twelfth Annual Exhibition of Paintings on China in London. In 1888, at Philadelphia's Pottery and Porcelain Exhibition, Rookwood was awarded first prize in the categories of modeled and decorated pottery and in underglaze decorated pottery. While other exhibitions were entered, the truly significant award came in 1889 at the Paris Exposition Universelle. There, in the face of strong competition, Rookwood, an American firm, won a gold medal for their wares. This award put the company on the map at home and abroad, assuring the firm of a strong future as a respected art pottery company.

Figure 83. Dull Finish potpourri jar with a reversible lid, decorated by Albert R. Valentien in 1886 with a bird flying past a branch. The rim and lid are accented with fired on gold. Base marks: ROOKWOOD in block letters, the date, shape number 277, an impressed Y for yellow clay, and the decorator's mark. *Courtesy of Mark Mussio, Cincinnati Art Galleries, LLC.*

Figure 84. Standard glaze pitcher with a pinched rim, decorated by Albert R. Valentien, 1889, featuring a praying Japanese elder in slip decoration that is perfectly rendered. 8" x 9". *Courtesy of David Rago Auctions.*

Rookwood and the Museums

As competition mounted among art pottery firms (and less expensive, commercial artwares began to cut into the market), Rookwood and other firms sought every advantage in building their reputations. Donating art pottery to the Smithsonian Institution was seen as a real opportunity to display wares to large numbers of potential consumers in a prestigious location.

As one might expect, the first pieces of art pottery received into the Smithsonian's collection came from the first and most successful of the art potteries, Rookwood. However, the original six Rookwood pieces came to the museum by an indirect route. Rather than the pottery firm donating the items directly, as many firms would, these came through the Women's Art Museum Association of Cincinnati. The Association traded the Rookwood art pottery wares, dating from 1885, for examples of Pueblo pottery from the Smithsonian's ethnology collection. The Pueblo pottery the Association acquired was donated to the Cincinnati Art Museum, established in 1881. In turn, the Cincinnati Art Museum was one source Rookwood decorators turned to for inspiration.

The Smithsonian Institution identifies Rookwood Pottery as the most famous of the late Victorian art potteries. Today, several Rookwood objects may be found on display in the Smithsonian's *Ceremonial Court.*

Edwin AtLee Barber purchased Rookwood ceramics for the Philadelphia Museum of Art as well. In recent years, collectors have added to Philadelphia's Rookwood collection. When visiting the Philadelphia Museum of Art, Rookwood art pottery is on view in Galleries 109 and 117, both in the American wing.

Closer to Rookwood's home, it is certainly no surprise that Rookwood art pottery may be found in the Cincinnati Wing of the Cincinnati Art Museum, along with the work of Mary McLaughlin and other local art potters. Examples of Rookwood's architectural ceramics will be found in The Fountain Room, including large wall plaques, mantels, and a working fountain.

During the 1880s, it became increasingly apparent that the location of the original Rookwood Pottery along the Ohio River and next to the crossing of the Little Miami Railroad at Eastern Avenue was less than ideal. At the best of times, this was a noisy, dirty place to work. In 1884, the Ohio River flooded, damaging the Pottery, bringing production to an expensive halt. In the 1890s, Rookwood Pottery moved to higher ground in a safer, quieter, more scenic location atop Mount Adams, overlooking downtown Cincinnati.

Rookwood's 1880s Objects

The following is a sampling of the various wares produced by Rookwood throughout the 1880s, organized by year and, within each year, by artist.

Figure 85. Early Dark Standard glaze baluster vase decorated by Albert R. Valentien with bright yellow mums and a flying wasp on a terra cotta ground, 1885. Base marks: stamped ROOKWOOD 1885, shape number 197D, and the artist's initials. 10.5" x 4.75". *Courtesy of David Rago Auctions.*

Figure 86. Early Dark Standard glaze lidded jar decorated by Albert R. Valentien with a turtle amidst blossoms, 1885. Back marks: stamped ROOKWOOD, 1885, artist's initials, and 47A. 9.5" x 6". *Courtesy of David Rago Auctions.*

Figure 87. Early Standard (Mahogany) glaze vase decorated by Albert R. Valentien in 1885 with crabs and lobster. Base marks: ROOKWOOD in block letters, the date, an impressed R for red clay, shape number 162 C, and the incised artist's initials. 8.5" h. *Courtesy of Mark Mussio, Cincinnati Art Galleries, LLC.*

Figure 88. Tall, early potpourri jar underglaze painted with a bird flying over bullrushes. Base marks: Rookwood, 1885, shape number 243, and W. 11" x 6". *Courtesy of David Rago Auctions.*

Figure 89. Early stoppered jug from 1885 decorated with white dogwood and star-shaped blossoms on a mottled indigo ground. Base marks: stamped ROOKWOOD 1885. 14" x 6.5". *Courtesy of David Rago Auctions.*

Figure 91. Early Standard glaze ridged three-corner pitcher painted by an unidentified artist with a stylized sun, 1886. Base marks: stamped ROOKWOOD, 1886, R, 259. 8.25" x 5.5". *Courtesy of David Rago Auctions.*

Figure 90. Early chocolate pot featuring glazed beige clay, 1885. Base marks: stamped ROOKWOOD, 1885, and 251. 8" x 6.5". *Courtesy of David Rago Auctions.*

Figure 92. Cameo glaze plate with a swirling pattern, decorated by Sallie Toohey in 1887 with a design of white roses on a branch. Base marks: flames mark, shape number 336, the designation W7, and the artist's cipher in black. 7" in diameter. *Courtesy of Mark Mussio, Cincinnati Art Galleries, LLC.*

Figure 93. Standard glaze vase decorated in 1887 by Albert Valentien, featuring whimsical yellow daisies on a well-shaded ground. Base marks: flames mark, shape number 330, an S for sage clay, an incised L for Light Standard glaze, and the artist's initials. 11.5" h. *Courtesy of Mark Mussio, Cincinnati Art Galleries, LLC.*

Figure 94. Gray Cameo glaze coffee pot and lid decorated by Anna Valentien in 1887 with blue morning glories accented with gold. Base marks: flames mark, shape number 251, impressed G for ginger clay, incised W for clear glaze, and the artist's signature. 8" h. *Courtesy of Mark Mussio, Cincinnati Art Galleries, LLC.*

Figure 96. Cameo glaze plate decorated by Amelia Sprague in 1888 with white mums on a cream-to-salmon background. Base marks: flames mark, shape number 386 B, impressed W for white clay, incised W for clear glaze, and the artist's incised initials. 8" in diameter. *Courtesy of Mark Mussio, Cincinnati Art Galleries, LLC.*

Figure 95. Dull Finish *ewer* decorated by an unknown artist, whose initials were "ME," in 1888, featuring white daisies with brown centers and accented with fired on gold. Base marks: flames mark, shape number 40 C, impressed W for white clay, artist's initials, and an S for smear glaze. 6.25" h. *Courtesy of Mark Mussio, Cincinnati Art Galleries, LLC.*

Figure 97. Imposing Light Standard glaze vase decorated in 1888 by Albert Valentien with stylized mums. Base marks: flames mark, shape number 339 B, impressed W for white clay, incised L for Light Standard glaze, and the artist's incised initials. 13" h. *Courtesy of Mark Mussio, Cincinnati Art Galleries, LLC.*

Figure 98. Impressive vase decorated by Albert R. Valentien in 1888 with prunus blossoms in pale blue against a medium blue ground with dark blue and gold passages of additional blossoms. Base marks: flames mark, shape number 180 C, W for white clay, incised S for smear (Dull Finish) glaze, and the artist's incised initials. 8" h. *Courtesy of Mark Mussio, Cincinnati Art Galleries, LLC.*

Figure 99. Commemorative commercial ware pitcher in a glossy, dark green glaze made in 1888 to honor the centennial of the founding of the City of Cincinnati, featuring the seals of the City and the State on either side. Base marks: early Rookwood symbol. 6.75" h. *Courtesy of Mark Mussio, Cincinnati Art Galleries, LLC.*

Figure 101. Light Standard glaze ewer decorated by Harriet Wilcox in 1889 with gooseberries. Base marks: flames mark. 8 1/2" h. *Courtesy of David Rago Auctions.*

Figure 100. Standard glaze pitcher decorated by Matt Daly in 1889 with bright green limes. Base marks: flames mark, special shape number S 843, impressed S for sage clay, incised L for Light Standard glaze, and the artist's initials. 11" h. *Courtesy of Mark Mussio, Cincinnati Art Galleries, LLC.*

Figure 102. Light Standard glaze chocolate pot decorated by Jeanette Swing in 1889 with golden chrysanthemum blossoms. Base marks: flames mark and the artist's initials. 9" x 6.5". *Courtesy of David Rago Auctions.*

Rookwood Pottery in the 1890s

As the new decade began, three significant events occurred at Rookwood within the first two years. Maria Longworth Storer had been disengaging herself from the business of Rookwood since her second marriage. She felt Rookwood Pottery was now strong enough to forge ahead without financial support from her family's wealth. Maria Storer presented her pottery company to William Taylor as a gift, leaving him to set the company's future course on his own.

Rookwood Pottery was incorporated as the Rookwood Pottery Company with William W. Taylor holding the positions of president and treasurer. Considering Rookwood Pottery now was held in international esteem, as proved by the gold medal from the 1889 Paris Exposition and French potters' instant imitation of the Rookwood Tiger Eye and Standard (christened "dark ware" by Taylor) glaze lines that had earned the award, the newly established board of directors felt it was time for a move to a bigger facility in a better neighborhood, away from railway lines and floods.

Figure 103. Monumental Standard glaze vase decorated by Matthew A. Daly in 1890 with dogwood flowers, stems, and leaves. Base marks: flames mark, shape number 393, W for white clay, incised L for Light Standard glaze, and the incised artist's initials. 25.5" h. *Courtesy of Mark Mussio, Cincinnati Art Galleries, LLC.*

Rookwood management worked hard to project the image that Rookwood Pottery produced handcrafted art in a studio setting in the best traditions of the Arts and Crafts Movement, as opposed to grinding out mass-produced shoddy wares in a factory setting. To that end, the new factory constructed in 1892 on the crest of Mount Adams in Eden Park was built in the English Tudor-revival style. This façade stated to all visitors (and there would be many) that here was a studio where craftsmen and women create art as in days of yore. An impressive display room was included in the facility and would soon do a brisk business.

The factory site was well located. Set close to Cincinnati's Art Academy and Art Museum, a close working relationship soon developed between the company and these esteemed organizations. William Taylor hired decorators graduating from the Academy and sent those de-signers to the museum searching for inspiration and de-signs. Set on fertile ground, a large flower garden was quickly grown on factory property, providing a quick reference source for designers. The decorators were sure to make good use of the gardens ... and the surrounding country-side ... as by the early 1890s alone over two hundred plants, both domestic and wild, had already been used in decoration at Rookwood.

Technological improvements came with the new factory. Three gas-fired kilns were installed, increasing Rookwood's production capacity significantly, allowing hundreds of pieces to be fired at once. With the new technology came a wave of innovation in wares and decorations, along with increases in quality control. The factory complex would be enlarged in 1899 and 1904 to keep up with consumer demands.

Figure 104. Two historical views of the Rookwood Pottery factory complex at Mount Adams in Cincinnati, Ohio, circa 1900. *Courtesy of the Library of Congress, Prints and Photographs Division, Detroit Publishing Company Collection.*

Figure 105. A very rare Rookwood white clay, unglazed souvenir shaped in the outline of a two-handled vase with the Rookwood conjoined flame logo on both sides. This rare souvenir was most likely made in 1891 for the upcoming opening of the new pottery building on Mt. Adams and given to visitors at the grand opening. 1.75" h. *Courtesy of Mark Mussio, Cincinnati Art Galleries, LLC.*

The 1890s would be a decade of growth for Rookwood. The company added thirty-seven additional decorators to the thirteen already working for the firm. Nine of the new decorators would remain with the company for over thirty years, including Lenore Asbury, Edward Timothy Hurley, Sara Sax, Carl Schmidt, and John Wareham.

During the 1880s, the company had been struggling to establish both a reputation and a market niche for itself. In the 1890s, Rookwood Pottery turned to standardization of its production processes to keep all those new decorators busy, to meet the rapidly growing demand for its wares, and to reduce costs at the same time. Over the course of the decade, Rookwood moved from hand thrown ceramics to molded forms. While throwing was not entirely abandoned, Rookwood had a growing list of retail agents and consumers seeking their more popular wares in large numbers. Although the company's advertisements continued to stress that Rookwood ceramics were handmade art pottery, more and more frequently the handcrafted aspect was limited to the decoration applied to artfully molded wares.

In another move to economize, Rookwood limited the body types (preferring white bodies) and glazes to reduce costs. Preferred glazes of the 1890s were transparent lead glazes that were easily tinted. Further economies were realized when decorative motifs were standardized. Flowers were to be painted in asymmetrical groupings on simple body forms to create the impression of informality in a Japanese style. This formulaic approach was nothing new; British potters had created a standard formula for their romantic views on transfer prints as early as the 1840s.

Figure 107. Iris glaze vase decorated by Edward T. Hurley in 1898 with large dogwood blossoms and stems. Base marks: flames mark, shape number 562, incised W for Iris glaze, the artist's incised initials, and a wheel-ground X. 9.5" h. *Courtesy of Mark Mussio, Cincinnati Art Galleries, LLC.*

Figure 106. Standard glaze sugar bowl decorated in 1896 by Lenore Asbury with wild roses climbing up and over the lid and down the opposite side. The bowl is embellished with butterfly handles and a butterfly finial. Base marks: flames mark, shape number 329, and the incised artist's initials. The lid is also initialed by Lenore Asbury. 4" h. *Courtesy of Mark Mussio, Cincinnati Art Galleries, LLC.*

Figure 108. Standard glaze two handled 1898 vase decorated by Carl Schmidt, depicting pretty yellow narcissus on a green to brown background. Base marks: flames mark, shape number 604E, and the artist's cipher. 5.75" h. *Courtesy of Mark Mussio, Cincinnati Art Galleries, LLC.*

Figure 109. Rare Standard glaze scenic vase painted in 1894 by John D. Wareham. The scene consists of the trunks of trees, bare in winter, silhouetted against an orange sky suggestive of sunset or sunrise, intermingled with highly detailed brush. Base marks: flames mark, shape number 749 C, W for white clay, an incised +, and the incised artist's monogram. 7" h. *Courtesy of Mark Mussio, Cincinnati Art Galleries, LLC.*

The Standard glaze line was Rookwood's major art pottery line of the 1890s. In the early 1890s, as the World's Columbian Exposition of 1893 in Chicago drew near, William Taylor sought ways to enrich the Standard line's appearance, making it more competitive at the Exposition. To that end, he worked out an arrangement with the Gorham Manufacturing Company. This Providence, Rhode Island, firm would provide silver overlay for Standard wares. William Taylor's confidence in Gorham was evident in the terms of the deal. Rookwood released all control over the Standard line wares sent to Gorham. Gorham applied silver decoration as they saw fit and shipped the finished wares off directly to Rookwood retail agents. The first Standard with silver overlay wares released appeared on the market in September 1892. While this experiment lasted a mere two years, it did provide some highly reflective Standard for the Columbian Exposition.

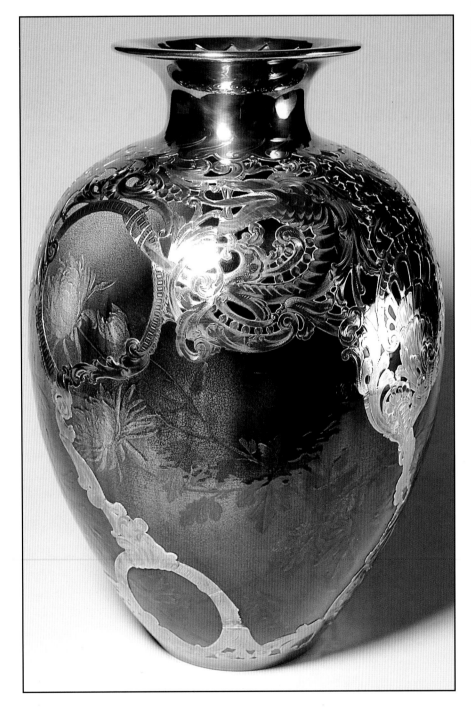

Figure 110. Monumental Rookwood Standard glaze vase with chrysanthemum decoration and lavish silver overlay by Gorham, produced in 1892. This is the largest silver overlay Rookwood vase that the Cincinnati Art Galleries had seen at the time of this writing. They speculate that it is possibly the largest existing American art pottery vase with silver overlay. Worked in with all the whirls and flourishes of silver are a large menacing dragon and a flying owl with an 8" wingspan. The silver completely encloses the collar and rim along with the foot, as well as most of the upper third of the vase. Base marks: flames mark, shape number 488 X, and an impressed W for white clay. The silver is engraved "R 751 Gorham Mfg. Co." where it curls under the foot. While no signature was found, Cincinnati Art Galleries states, "Only two artists, Albert Valentien and Kataro Shirayamadani, would have been allowed to work on such a large vessel, but the mark, which undoubtedly would have been on the side of the vase, may well be covered by the overlay." 24" h. *Courtesy of Mark Mussio, Cincinnati Art Galleries, LLC.*

Figure 111. Standard glaze vase decorated by John Dee Wareham, circa 1892, with spider mum. Silver overlay decoration was provided by Gorham. Base marks: flames mark, shape number 488 E, an impressed W for white clay, and the incised artist's monogram. The silver is marked "Gorham Mfg. Co. R 1361." 6" h. *Courtesy of Mark Mussio, Cincinnati Art Galleries, LLC.*

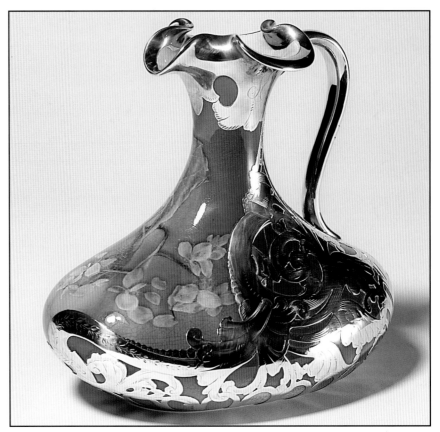

Figure 113. Flat-sided Standard glaze ewer with extensive leaf and flower decoration by Harriet Wilcox and equally extensive Gorham silver overlay, all done in 1893. Base marks: flames mark, shape number 684, W for white clay, and the artist's incised initials. The silver overlay is marked "R 1446 Gorham Mfg. Co." 8.25" h. x 8.75" w. *Courtesy of Mark Mussio, Cincinnati Art Galleries, LLC.*

Figure 112. Standard glaze cylindrical 1883 vase, titled *Edelweiss*, decorated by Bruce Horsfall, featuring a golden-haired maiden dropping blossoms. Half of the vase is covered in Gorham floral silver overlay. Base marks: flames mark, B-, the title *Edelweiss*, shape number 589C W. 12.75" x 3.75". *Courtesy of David Rago Auctions.*

Figure 114. Standard glaze two-handled vase decorated with flowering Hawthorne by Constance Baker in 1894. Gorham added ornate silver floral overlay. Base marks: flames mark, shape number 533 D, an incised W for white clay, and the artist's incised initials. The silver overlay is marked "Gorham Mfg. Co. 999/1000 fine R-1902." 8.75" h. *Courtesy of Mark Mussio, Cincinnati Art Galleries, LLC.*

At the Columbian Exposition, Rookwood Pottery displayed the silver enhanced Standard wares, items decorated with Pueblo and Great Plains Native American portraitures, and introduced plaques. In enhancing Rookwood's reputation, two events of equal significance occurred during the Exposition: Rookwood wares were awarded high honors by the judges and they drew the attention and praise of ceramics scholar Edwin AtLee Barber.

Rookwood produced a number of portraits featuring romanticized views of Native-Americans and African-Americans. These were images inspired by the "noble savage" myth popular in the day. Both races were viewed as living closer to nature, surviving by instinct rather than intellect, and unencumbered by the concerns of "civilized society." Of the nation's interest in Native-Americans in the 1890s, in "Rookwood Pottery: The Glorious Gamble" Kenneth Trapp would write in 1992, "The fascination with Native-American people from the Great Plains and the Southwest was fed by western pulp novels, by the canvases of the Cincinnati painters Henry Francis Farny and Joseph Henry Sharp, both of whom traveled to the West to paint Native-Americans, and of course by the Buffalo Bill Wild West shows that made periodic visits to the Queen City." (Trapp 1992, 19)

Figure 115. Very unusual Standard glaze plaque featuring the portrait of a cheerful young woman, painted by Matt Daly in 1896. On the back of the plaque is painted: "Matt Daly Rookwood Pottery 1896" in brown slip. 4" x 4.5". *Courtesy of Mark Mussio, Cincinnati Art Galleries, LLC.*

Additionally, Rookwood produced contemporary German and Old Masters portraits, along with notable individuals and an assortment of animals to round out the presentation. The popularity of Rookwood's hand-painted portraiture was tied with consumer's enthusiasms for the Standard Glaze line—the interest in both waned at the turn of the twentieth century.

Figure 116. Standard glaze three-handled tyg painted by Grace Young in 1898, featuring the portrait of a young Native American. Base marks: flames mark, shape number 830D, and the artist's initials. 6" x 8". *Courtesy of David Rago Auctions.*

Figure 117. Imposing Standard glaze tankard produced in 1899 and decorated by Grace Young, recognized as Rookwood's "Portrait Diva." It is adorned with a smiling African-American boy. Base marks: flames mark, shape number 656, and Ms. Young's cipher. 9.5" h. *Courtesy of Mark Mussio, Cincinnati Art Galleries, LLC.*

New glazes were added in 1894, including Aerial Blue, Iris, and Sea Green. Of the three lines, Aerial Blue was fated never to be placed in full production. Iris and Sea Green would be successfully produced for over a decade.

Figure 118. Early Iris glaze vase decorated by Olga Reed in 1896 with flying swallows over a shaded blue and gray background. Base marks: flames mark, shape number 589F, an incised W for Iris glaze, and the incised decorator's initials. 7.5" h. *Courtesy of Mark Mussio, Cincinnati Art Galleries, LLC.*

Figure 119. Sea Green vase adorned with white poppies created by Constance Baker in 1896, and then covered with the Sea Green glaze. Base marks: flames mark, shape number 799, an incised G for the glaze choice, and the incised artist's initials. 8.5" h. *Courtesy of Mark Mussio, Cincinnati Art Galleries, LLC.*

In 1894, Shirayamadani returned from a trip to Japan he had undertaken the previous year seeking new techniques for Rookwood. Returning with him was a Japanese metalworker, E.H. Asano. With Asano's guidance, Rookwood opened a metal department for the manufacture of decorative fittings. By 1896, the metal department was reduced to the production of pewter mounts and lids for steins. Metalworking proved too expensive for Rookwood to maintain and the department was quickly closed.

However, the closure of the metal department would not stop Shirayamadani and several other decorators from experimenting with electro-plated copper and silver designs on ceramics. These were produced from roughly 1897 to 1903. Among the electro-plated embellishments created were underwater creatures (crabs, frogs, octopus, seahorses), water lilies, cattails, leaves, and rocks. While the eletro-plating process proved too expensive, it did allow Shirayamadani and his associates to produce some eye-catching work for several international expositions, including the Paris Exposition of 1900, St. Petersburg, Russia, and Buffalo, New York, of 1901, and the Turin Exposition of 1902.

Figure 120. Standard glaze stein with pewter mount for the lid dated to 1896. The pewter mount is decorated with a whimsical frog. Matthew Daly painted the portrait of author Nathaniel Hawthorne. Base marks: flames mark, shape number 820, the decorator's signature and the title "Portrait of Nath'l Hawthorne." 9.25" h. *Courtesy of Mark Mussio, Cincinnati Art Galleries, LLC.*

Figure 121. Sea Green glaze pitcher from 1898, decorated by Artus Van Briggle with a brown lily climbing the side. Base marks: flames mark, shape number 833D, an incised G for Sea Green glaze, a triangular-shaped esoteric mark, a wheel-ground X, and the the incised decorator's initials. 7.75" h. *Courtesy of Mark Mussio, Cincinnati Art Galleries, LLC.*

In 1896, decorator Artus Van Briggle would begin experimenting with mat (or "dead") glazes. He was trying to recreate glazes he had seen on Chinese ceramics while visiting Paris over the past two years. These early experiments with mat glazes would lead to a very significant and enduring glaze line in 1904, Vellum.

With a well-established, strong reputation and a growing stock of innovative glaze lines, Rookwood Pottery was in good shape as it headed into the twentieth century.

Rookwood's 1890s Objects

The following is a sampling of the various wares produced by Rookwood throughout the 1890s, organized by year and, within each year, by artist.

Figure 122. Large Light Standard glaze 1890 bulbous vase painted by Matthew A. Daly with branches of peaches on a shaded ground. Base marks: flames mark, shape number 488FW, the artist's initials, and L for Light Standard glaze. 10" x 8". *Courtesy of David Rago Auctions.*

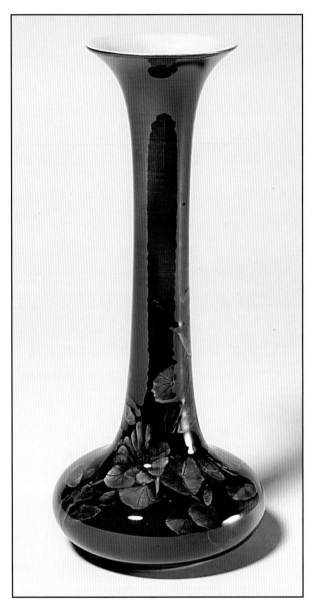

Figure 123. Standard glaze tankard decorated with orange poppies by Anna Marie Valentien in 1890. The decorator requested a Light Standard glaze, which makes the foliage show up well. Base marks: flames mark, shape number 564D, an impressed W for white clay, the artist's incised initials, and an L indicating Light Standard glaze. 8.5" h. *Courtesy of Mark Mussio, Cincinnati Art Galleries, LLC.*

Figure 124. Standard glaze vase decorated by Anna Marie Valentien in 1890 with flowering nasturtiums, leaves, and vines. Base marks: flames mark, shape number 553 C, an impressed W for white clay, an incised L for Light Standard glaze, and the decorator's incised initials. 12" h. *Courtesy of Mark Mussio, Cincinnati Art Galleries, LLC.*

Figure 125. Two amusing Standard glaze mugs dated to 1890, featuring Grace Young's imaginative "fairy tale creatures." On the left, the figure earnestly discusses affairs with a spider while kneeling. On the right, the figure enjoys watermelon while a frog looks on. Base marks: flames mark, shape number 587, an incised L for Light Standard glaze, an impressed W for white clay, and the artist's signature. 4.5" h. each. *Courtesy of Mark Mussio, Cincinnati Art Galleries, LLC.*

Figure 126. Standard glaze baluster vase decorated by Edward Diers with golden maple leaves in 1891. Base marks: flames mark, shape number 605, and the decorator's initials. 5" x 3.25". *Courtesy of David Rago Auctions.*

Figure 127. Novel twin handled "Japanese crock" adorned with Virginia creeper painted in 1891 by William McDonald. The shape was in a Japanese style created by Maria Longworth Nichols that included applied handles and rim incising. Base marks: flames mark, shape number 42, W for white clay, incised L for Light Standard glaze, and the artist's incised initials. 7.5" h. *Courtesy of Mark Mussio, Cincinnati Art Galleries, LLC.*

Figure 128. Standard glaze vase with two delicate handles dated to 1891 and decorated by Mary Nourse with detailed clover flowers and leaves. Base marks: flames mark, shape number 77C, the artist's initials, incised L for Light Standard glaze, and impressed W for white clay. 5" h. *Courtesy of Mark Mussio, Cincinnati Art Galleries, LLC.*

Figure 129. Standard glaze vase decorated in 1891 by Sallie Toohey with an autumn leaves motif against a shaded brown ground. Base marks: flames mark, shape number 402, impressed W for white clay, incised L for Light Standard glaze, and the incised artist's monogram. 6" h. *Courtesy of Mark Mussio, Cincinnati Art Galleries, LLC.*

Figure 130. Large Standard glaze ewer decorated with blackberries, vines, and leaves by Anna Valentien in 1891. Base marks: flames mark, shape number 468 B, incised L for Light Standard glaze, impressed W for white clay, and the artist's incised initials. 10.75" h. *Courtesy of Mark Mussio, Cincinnati Art Galleries, LLC.*

Figure 131. Small Standard glaze 1891 vase with embossed and hand painted sprigs and white berries decoration by an unknown artist. Base marks: flames logo and shape number 162. 5" h. *Courtesy of Bob Shores and Dale Jones.*

Figure 132. Standard glaze ewer from 1891 decorated by an unknown artist with blue violets and heart-shaped leaves. Base marks: flames logo, shape number 486D, and an impressed W for white clay. *Courtesy of Mark Mussio, Cincinnati Art Galleries, LLC.*

Figure 133. Standard glaze mug decorated in 1891 by an unidentified artist with a brown and white hunting dog chasing a fox into his den. Base marks: flames mark, shape number 587, and a W for white clay. 4.5" h. *Courtesy of Mark Mussio, Cincinnati Art Galleries, LLC.*

Figure 134. Impressive early Standard glaze 1892 spherical swirled vase with a ruffled rim and painted by Matthew A. Daly with orange poppies. Base marks: flames mark, shape number 612A, W for white clay, and the artist's initials. 8.5" x 8". *Courtesy of David Rago Auctions.*

Figure 135. Early Light Standard glaze 1892 ewer painted by Matthew A. Daly with branches of bell flowers in orange and yellow. Base marks: flames mark, shape number 387Bm, W for white clay, the artist's initials, and an L for Light Standard glaze. 12.75" x 6.5". *Courtesy of David Rago Auctions.*

Figure 136. Gorham silver-overlaid Standard glaze pitcher painted by Kate C. Matchette, 1892, with branches of green leaves and blossoms, with birds building a nest amidst winding vines and blossoming branches. 9" x 4.5". *Courtesy of David Rago Auctions.*

Far left:
Figure 137. Gorham silver-overlaid Standard glaze vase with a pinched rim, painted by Mary Nourse with yellow roses and green leaves on brown ground in 1892. The Gorham silver features a vine scroll and stylized foliage patterns. 6.25" x 3.25". *Courtesy of David Rago Auctions.*

Left:
Figure 138. Light Standard glaze vase with two delicate handles dated to 1892 and decorated by Mary Nourse with poppy blooms, buds, and stems. Base marks: flames mark, incised artist's initials, shape number 77C, incised L for Light Standard glaze, and impressed W for white clay. 5" h. *Courtesy of Mark Mussio, Cincinnati Art Galleries, LLC.*

Figure 139. Standard glaze vase decorated in a water lily design in 1892 by Kataro Shirayamadani. Base marks: flames mark, shape number 664B, an incised W, and the artist's incised signature. 11" h. *Courtesy of Bob Shores and Dale Jones.*

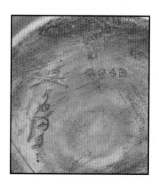

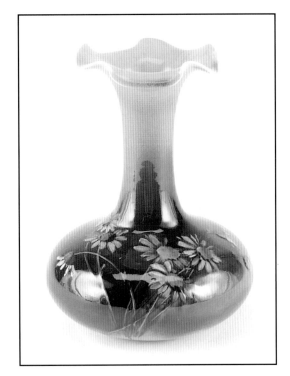

Figure 140. Light Standard glaze bottle-shaped vase with a ruffled rim. The yellow daisies decoration was painted by Jeanette Swing in 1892. Base marks: flames mark. 7". *Courtesy of David Rago Auctions.*

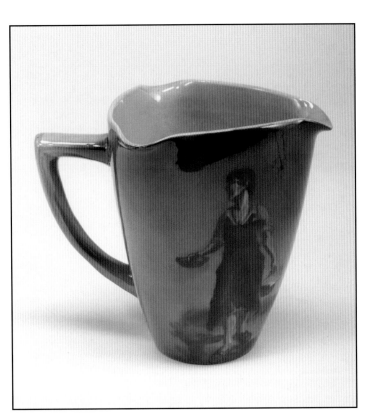

Figure 141. Standard glaze three-sided pitcher painted by Harriet Wilcox with a peasant holding a bowl and a pitcher of wine, 1892. Base marks: flames mark, shape number 259C, a W indicating white clay, and the artist's initials. 6" x 7.5". *Courtesy of David Rago Auctions.*

Figure 142. Standard glaze ewer with delicate handle, made in 1892, and carefully decorated with a jonquil flower and leaves; however, the artist failed to sign the piece. Base marks: flames mark, shape number 496C, and an impressed W designating white clay. 10.25" h. *Courtesy of Mark Mussio, Cincinnati Art Galleries, LLC.*

Figure 143. Standard glaze vase, 1892, decorated with cherries among leaves by an unidentified decorator. Base marks: flames mark, shape number 654C, and an impressed W for white clay. 5.5" h. *Courtesy of Mark Mussio, Cincinnati Art Galleries, LLC.*

Figure 144. Standard glaze vase decorated with branches of yellow roses in 1892 by an unidentified artist. Base marks: flames mark, shape number 614B, and a W for white clay. 14" x 7". *Courtesy of David Rago Auctions.*

Figure 145. Standard glaze tall bottle-shaped 1893 vase decorated by Matthew A. Daly with orange chrysanthemums. Base marks: flames mark, the artist's initials, shape number 644C, and a W indicating white clay. 14.5" x 4". *Courtesy of David Rago Auctions.*

Figure 146. Light Standard glaze bulbous 1893 vase decorated with yellow daisies by Sadie Markland. Base marks: flames mark, shape number 40, a W for white clay, and the artist's initials. 5.25" x 3.25". *Courtesy of David Rago Auctions.*

Figure 147. Standard glaze bowl decorated by Mary Nourse in 1893 with raspberries. Base marks: flames mark, shape number 427, an impressed W for white clay, an incised L for Light Standard glaze, and the artist's incised initials. 3.25" h. x 9" in diameter. *Courtesy of Mark Mussio, Cincinnati Art Galleries, LLC.*

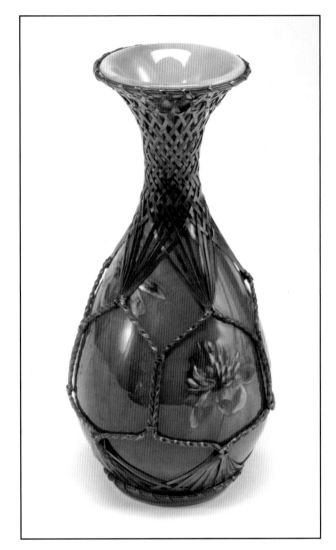

Figure 148. Silver-overlaid 1893 Standard glaze bottle-shaped vase covered in woven sterling bands and decorated by Caroline Steinle with clover blossoms and leaves. Base marks: flames mark, shape number 381C, a W for white clay, the artist's initials, and STERLING. 6.75" x 3.25". *Courtesy of David Rago Auctions.*

Figure 149. Light Standard glaze miniature 1893 pillow vase decorated by Caroline Steinle with yellow clover blossoms. Base marks: flames mark. 4". *Courtesy of David Rago Auctions.*

Figure 150. Standard glaze vase decorated by Constance Baker in 1894 with nicely detailed thistles. Base marks: flames mark, shape number 611 D, an impressed W for white clay, and the artist's incised initials. 8.5" h. *Courtesy of Mark Mussio, Cincinnati Art Galleries, LLC.*

Figure 151. Standard glaze bottle-shaped 1894 vase painted by Constance Baker with dogwood branches. Base marks: flames mark and the artist's initials. 8". *Courtesy of David Rago Auctions.*

Figure 152. Standard glaze pillow vase decorated in 1894 by Charles Dibowski, featuring a portrait of a man wearing a wig. Base marks: flames mark and the artist's cipher. 5.75" x 5". *Courtesy of David Rago Auctions.*

Figure 153. Standard glaze vase decorated in 1894 by Kate Matchette with flowers similar to forget-me-nots, with leaves and stems. Base marks: flames mark, shape number 162D, an impressed W for white clay, and the artist's incised initials. 5" h. *Courtesy of Mark Mussio, Cincinnati Art Galleries, LLC.*

Figure 154. Standard glaze 1894 ewer decorated with lifelike white dogwood blossoms by Mary Nourse. Base marks: flames mark, shape number 715 DD, an impressed W for white clay, an incised L for Light Standard glaze, and the artist's incised initials. 6" h. *Courtesy of Mark Mussio, Cincinnati Art Galleries, LLC.*

Figure 155. Standard glaze vase from 1894, decorated by Anna Marie Valentien with yellow jonquils. Base marks: flames mark, shape number 562, an impressed W for white clay, and the artist's incised initials. 9.5" h. *Courtesy of Mark Mussio, Cincinnati Art Galleries, LLC.*

Figure 156. Standard glaze vase with leaf and berry decoration decorated by Charles Dibowski in 1895. Base marks: flames mark, shape number 781, an incised L for Light Standard glaze, and the artist's incised monogram. 9.75" h. *Courtesy of Mark Mussio, Cincinnati Art Galleries, LLC.*

Figure 157. Standard glaze long-necked 1895 ewer decorated by Charles Dibowski with ivory trefoils and blackberries. Base marks: flames mark. 6.5". *Courtesy of David Rago Auctions.*

Figure 158. Standard glaze ewer by Amelia B. Sprague, 1895, with slip-relief holly leaves and berries. Base marks: flames mark and artist signed. 8" x 6". *Courtesy of David Rago Auctions.*

Figure 160. Standard glaze vase decorated with mushrooms in 1896 by Rose Fechheimer. Base marks: flames mark, shape number 654 C, and the decorator's incised initials. 5" h. *Courtesy of Mark Mussio, Cincinnati Art Galleries, LLC.*

Figure 159. Standard glaze ewer decorated by Matthew Daly in 1896 with a flowering blackberry bush. Base marks: flames mark, shape number 495 A, and the incised artist's initials. *Courtesy of Mark Mussio, Cincinnati Art Galleries, LLC.*

Figure 161. Standard glaze squat pitcher decorated with yellow lotus blossoms and leaves by Bruce Horsfall in 1896. Base marks: flames mark. 7" x 9.5". *Courtesy of David Rago Auctions.*

Figure 162. Impressive Standard glaze three-handled tyg decorated by Sturgis Laurence, 1896, with a portrait of Rip Van Winkle on a green and brown ground. 8" x 10". *Courtesy of David Rago Auctions.*

Figure 163. Standard glaze bottle-shaped vase painted by Elizabeth Lincoln with holly branches in 1896. Base marks: flames mark. 7" h. *Courtesy of David Rago Auctions.*

Figure 164. Standard glaze sugar bowl (missing its lid) with a colorful decoration of red holly berries and green leaves, painted by Elizabeth Lincoln in 1896. Base marks: flames mark, shape number 692, and the artist's incised initials. 3" h. *Courtesy of Mark Mussio, Cincinnati Art Galleries, LLC.*

Figure 165. Standard glaze tall tapered pitcher decorated by Mary Nourse with palm fronds, 1896. Base marks: flames mark and the artist's initials. 9.75" x 5". *Courtesy of David Rago Auctions.*

Figure 166. Standard glaze creamer decorated in 1896 by Carrie Steinle, featuring pansies, leaves, and stems on a graduated brown background. Base marks: flames mark, the artist's incised initials, and shape number 630. 3.25" h. *Courtesy of Mark Mussio, Cincinnati Art Galleries, LLC.*

Figure 167. Standard glaze coffee pot with red poppies painted by Constance Baker in 1897. Base marks: flames mark, shape number 773m and the artist's incised initials. 8.25" h. *Courtesy of Mark Mussio, Cincinnati Art Galleries, LLC.*

Figure 168. Standard glaze two-handled vase decorated in 1897 with yellow jonquils and green stems and leaves on the shaded brown-to-yellow ground by Mary Nourse. Base marks: flames mark, shape number 459 C, an incised L for Light Standard glaze, and the artist's incised initials. An old label affixed to the bottom provides the date and the decorator's (misspelled) name. 6.5" h. *Courtesy of Mark Mussio, Cincinnati Art Galleries, LLC.*

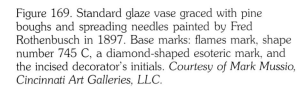

Figure 169. Standard glaze vase graced with pine boughs and spreading needles painted by Fred Rothenbusch in 1897. Base marks: flames mark, shape number 745 C, a diamond-shaped esoteric mark, and the incised decorator's initials. *Courtesy of Mark Mussio, Cincinnati Art Galleries, LLC.*

Figure 170. Standard glaze vase decorated in 1897 by Anna Marie Valentien with ripe milkweed pods and seeds. Base marks: flames mark, shape number 556 C, a diamond-shaped esoteric mark, and the decorator's incised initials. 11" h. *Courtesy of Mark Mussio, Cincinnati Art Galleries, LLC.*

Figure 172. Standard glaze ewer decorated with autumnal oak leaves by Sallie Coyne in 1898. Base marks: flames mark, shape number 611C, and the decorator's incised monogram. 9.5" h. *Courtesy of Mark Mussio, Cincinnati Art Galleries, LLC.*

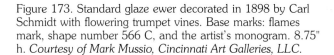

Figure 171. Standard glaze tall pitcher painted by Constance Baker with a green apple on branch, 1898. Base marks: flames mark, shape number 781B, and the artist's initials. 11.5" x 5". *Courtesy of David Rago Auctions.*

Figure 173. Standard glaze ewer decorated in 1898 by Carl Schmidt with flowering trumpet vines. Base marks: flames mark, shape number 566 C, and the artist's monogram. 8.75" h. *Courtesy of Mark Mussio, Cincinnati Art Galleries, LLC.*

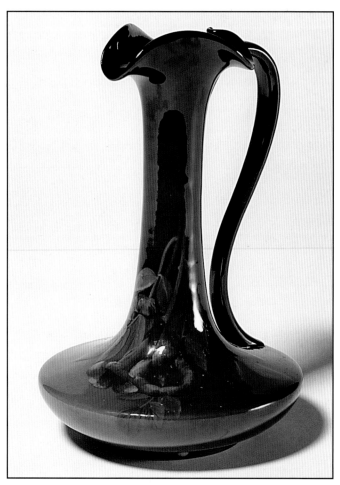

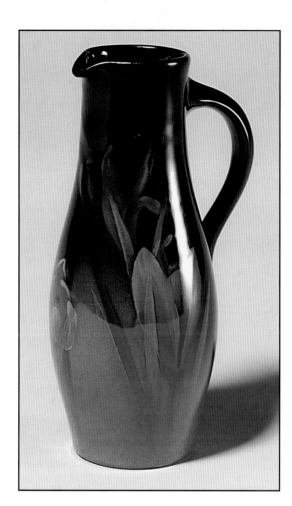

Figure 174. Standard glaze ewer decorated in 1898 by Carl Schmidt, featuring blue crocus flowers and leaves on a shaded brown background. Base marks: flames mark, the artist's signature, and shape number 838F. 5" h. *Courtesy of Mark Mussio, Cincinnati Art Galleries, LLC.*

Figure 175. Monumental Standard glaze vase with hollyhock decoration by Kataro Shirayamadani, produced in 1898 on a Special shape. Base marks: flames mark, Special shape number S 1409 A, and the artist's incised cipher. 20.75" h. *Courtesy of Mark Mussio, Cincinnati Art Galleries, LLC.*

Figure 176. Standard glaze baluster vase by Kataro Shirayamadani in 1898 with modeled and slip-painted orange lotus blossoms and large green leaves. Base marks: flames mark, shape number S1411C, and the artist's cipher. 13" x 8". *Courtesy of David Rago Auctions.*

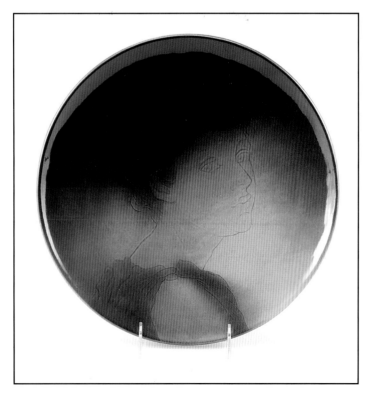

Figure 177. Rare Standard glaze charger by Anna Marie Valentien, 1898, painted with a portrait of a young woman with outlined features in brown and yellow-green glazes. Base marks: red crayon numbers on base, deaccessioned from the Cincinnati Museum. 12.25" in diameter. *Courtesy of David Rago Auctions.*

Figure 178. Standard glaze vase decorated by Lenore Asbury in 1899 with an autumn leaves motif. The vase was then covered by the Alvin Manufacturing Company with heavy, intricate sterling silver overlay consisting of roses, vines, and leaves. Base marks: flames mark, shape number 588 B, and the decorator's incised initials. The silver is marked "999/1000 Fine Patented" with a shield containing the Alvin logo in the center. 12" h. *Courtesy of Mark Mussio, Cincinnati Art Galleries, LLC.*

Figure 179. Standard glaze vase decorated by
Lenore Asbury in 1899 with delicate flowers amidst
leaves and branches. Base marks: flames mark,
shape number 387 C, and the incised decorator's
initials. 10.25" h. *Courtesy of Mark Mussio, Cincinnati Art Galleries, LLC.*

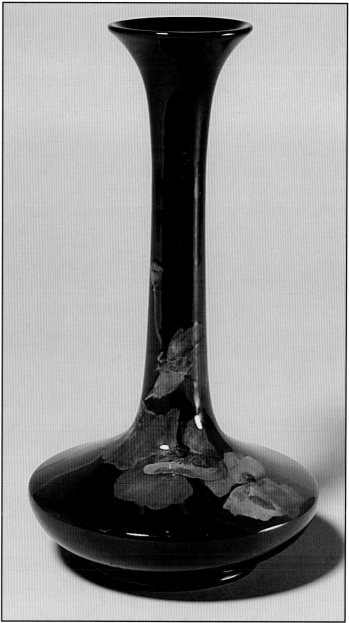

Figure 180. Standard glaze vase decorated in 1899 by Amelia
Browne Sprague with blooming orange poppies. Base marks: flames
mark, shape number 566 B, an unusual esoteric mark, incised artist's
initials, and a Davis Collamore & Co. (a retail agent) label. 12.25" h.
Courtesy of Mark Mussio, Cincinnati Art Galleries, LLC.

Figure 181. Tapering Standard glaze vase, dated to 1899, and decorated by Olga Geneva Reed with an array of oak leaves on a shading brown background. Base marks: flames mark, shape number 806B, and the artist's incised signature. 10.5" h. *Courtesy of Mark Mussio, Cincinnati Art Galleries, LLC.*

Figure 182. Imposing Standard glaze vase decorated by Kataro Shirayamadani in 1899 with orange trumpet creepers and green leaves. Base marks: flames mark, shape number 339 B, and the artist's incised Japanese signature. 13" h. *Courtesy of Mark Mussio, Cincinnati Art Galleries, LLC.*

Chapter Two

Rookwood Pottery
of the Twentieth Century

Rookwood Pottery in 1900

Outside Japan and China, we do not know where any colors and glazes are to be found finer than those which come from Rookwood Pottery.
—*Crockery and Glass Journal*, 1901 (Levy 2003)

During the early decades of the twentieth century, Rookwood Pottery would face stiff competition from many new art potters arriving on the scene. Rookwood's underglaze slip-decorated wares were widely copied, both in the United States and overseas in Britain and Europe.

Figure 183. Colorful Iris glaze vase adorned in 1900 by Edward Diers with a spray of blue crocuses and green ensiform leaves on a shaded blue background. Base marks: flames mark, shape number 914E, an incised W for Iris glaze, and the decorator's incised monogram. 5.25" h. *Courtesy of Mark Mussio, Cincinnati Art Galleries, LLC.*

In 1900, Rookwood Pottery would have roughly forty decorators on staff. Instituted by Taylor in the nineteenth century and continued into the twentieth was a program sending decorators abroad to study. These traveling decorators brought back fresh ideas to stretch Rookwood's decoration and shapes repertoire. The company would continue to develop new techniques. As the first decade of the twentieth century rolled by, Rookwood Pottery increased the volume of molded bodies produced for economy's sake. Still the company would promote their wares as art as the pottery continued to be unique in decoration and artist signed.

In 1902, Thorstein Veblen spoke to the virtues of handmade versus machine made wares as applied to Arts and Crafts ideals in his article "Arts and Crafts" in *The Journal of Political Economy*. He wrote, "At its inception the [Arts and Crafts] movement was a romanticism ... Archaism and sophistication came of a revulsion against the besetting ugliness of what was present before the eyes of the leaders. The absolute dearth of beauty in the philistine present forced them to hark back to the past. The enduring characteristic is rather an insistence on sensuous beauty of line and color and on visible serviceability in all objects which it touches. And these results can be attained in fuller measure through the technological expedients of which the machine process disposes than by any means within the reach of the industry of a past age." (Veblen 1902, 111) In time, Rookwood's management would come to agree with this point of view.

Figure 184. Iris glaze vase decorated with pink pansies and green foliage on a mauve to pale green to cream ground by Sara Sax in 1900. Base marks: impressed flames mark, shape number 667, an incised W for Iris glaze, and the artist's monogram. 6.5" h. *Courtesy of Mark Mussio, Cincinnati Art Galleries, LLC.*

The Paris Exposition Universelle of 1900 would prove very profitable to Rookwood. Taylor turned the decorators loose to produce special exposition pieces, including the previously mentioned electro-plated wares. Under normal circumstances, a decorator could complete two or three items each day. However, decorating the exposition pieces each required days or weeks of work. Experimentation increased to improve decorative treatments and production methods. As a result, Rookwood wares were awarded the highly sought Grand Prix from the judges in Paris. William Taylor himself was awarded the Chevalier of the Legion of Honor, and individual awards were given to Albert Valentien and Stanley G. Burt. No doubt encouraged by the results, Rookwood would send exhibits to many expositions throughout the decade. In fact, in no other decade would Rookwood travel so far or attend so many expositions.

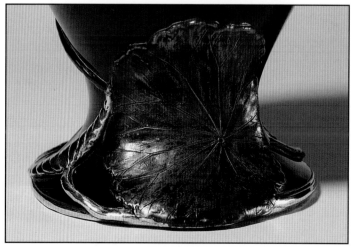

Figure 185. Rare and extremely important Black Iris glaze vase with electroplated metal mounts decorated by Kataro Shirayamadani in 1900, quite possibly for the Paris Exposition. Decoration consists of caramel colored flying cranes and black clouds; the applied metal consists of both copper and silver electroplate over deeply carved lotus blossoms and pads, the combination being nearly unheard of in Rookwood's brief period of electrodepositing. Base marks: flames mark, Special Shape number S 1523, and the artist's incised cipher. 14.5" h. *Courtesy of Mark Mussio, Cincinnati Art Galleries, LLC.*

Beginning in 1900, Rookwood produced mat glazes in line with consumers changing tastes and desire for simplicity. These mat glazes were not formally introduced to the buying public until 1902, when they first appeared in a promotional pamphlet. At this point the mat glazes were listed as a single finish, with no distinction made for either the decoration or the nature of the various mat glazes. Also listed in the catalog was architectural faience.

Figure 186. Mat glaze ewer produced in 1902 and decorated by Leona Van Briggle with unusually colored crabapple blossoms. Base marks: flames mark, date, shape number 843C, and the artist's incised signature. 6" h. *Courtesy of Mark Mussio, Cincinnati Art Galleries, LLC.*

Rookwood Tiles and Plaques

In 1902 Rookwood ventured into the world of tile making and architectural faience with the establishment of the architectural faience department. Rookwood's tiles would be adorned with mat glazes in a wide variety of colors and hues, including special order colors. In 1903, the company received its first large commissions, designing tiles for four of New York City's subway stations. Successful completion of that project led to commissions for tile work from famous hotels nationwide. Rookwood's tile work was especially popular with those hotels catering to famous socialites. At times, hundreds of tiles were used to create complete murals. Rookwood tiles and plaques were also to be found in many private homes, often decorating fireplace mantels and bathrooms.

Also produced in the architectural faience department were garden pottery wares, including fountains, sundial pedestals, urns, and window boxes. Some of these garden items were obviously quite large. Clement J. Barnhorn was responsible for designs of many of the panels and fountains produced. By 1920, however, Rookwood management would find their architectural faience department losing ground to larger companies with machinery more suited to large-scale tile production.
(Following 3 pages)

Figure 187. Architectural Faience three tile tableau with striking colors featuring tall trees with purple mountains in the background across a blue body of water. This tableau was removed from a fireplace in Cincinnati. Newly created oak Arts & Crafts frame. 12" x 36". *Courtesy of Mark Mussio, Cincinnati Art Galleries, LLC.*

Figure 188. Fine and rare tile backsplash in the Arts and Crafts/Gothic style with indigo diagonal tiles, beige surround, and a green tree at the top covered in a large amber ribbon. 43" x 30.5". *Courtesy of David Rago Auctions.*

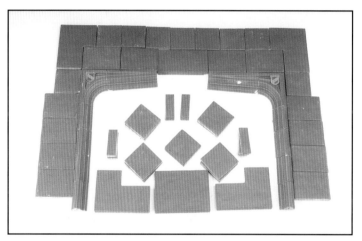

Figure 189. Architectural Faience fireplace surround comprised of sixty-two tiles covered in Mat Green glaze, the corners with a heraldic design in blue and brown. The keystone tile is missing. Back marks: stamped RP and numbers. *Courtesy of David Rago Auctions.*

Figure 190. Rookwood Faience fireplace surround of twenty-five tiles covered in mottled brown glaze, the corners with a heraldic design in blue and amber. Back marks: stamped RP and numbers. *Courtesy of David Rago Auctions.*

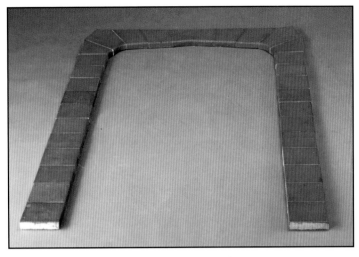

Figure 191. Rare Rookwood Faience door surround of thirty-one tiles covered in Mat Green glaze. Back marks: stamped ROOKWOOD FAIENCE with numbers. Exterior: 78" x 48", interior center: 72" x 36". Individual tiles: 6" square and some shaped. *Courtesy of David Rago Auctions.*

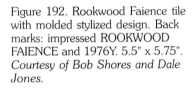

Figure 192. Rookwood Faience tile with molded stylized design. Back marks: impressed ROOKWOOD FAIENCE and 1976Y. 5.5" x 5.75". *Courtesy of Bob Shores and Dale Jones.*

Figure 193. Rookwood Faience tile with molded stylized rose design. Back marks: impressed ROOKWOOD FAIENCE and 1684Y. 5.5" x 5.75". *Courtesy of Bob Shores and Dale Jones.*

Figure 194. Rare Rookwood Faience 8" tile embossed with a medallion of seahorses in brown and green on a turquoise and green ground. Back marks: stamped ROOKWOOD FAIENCE and 1234. *Courtesy of David Rago Auctions.*

Figure 195. Rookwood Faience tile embossed with purple magnolia blossom and turquoise leaves on pink ground. 6" square. *Courtesy of David Rago Auctions.*

Figure 196. Unusual floor tile with griffin in brown clay against dark Mat Red glaze. Back marks: stamped RP and 366. 9" square. *Courtesy of David Rago Auctions.*

Figure 199. Rookwood Faience tile embossed with a swan in Mat Ivory glaze on a blue-gray and blue-green crystalline ground. Back marks: stamped RP375. 6" square. *Courtesy of David Rago Auctions.*

Figure 197. Fine and unusual diamond-shaped tile with two tall ships in brown and caramel on green waves against blue sky. Back marks: stamped RP, 417, and G352. 8". *Courtesy of David Rago Auctions.*

Figure 200. Fine Scenic Vellum plaque, titled *Evening*, decorated by Fred Rothenbusch with a landscape of trees in front of a light green sky. Mounted in the original frame and paper labels. Plaque: 8" x 10". *Courtesy of David Rago Auctions.*

Figure 198. Fine and large tile decorated in cuenca with a tall ship in front of a cloud-filled sky. Mounted in an Arts & Crafts frame. 12" square. *Courtesy of David Rago Auctions.*

In 1904, Rookwood displayed five new types of mat glazed wares: Mat Glaze Painting, Conventional Mat Glaze, Incised Mat Glaze, Modeled Mat Glaze, and Vellum. Of these, Incised Mat featured simple incised, geometric shapes inspired by Navajo and Hopi Indian designs which were fascinating Americans at that time. Incised Mat also represented shift from the company's traditional approach to art. Decorators did not apply the designs to this ware. In a purposeful effort to reduce costs and reach a broader consumer market, these decorations were applied either by factory workers or they could be included in the design of the mold itself. Rookwood would not resort to designs in the mold until the 1920s when the need for economical production grew more dire.

While experts at the St. Louis Exposition did not recognize Vellum for the technical achievement that it was, considering it a mere novelty, this sophisticated glaze was a melding of mat finish with a transparent gloss glaze. While the other four mat glazes were too thick and opaque to allow much beyond limited decoration in modeling or broad painting, Vellum was a soft transparent mat glaze allowing underglaze slip painting. This glaze also gently diffuses light, making the underglaze decoration appear soft.

Figure 201. Incised Mat glaze vase with grape decoration, which wraps around the vase, decorated by Sallie Coyne in 1904. Base marks: flames mark, the date, shape number 768 DZ, an impressed arrow-shaped esoteric mark, and the impressed artist's monogram. 9" h. *Courtesy of Mark Mussio, Cincinnati Art Galleries, LLC.*

Figure 202. Early Vellum glaze vase decorated by Edward T. Hurley in 1904 with four fish in differing attitudes around the circumference of the vase. Base marks: flames mark, the date, shape number 30 F, three short parallel incised lines, a V for Vellum, and the decorator's incised initials. 6" h. *Courtesy of Mark Mussio, Cincinnati Art Galleries, LLC.*

Vellum was used to create broad, artistic landscapes, including sunsets, snow scenes, and forested landscapes. In fact, Scenic Vellum landscapes fell into three general categories, each further afield from Rookwood's Cincinnati home: Ohio River Valley meadows, wooded fields, or hills; the snowcapped Rocky Mountains of the American West; and romantic scenes of Venice. Vellum was applied to good effect on Rookwood's flat wall plaques produced in the architectural faience department. Weight and durability limited the size of these plaques, although larger arrangements with several plaques were also made. Plaques received oak frames and romantic titles (on the back) before leaving the factory. These plaques were also artist signed (front or back) and designated among the marks with the letter "V" impressed or incised on the back.

Also introduced in 1904 was Rookwood's first numbered paperweight in the form of an owl. A rook would be added in 1908. The company's very first paperweight had been part of a desk set manufactured in 1894. While Rookwood would make a number of paperweights between 1904 and 1925, production would not begin in earnest until 1929. Over the years, eighty-three different numbered paperweight shapes were produced, along with six additional special shapes. Various animal figures as paperweights, bookends, and other useful household items would be sold from the 1900s through the 1950s to extend Rookwood's reach deeper into the consumer market.

Figure 203. Fine and unusual Scenic Vellum flaring vase with forest scene painted in fall colors by Edward T. Hurley in 1908. Base marks: flames mark, the date, shape number 1369D. 9" x 5". *Courtesy of David Rago Auctions.*

Figure 204. Large Scenic Vellum plaque by Edward T. Hurley, titled *The Birches.* It is mounted in the original frame, covering its back. Front marks: flames mark paper label, title label, and the decorator's initials. Plaque: 14" x 9". *Courtesy of David Rago Auctions.*

Figure 205. Large Scenic Vellum plaque decorated by Edward T. Hurley, titled *Birches and the Lake*. It is mounted in the original frame, covering its back. Artist's initials on front; title label on back. Plaque: 11.75" x 8.5". *Courtesy of David Rago Auctions.*

Figure 206. Scenic Vellum plaque decorated by Lorinda Epply, titled *A Quiet Scene*, with birch and elm trees in a verdant landscape. It is mounted in the original frame. Marks: flames mark, title, and artist label. Plaque: 5.75" x 7.75". *Courtesy of David Rago Auctions.*

Rookwood's 1900s Objects

The following is a sampling of the various wares produced by Rookwood throughout the first decade of the twentieth century, organized by year and, within each year, by artist.

Figure 207. Striking, unusual silver-overlaid Standard glaze spherical inkwell on an oval pen tray, decorated by Constance A. Baker with clover blossoms, leaves, and a feather. The inkwell is completely covered in sterling arabesques, dating to 1900. Back marks: flames mark, shape number 586C, and the artist's initials. 3.5" x 10". *Courtesy of David Rago Auctions.*

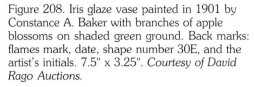

Figure 208. Iris glaze vase painted in 1901 by Constance A. Baker with branches of apple blossoms on shaded green ground. Back marks: flames mark, date, shape number 30E, and the artist's initials. 7.5" x 3.25". *Courtesy of David Rago Auctions.*

Figure 209. Standard glaze ewer painted by Sallie Coyne in 1900 with hawthorn flowers, thorns, and leaves. Base marks: flames mark, shape number 874, and the artist's incised mark. 9" h. *Courtesy of Mark Mussio, Cincinnati Art Galleries, LLC.*

Figure 210. Rare Sea Green cabinet vase painted with white snowdrops by Sallie Coyne in 1901. Base marks: flames mark, the date, shape number 654E, and the artist's initials. 3.25" x 2.5". *Courtesy of David Rago Auctions.*

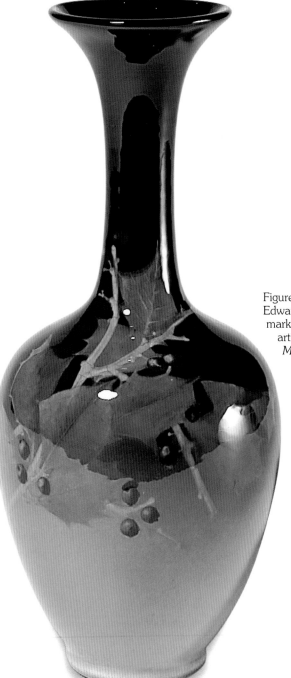

Figure 211. Standard glaze vase decorated in 1900 by Edward T. Hurley with holly berries and leaves. Base marks: flames mark, shape number 781 B, and the artist's incised initials. 11.75" h. *Courtesy of Mark Mussio, Cincinnati Art Galleries, LLC.*

Figure 212. Standard glaze mug decorated by Elizabeth Lincoln in 1900 featuring an appropriate hops motif. The initials "W.F.G." have been added to the front of the mug in brown slip. Base marks: flames mark, shape number 587 C, and the decorator's initials. 4.5" h. *Courtesy of Mark Mussio, Cincinnati Art Galleries, LLC.*

Figure 213. Standard glaze vase decorated by Clara Lindeman in 1900 with cherries hanging from branches. Base marks: flames mark, shape number 734D, and the decorator's incised initials. 6.75" h. *Courtesy of Mark Mussio, Cincinnati Art Galleries, LLC.*

Figure 214. Striking Sea Green vase upon which, in 1900, Fred Rothenbusch arrayed overlapping palm fronds upon a black background. Base marks: flames mark, shape number 741C, an incised G connoting the glaze choice, and the artist's incised initials. 5.5" h. *Courtesy of Mark Mussio, Cincinnati Art Galleries, LLC.*

Figure 215. Rare Iris glaze vase with finely detailed clover and three busy bees gathering nectar painted in 1900 by Carl Schmidt. Base marks: flames mark, the date, shape number 924, an incised W for white (Iris) glaze, and the incised artist's monogram. Cincinnati Art Galleries states, "Schmidt was still a few years away from becoming one of Rookwood's most trusted artists. This piece, smaller and with the early incised monogram, is one of several with clover and bees done by Schmidt around 1900 and is a precursor of his fabulous work to come. Superior art and composition." 5.25" h. *Courtesy of Mark Mussio, Cincinnati Art Galleries, LLC.*

Figure 216. Standard glaze vase decorated with blooming yellow tulips and green leaves in 1900 by Carl Schmidt. Base marks: flames mark, shape number 565, and the artist's monogram. 7.5" h. *Courtesy of Mark Mussio, Cincinnati Art Galleries, LLC.*

Figure 217. Standard glaze tyg decorated by Amelia Sprague with bunches of ripe grapes in 1900. Base marks: flames mark, shape number 859 B, and the artist's conjoined initials. 7.75" h. *Courtesy of Mark Mussio, Cincinnati Art Galleries, LLC.*

Figure 218. Standard glaze vase with detailed nasturtiums painted by Carrie Steinle in 1900. Base marks: flames mark, shape number 792D, and the decorator's incised initials. 7" h. *Courtesy of Mark Mussio, Cincinnati Art Galleries, LLC.*

Figure 219. Exceptional bronze-overlaid Sea Green bulbous vase decorated in 1900 by Anne Marie Valentien, featuring a languid nude wrapped around its middle and rim, covered in verdigris patina over a green glazed ground. Base marks: flames mark, shape number 128Z, and the artist's initials. 5.25" x 4.25". *Courtesy of David Rago Auctions.*

Figure 220. Standard glaze vase painted in 1900 by Grace Young, titled *High Hawk (Sioux)*, featuring a young Native American in full headdress. This is among Grace Young's best work. Base marks: flames mark, shape number 900B, the artist's initials, and the title *HIGH HAWK SIOUX*. 9" x 5.5". *Courtesy of David Rago Auctions.*

Figure 221. Standard glaze tankard painted in 1900 by Grace Young with a Native American portrait, titled *White Man Bear, Sioux*, with the handle and rim overlaid in silver. Base marks: flames mark, shape number 775, the artist's initials, and the title. 7.5" x 6". *Courtesy of David Rago Auctions.*

Figure 222. Iris glaze vase with blue wood lilies painted by Edward Diers in 1901. Base marks: flames mark, the date, shape number 924, an incised W for Iris glaze, and the artist's initials. 5.5" h. *Courtesy of Mark Mussio, Cincinnati Art Galleries, LLC.*

Figure 223. Standard glaze ewer with nasturtium decoration painted by Edward Diers in 1901. Base marks: flames mark, date, shape number 718, and the artist's incised monogram. 7.5" h. *Courtesy of Mark Mussio, Cincinnati Art Galleries, LLC.*

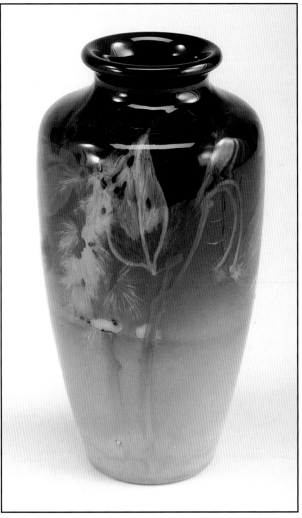

Figure 224. Standard glaze ovoid vase painted by Edward Diers with milkweed pods in 1901. Base marks: second mark for two high-water marks and glaze misses, flames mark, date, shape number 614E, and the artist's initials. 8" x 3.75". *Courtesy of David Rago Auctions.*

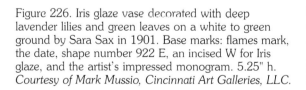

Figure 225. Standard glaze vase decorated by Mary Nourse in 1901, featuring lotus blossoms and lily pads over a background that shades through yellow, green, and brown. Base marks: flames mark, the date, shape number 903B, and the artist's initials underlined. 9.75" h. *Courtesy of Mark Mussio, Cincinnati Art Galleries, LLC.*

Figure 226. Iris glaze vase decorated with deep lavender lilies and green leaves on a white to green ground by Sara Sax in 1901. Base marks: flames mark, the date, shape number 922 E, an incised W for Iris glaze, and the artist's impressed monogram. 5.25" h. *Courtesy of Mark Mussio, Cincinnati Art Galleries, LLC.*

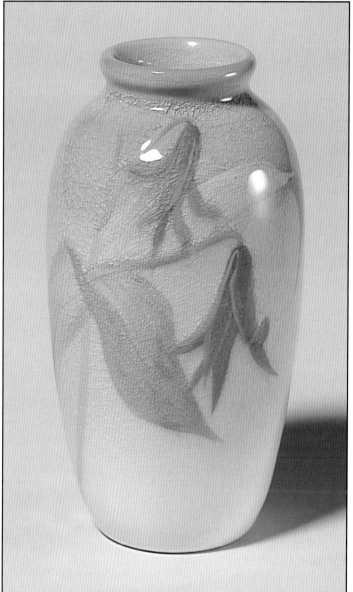

Figure 227. Rare Carved Mat glaze vase with electroplated copper applied over the carved areas featuring five carved panels, each with a dandelion leaf, each panel connected at the shoulder by the dandelion blooms, which encircle the vase. This is the work of Kataro Shirayamadani in 1901. Base marks: flames mark, the date, shape number 927 E, and the artist's incised cipher. 6.75" h. *Courtesy of Mark Mussio, Cincinnati Art Galleries, LLC.*

Figure 228. Painted Mat baluster vase decorated in 1901 by Anna M. Valentien with branches of brown leaves and pink berries on a celadon ground. Base marks: second mark for glaze misses, flames mark, the date, shape number 3EZ, and the artist's initials. 5.75" x 4.75". *Courtesy of David Rago Auctions.*

Figure 230. Vellum bulbous vase, 1901, with thick blue glaze dripping over a brown mottled ground. Base marks: flames mark, the date, Rookwood Museum paper label. 5" x 4.5". *Courtesy of David Rago Auctions.*

Figure 229. Rare embossed Painted Mat vase with yellow and red chrysanthemums on a black ground decorated in 1901 by Harriet Wilcox. Base marks: flames mark, the date, shape number 886 Z, and the artist's initials in black slip. *Courtesy of Mark Mussio, Cincinnati Art Galleries, LLC.*

Figure 231. Standard glaze vase with Art Nouveau red poppies painted in 1902 by Matthew A. Daly. Base marks: flames mark, the date, shape number 804 C, an incised Y for yellow (Standard) glaze, and the decorator's incised full signature. 12.75" h. *Courtesy of Mark Mussio, Cincinnati Art Galleries, LLC.*

Figure 232. Standard glaze vase decorated by Matthew A. Daly in 1920, featuring yellow jonquils encircling the body. Base marks: flames mark, the date, shape number 901B, a Y for yellow tinted glaze, and the artist's signature, "M.A. Daly." 11.25" h. *Courtesy of Mark Mussio, Cincinnati Art Galleries, LLC.*

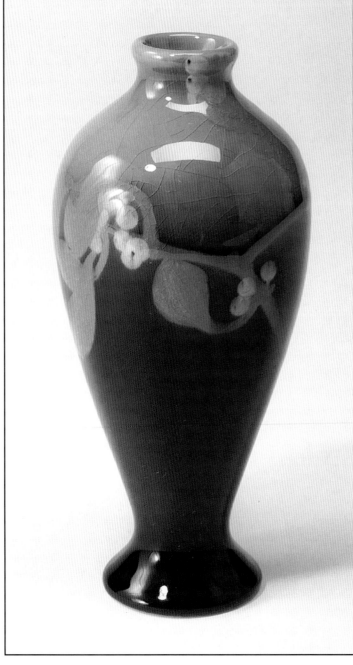

Figure 233. Iris glaze baluster vase painted by Rose Fechheimer in 1902, displaying grey mistletoe on a caramel-to-indigo ground. Base marks: flames mark, the date, shape number 842C, W, and the artist's initials. 7" x 3". *Courtesy of David Rago Auctions.*

Figure 234. Standard glaze vase decorated in 1902 by Edward T. Hurley with a realistically painted brown and white cat. Base marks: flames mark, the date, shape number 900D, and the artist's incised initials. 6.25" h. *Courtesy of Mark Mussio, Cincinnati Art Galleries, LLC.*

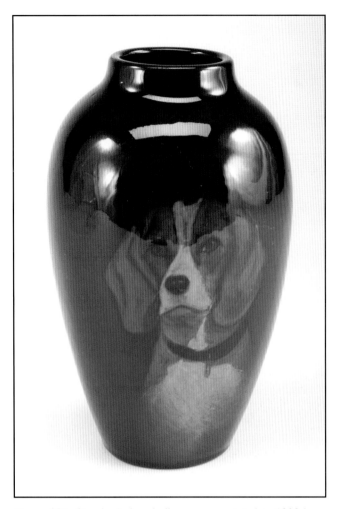

Figure 235. Standard glaze bulbous vase painted in 1902 by Edward T. Hurley with a portrait of a beagle. Base marks: flames mark, the date, shape number 900B, and the artist's initials. 9" x 5.5". *Courtesy of David Rago Auctions.*

Figure 237. Iris glaze vase with bright yellow parrot tulips on a nearly black ground painted in a stylish Art Nouveau manner in 1902 by Sara Sax. Three large flowers in various stages of bloom cover about two thirds of the vase. Base marks: flames mark, the date, shape number 907 D, an incised W for white (Iris) glaze, and the artist's impressed monogram. 10.5" h. *Courtesy of Mark Mussio, Cincinnati Art Galleries, LLC.*

Figure 236. Standard glaze ewer cast in 1902 and decorated by Laura Lindeman with clover flowers and leaves. Base marks: flames mark, the date, shape number 584C, and the artist's incised initials. 5.5" h. *Courtesy of Mark Mussio, Cincinnati Art Galleries, LLC.*

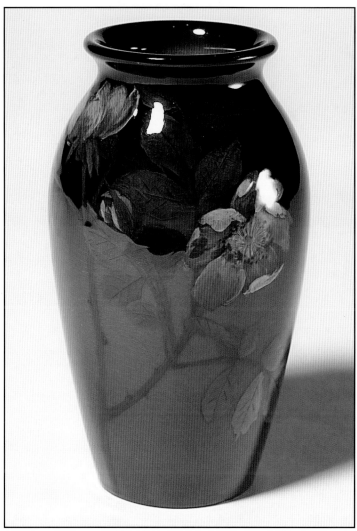

Figure 238. Standard glaze vase decorated by Carrie Steinle in 1902, featuring orange wild roses with green leaves, and branches. Base marks: flames mark, the date, shape number 568C, and the decorator's incised initials. 7" h. *Courtesy of Mark Mussio, Cincinnati Art Galleries, LLC.*

Figure 240. Colorful Iris glaze vase with large, mauve chrysan-themums with green stems and leaves painted in 1902 by John Dee Wareham. Base marks: flames mark, the date, shape number 905 B, and the artist's incised initials. 14.5" h. *Courtesy of Mark Mussio, Cincinnati Art Galleries, LLC.*

Figure 239. Silver-overlaid Standard glaze vase painted with roses by Leona Vera Van Briggle and overlaid with star-shaped blossoms in 1902. Base marks: flames mark, the date, shape number 905E, and the artist's initials. 6.75" x 3.75". *Courtesy of David Rago Auctions.*

Figure 241. Standard glaze vase painted by Lenore Asbury with milkweed pods in 1903. Base marks: flames mark and the artist's initials. 12" x 4.75". *Courtesy of David Rago Auctions.*

Figure 243. Standard glaze cylindrical vase painted in 1903 by Edith Felton with daisies. Base marks: flames mark and the artist's initials. 5.5" x 3". *Courtesy of David Rago Auctions.*

Figure 242. Iris glaze ovoid vase painted in 1903 by Rose Fechheimer with a grapevine in purple and red on a white ground. Base marks: flames mark, the date, shape number 922C, W, and the artist's initials. 8.25" x 4.5". *Courtesy of David Rago Auctions.*

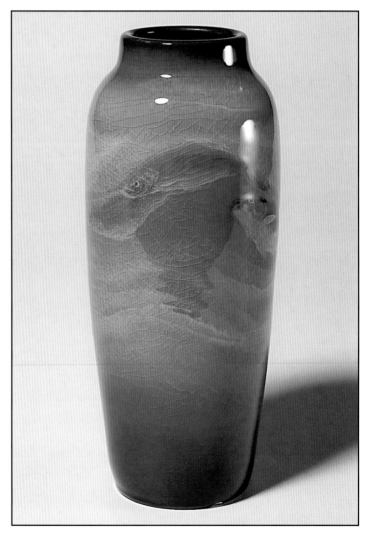

Figure 244. Sea Green vase decorated with five swimming fish by Edward T. Hurley in 1903. The fish are accented by undulating currents. Base marks: flames mark, the date, shape number 907D, an incised G for Sea Green glaze, an impressed 199, and the artist's incised initials. 10" h. *Courtesy of Mark Mussio, Cincinnati Art Galleries, LLC.*

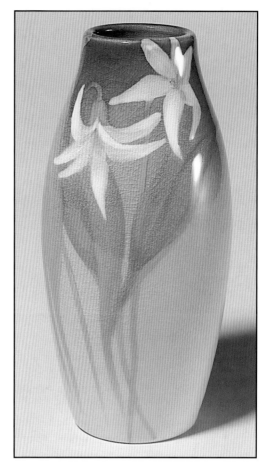

Figure 246. Iris glaze vase depicting white flowers and green leaves and stems on a graduated green ground painted by Laura Lindeman in 1903. Base marks: flames mark, the date, shape number 931D, an incised W for Iris glaze, and the decorator's incised initials. *Courtesy of Mark Mussio, Cincinnati Art Galleries, LLC.*

Figure 245. Rare Iris glaze tall vase painted in 1903 by Sturgis Lawrence with white sailboats on blue water under white clouds. Base marks: second mark for crazing at the shoulder, flames mark, the date, shapes number 904C, and the artist's initials. 11.75" x 4.25". *Courtesy of David Rago Auctions.*

Figure 247. Iris glaze ovoid vase painted by Laura Lindenman with yellow cornflowers, 1903. Base marks: flames mark. 7.5" h. *Courtesy of David Rago Auctions.*

Figure 248. Standard glaze vase with goldenrod plants painted by Marianne Mitchell in 1903. Base marks: flames mark, the date, shape number 614 E and the decorator's incised monogram. 8" h. *Courtesy of Mark Mussio, Cincinnati Art Galleries, LLC.*

Figure 249. Large Standard glaze ovoid vase painted by Mary Nourse with autumn oak leaves, 1903. Base marks: flames mark and the decorator's initials. 10" x 5". *Courtesy of David Rago Auctions.*

Figure 250. Tall Iris glaze vase painted in 1903 by Olga Geneva Reed with yellow and orange bachelors' buttons. Base marks: flames mark, the date, shape number 901, the artist's initials, W, and an X second mark. 11.75" x 5". *Courtesy of David Rago Auctions.*

Figure 251. Iris glaze vase with purple violets painted by Fred Rothenbusch in 1903. Base marks: flames mark, the date, shape number 483, an incised W for Iris glaze, and the decorator's incised initials. 6.25" h. *Courtesy of Mark Mussio, Cincinnati Art Galleries, LLC.*

Figure 252. Iris glaze vase with white Easter lilies painted in 1903 by Carl Schmidt. There are two long stalks with flowers, the stalk in the front having three lilies and the other bearing two. Base marks: flames mark, the date, shape number 907 C, an incised W for white (Iris) glaze, and the artist's impressed monogram. 14" h. Cincinnati Art Gallieries reported, "This vase was re-discovered by appraisers on the BBC version of 'Antiques Roadshow' ..." *Courtesy of Mark Mussio, Cincinnati Art Galleries, LLC.*

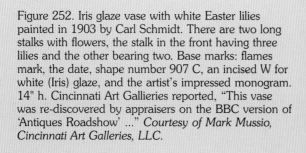

Figure 253. Iris glaze vase painted by Lenore Asbury with yellow tulips in 1904. Base marks: flames mark, the date, shape number 892C, W, and the decorator's initials. 8.75" x 4.25". *Courtesy of David Rago Auctions.*

Figure 254. Sea Green vase displays blooming magnolia flowers, leaves, and branches painted by Constance Baker in 1904. Base marks: flames mark, the date, shape number 900 C, an incised G for Sea Green glaze, and the decorator's initials. 7.5" h. *Courtesy of Mark Mussio, Cincinnati Art Galleries, LLC.*

Figure 255. Standard glaze squat vessel painted in 1904 by Irene Bishop with golden primrose blossoms. Base marks: flames mark, the date, shape number 919E, and the artist's initials. 4" x 4". *Courtesy of David Rago Auctions.*

Figure 256. Standard glaze vase with black-eyed susans painted by Caroline Bonsall in 1904. Base marks: flames mark, the date, shape number 604 D, and the artist's incised initials. 6.75" h. *Courtesy of Mark Mussio, Cincinnati Art Galleries, LLC.*

Figure 257. Sea Green vase with four swimming fish created in 1904 by Edward T. Hurley. Base marks: flames mark, the date, shape number 901 C, an incised G for Sea Green glaze, and the artist's incised initials. 8.5" h. *Courtesy of Mark Mussio, Cincinnati Art Galleries, LLC.*

Figure 258. Two Standard glaze vases: one vase painted by Elizabeth Lincoln with orange roses, dating from 1904 (mark on the base with an X as a second for scaling at the rim); the other decorated in 1907 by Laura Lindeman with lily-of-the-valley. Both examples are marked. 4.25" x 6.5". *Courtesy of David Rago Auctions.*

Figure 259. Iris glaze vase featuring yellow dandelions and green leaves on a shaded cream-to-brown ground painted in 1904 by Clara Lindeman. Base marks: flames mark, the date, shape number 906E, an incised W for Iris glaze, and the artist's initials. 4" h. *Courtesy of Mark Mussio, Cincinnati Art Galleries, LLC.*

Figure 261. Iris glaze vase painted by Fred Rothenbusch with purple crocuses in 1904. Base marks: flames mark, the date, shape number 941C, W, and the artist's initials. 9.5" x 3.25". *Courtesy of David Rago Auctions.*

Figure 260. Iris glaze vase with purple pansies and green leaves and stems on a lavender to shaded gray ground painted by Fred Rothenbusch in 1904, and accented with a simple silver collar at the rim. Base marks: flames mark, the date, shape number 838C, an incised W for Iris glaze, and the artist's cipher. 7.5" h. *Courtesy of Mark Mussio, Cincinnati Art Galleries, LLC.*

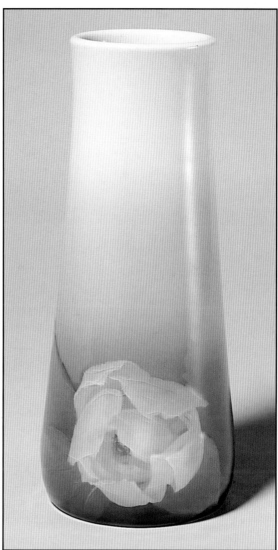

Figure 262. Sara Sax adorned this tall Iris glaze vase with white magnolia flowers, green leaves, and brown branches on a nicely shaded gray to cream background in 1904. Base marks: flames mark, the date, shape number 950C, an incised W for Iris glaze, the decorator's impressed monogram, and a wheel-ground X to indicate this item is a second (probably due to some glaze peppering, mostly in the rim area). 10.25" h. *Courtesy of Mark Mussio, Cincinnati Art Galleries, LLC.*

Figure 263. Iris glaze vase with white parrot tulip painted in 1904 by Sara Sax. Base marks: flames mark, the date, shape number 907 E, an incised W for white (Iris) glaze, and the artist's impressed monogram. 8.5" h. *Courtesy of Mark Mussio, Cincinnati Art Galleries, LLC.*

Figure 264. Standard glaze vase, dated 1904, decorated by Carrie Steinle with yellow daffodils on a shaded surface. Base mark: flames mark, the date, shape number 925E, and the artist's incised signature. 6.5" h. *Courtesy of Mark Mussio, Cincinnati Art Galleries, LLC.*

Figure 266. Commemorative plaque made in 1904 for an Elks convention displaying the molded head of a proud elk against the background of a clock and the notation "B.P.O.E. Cincinnati, 1904" on the face. It is covered with a purple high glaze. Base marks: flames mark, the date, and shape number 744 Z. The Z designation is indicative of mat glaze items, but every known example of this has been covered with the glossy purple finish. *Courtesy of Mark Mussio, Cincinnati Art Galleries, LLC.*

Figure 265. Iris glaze vase decorated in 1904 by Albert Valentien, depicting life-sized goldenrod plants fully encircling the tall vase. Base marks: flames mark, the date, shape number 904 A, and the decorator's full signature. 17" h. *Courtesy of Mark Mussio, Cincinnati Art Galleries, LLC.*

Figure 267. Iris glaze vase painted in 1905 by Irene Bishop with a branch of purple wisteria. Base marks: flames mark, the date, shape number 950D, IV, and W. 8.25" x 3.5". *Courtesy of David Rago Auctions.*

Figure 268. Standard glaze vase with yellow day lilies painted by Caroline Bonsal in 1905. Base marks: flames mark, the date, shape number 937 and the decorator's incised initials. 9" h. *Courtesy of Mark Mussio, Cincinnati Art Galleries, LLC.*

Figure 269. Slender Iris glaze vase displaying pink nasturtiums and sinuous green leaves and vines on a yellow to blue ground decorated by Edward Diers in 1905. Base marks: flames mark, the date, shape number 941 D, an incised W for Iris glaze, and the artist's incised initials. 8" h. *Courtesy of Mark Mussio, Cincinnati Art Galleries, LLC.*

Figure 270. Petite Sea Green vase decorated by Elizabeth Lincoln in 1905 with green branches and leaves and yellow rose hips encircling the upper portion of the piece. Base marks: flames mark, the date, shape number 942E, an incised G for the Sea Green glaze, a wheel-ground X indicating this item is a second, and the artist's initials. 4.25" h. *Courtesy of Mark Mussio, Cincinnati Art Galleries, LLC.*

Figure 271. Painted Mat vase with Virginia creeper leaves, vines, and berries painted in 1905 by Olga Geneva Reed. All decoration is done in a rose shade against a maroon ground. Base marks: flames mark, the date, shape number 892 C, an impressed V, and the artist's initials in black slip. 8.75" h. *Courtesy of Mark Mussio, Cincinnati Art Galleries, LLC.*

Figure 272. Iris glaze vase decorated in 1905 by Fred Rothenbusch with pink carnation flowers and buds with green leaves and stems on a nicely shaded ground. Base marks: flames mark, the date, shape number 904E, an incised W for Iris glaze, and the decorator's incised monogram. *Courtesy of Mark Mussio, Cincinnati Art Galleries, LLC.*

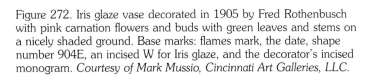

Figure 273. Iris glaze vase adorned with white daisies on a subtly shaded background, decorated by Sara Sax in 1905. Base marks: flames mark, the date, shape number 904D, an incised W for Iris glaze, and the artist's monogram. 7.75" h. *Courtesy of Mark Mussio, Cincinnati Art Galleries, LLC.*

Figure 274. Slender Iris glaze vase displaying three white trout lilies with green leaves and stems on a white to lavender ground, decorated by Sara Sax in 1905. Base marks: flames mark, the date, shape number 941 D, an incised W for Iris glaze, and the decorator's monogram. 8" h. *Courtesy of Mark Mussio, Cincinnati Art Galleries, LLC.*

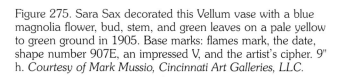

Figure 275. Sara Sax decorated this Vellum vase with a blue magnolia flower, bud, stem, and green leaves on a pale yellow to green ground in 1905. Base marks: flames mark, the date, shape number 907E, an impressed V, and the artist's cipher. 9" h. *Courtesy of Mark Mussio, Cincinnati Art Galleries, LLC.*

Figure 277. Rare Carved Mat vase with three dimensional cherry blossoms done in 1905 by Kataro Shirayamadani. The lifelike flowers are executed in red, green, and yellow on a rose ground with blackened areas for contrast. Base marks: flames mark, the date, shape number 919 E, and the artist's incised cipher. 4" h. Cincinnati Art Galleries relate, "Shirayamadani mostly worked on larger carved forms during this period which were often to be designed as lamps. Smaller, organic vase forms are rare …" *Courtesy of Mark Mussio, Cincinnati Art Galleries, LLC.*

Figure 276. Iris glaze vase with two large blue and white irises painted in 1905 by Carl Schmidt. Base marks: flames mark, the date, shape number 951 C, an incised W for white (Iris) glaze, and the decorator's impressed monogram. 10.25" h. This piece was once owned by Carl Schmidt's daughter, Dorothy Potts. *Courtesy of Mark Mussio, Cincinnati Art Galleries, LLC.*

Figure 278. Standard glaze vase decorated with orange wild roses painted by Carrie Steinle in 1905. Base marks: flames mark, the date, shape number 901D, and the artist's incised monogram. 7" h. *Courtesy of Mark Mussio, Cincinnati Art Galleries, LLC.*

Figure 281. Incised Mat vase decorated in 1906 by Rose Fechheimer using an oak leaves and acorns motif around the shoulder of the vase. The vessel was then colored with maroon and green mat glazes. Base marks: flames mark, the date, shape number 881D, and the designer's incised signature. 5.5" h. *Courtesy of Mark Mussio, Cincinnati Art Galleries, LLC.*

Figure 279. Production comport glazed in green and brown with molded vertical line decoration, potted in 1905. Base marks: flames mark, the date, and shape number S1781C. 7" h. *Courtesy of Bob Shores and Dale Jones.*

Figure 280. Mat glaze three-handled loving cup in the Arts and Crafts style with molded, sinuous design under a red to blue mat glaze, 1905. Base marks: flames mark, the date, shape number 830B, an impressed V, and a wheel-ground X indicating this is a second, probably for an irregular 1.5" glaze miss near one of the handles. 7.25" h. *Courtesy of Mark Mussio, Cincinnati Art Galleries, LLC.*

Figure 282. Carved Mat ovoid vase by Rose Fechheimer with water lilies in red and green on a rich brown and green frothy ground, 1906. Base marks: flames mark, the date, an illegible shape number, and the artist's initials. 7.75" x 4". *Courtesy of David Rago Auctions.*

Figure 283. Iris glaze scenic vase decorated by Edward T. Hurley in 1906. Hurley has artfully arranged pine trees near the edge of a body of water, utilizing bright shades of blue, green, and brown. Tiny seagulls can be seen gliding by. Base marks: flames mark, the date, an incised W for Iris glaze, and the artist's incised initials. 7.75" h. *Courtesy of Mark Mussio, Cincinnati Art Galleries, LLC.*

Figure 284. Iris glaze ovoid vase painted by Elizabeth Lincoln with rooks in flight on a lavender ground, 1906. Base marks: flames mark, the date, shape number 900C, W, and the artist's cipher. 7.5" x 4.5". *Courtesy of David Rago Auctions.*

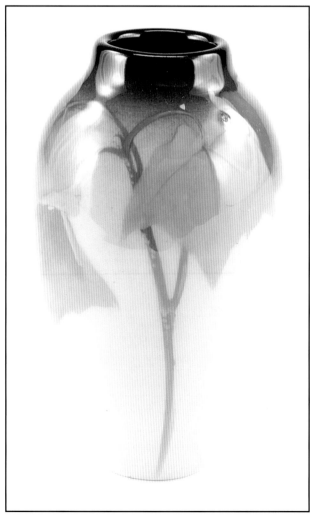

Figure 285. Iris glaze bulbous vase finely painted by Sara Sax with autumn leaves, 1906. Base marks: flames mark, the date, shape number 900D, and the artist's cipher. 6.5" x 3.5". *Courtesy of David Rago Auctions.*

Figure 286. Vellum vase painted in 1906 by Carl Schmidt with blue irises. Base marks: flames mark, the date, shape number 950C, and the artist's initials. 10.25" x 4.25". *Courtesy of David Rago Auctions.*

Figure 288. Iris glaze vase with four swifts on a branch under green foliage, decorated in 1906 by an unidentified artist. Base marks: an X indicating this is a second (for glaze inconsistencies and an underglaze chip on the top rim) flames mark, date, illegible artist's signature. 7" x 5". *Courtesy of David Rago Auctions.*

Figure 287. Painted Mat vase decorated in 1906 with a pine cone motif by Harriet Wilcox. Base marks: flames mark, the date, shape number 950B, and the artist's initials in black slip. *Courtesy of Mark Mussio, Cincinnati Art Galleries, LLC.*

Figure 289. Early production vase impressed with a stylized arrow pattern under a rich green glaze, 1906. Base marks: flames mark and date. 7.5" h. *Courtesy of David Rago Auctions.*

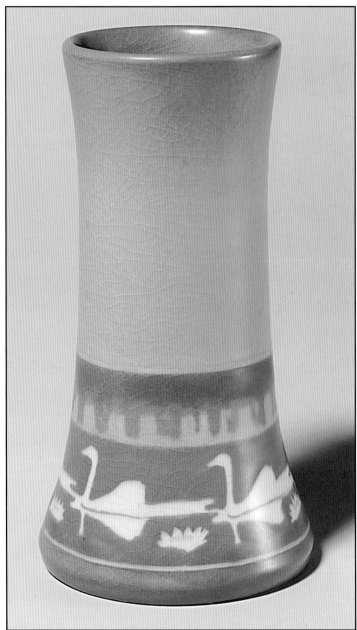

Figure 290. Iris glaze vase with daffodil decoration done by Sallie Coyne in 1907. Most of the decoration is on the front of the vase with tall, thin stalks ending in graceful flowers. Base marks: flames mark, the date, shape number 482, an incised W for white (Iris) glaze, and the artist's incised monogram. 9.75" h. *Courtesy of Mark Mussio, Cincinnati Art Galleries, LLC.*

Figure 291. Unusual Vellum glaze scenic vase decorated in 1907 by Edward Diers with a repeating band of stylized swans reflecting in the water with trees in the background and water lilies in the foreground. Base marks: flames mark, the date, shape number 1358, an impressed V, an incised V for Vellum glaze, and the artist's incised initials. 8.5" h. *Courtesy of Mark Mussio, Cincinnati Art Galleries, LLC.*

Figure 292. Carved Matt fruit bowl with a rolled rim. The piece was incised by Cecil Duell in 1907 with stylized bunches of green grapes on an indigo ground. Base marks: flames mark, the date, shape number 957C, and the artist's initials. 3.25" x 8". *Courtesy of David Rago Auctions.*

Figure 293. Iris glaze vase with blackberry decoration created in 1907 by Fred Rothenbusch. A vine encircles the collar of the vase while leaves, berries and canes descend from it. Base marks: flames mark, the date, shape number 905 C, an incised W for white (Iris) glaze, and the artist's incised monogram. 10" h. *Courtesy of Mark Mussio, Cincinnati Art Galleries, LLC.*

Figure 294. Unusual and distinctive Vellum vase divided into three panels, each featuring an identical view of a very stylized Scottish thistle. This decoration is the work of Sara Sax in 1907. Base marks: flames mark, the date, shape number 952 E, an impressed V, an incised V for Vellum glaze, and the artist's impressed monogram. 7.5" h. *Courtesy of Mark Mussio, Cincinnati Art Galleries, LLC.*

Figure 295. Iris glaze ovoid vase decorated by Sara Sax with grey roses in a shaded pink-to-green ground, 1907. Base marks: flames mark, the date, shape number, 932C, W, and the artist's cipher. 9.75" x 4". *Courtesy of David Rago Auctions.*

Figure 296. Iris glaze vase painted by Carl Schmidt in 1907 with lifelike mushrooms. Base marks: flames mark, the date, shape number 917 C, a W for Iris glaze, and the artist's monogram. 7" h. *Courtesy of Mark Mussio, Cincinnati Art Galleries, LLC.*

Figure 297. Spectacular Iris glaze vase composed in 1907 by Kataro Shirayamadani, adorned a pair of black ducks skimming over the marshland. Base marks: flames mark, the date, shape number 935C, an incised W for Iris glaze, and the artist's incised Japanese signature. 9" h. *Courtesy of Mark Mussio, Cincinnati Art Galleries, LLC.*

Figure 298. Fine and rare Iris glaze cylindrical vase painted by Kataro Shirayamadani in 1907 with a landscape in celadon against a black-to-ivory sky. Base marks: flames mark, the date, shape number 952E, and the artist's Japanese cipher. 7" x 3.25". *Courtesy of David Rago Auctions.*

Figure 299. Standard glaze vase depicting a woodland plant, perhaps lyre-leaved sage, painted in 1907 by Carrie Steinle. Base marks: flames mark, the date, shape number 950D, and the artist's incised signature. 8.25" h. *Courtesy of Mark Mussio, Cincinnati Art Galleries, LLC.*

Figure 300. Iris glaze vase decorated by Katherine Van Horne in 1907 displaying green grapes and leaves on a light to dark gray background. Base marks: flames mark, the date, shape number 900D, an incised W for Iris glaze, and the artist's incised monogram. 6.25" h. *Courtesy of Mark Mussio, Cincinnati Art Galleries, LLC.*

Figure 301. Production pitcher embossed with triangles under a good frothy mint green glaze, 1907. Base marks: flames mark and the date. 4.5". *Courtesy of David Rago Auctions.*

Figure 303. Colorful Iris glaze vase decorated with white flowers with yellow centers and green leaves and stems on a yellow to peach to gray ground by Sallie Coyne in 1908. Base marks: flames mark, the date, shape number 905D, an incised W for Iris glaze, and the artist's monogram. 7.75" h. *Courtesy of Mark Mussio, Cincinnati Art Galleries, LLC.*

Figure 302. Iris glaze vase with red nasturtium decoration done in 1908 by Lenore Asbury. Base marks: flames mark, the date, shape number 604 D, an incised W for white (Iris) glaze, and the artist's incised initials. 7" h. *Courtesy of Mark Mussio, Cincinnati Art Galleries, LLC.*

Figure 304. Vellum ovoid vase painted in 1908 by Edward Diers with clusters of blue berries hanging from delicate vines against a blush ground. Base marks: flames mark, the date, shape number 1126C, V, and the artist's initials. 9.25" x 5.25". *Courtesy of David Rago Auctions.*

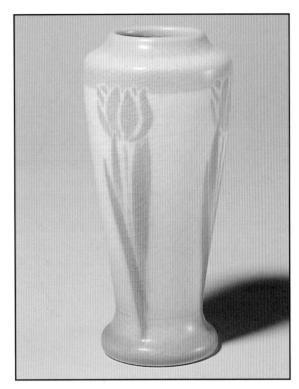

Figure 305. Pleasant 1908 Vellum glaze vase encircled with stylized pink tulips and green leaves by Elizabeth Lincoln. Base marks: flames mark, the date, shape number 1358E, a V for Vellum glaze, and the decorator's initials. 7" h. *Courtesy of Mark Mussio, Cincinnati Art Galleries, LLC.*

Figure 307. Painted Mat cylindrical vase painted in 1908 by Elizabeth Noonan with blue and blue-green rooks in flight. Base marks: flames mark, the date, shape number 952E, V, and the artist's initials. 7.5" x 3.5". *Courtesy of David Rago Auctions.*

Figure 308. Vellum footed squat bowl in 1908 by Mary Nourse in turquoise-to-indigo. Base marks: flames mark and the date. 2.75" x 5.25". *Courtesy of David Rago Auctions.*

Figure 306. Iris glaze vase with cherry blossoms sprouting from a gnarled limb, the work of Clara Lindeman in 1908. The finely detailed pink and white blooms contrast nicely with their host twigs, all done in a very Japanese manner. Base marks: flames mark, the date, shape number 900 C, an incised W for white (Iris) glaze, and the artist's incised initials. 8.25" h. Cincinnati Art Galleries states, "This is one of the nicest examples by Clara Lindeman we have seen." *Courtesy of Mark Mussio, Cincinnati Art Galleries, LLC.*

Figure 309. Iris glaze vase with boldly painted magnolia executed in 1908 by Sara Sax. Base marks: flames mark, the date, shape number 604 D, an incised W for white glaze, and the artist's impressed monogram. 7" h. *Courtesy of Mark Mussio, Cincinnati Art Galleries, LLC.*

Figure 311. Mat glaze production vase from 1908 with decoration of highly molded bearded irises at the top with stems descending. This early production vase has been covered with a blue-green mat glaze. Base marks: flames mark, the date, shape number 1003, and an impressed V. 8.5" h. *Courtesy of Mark Mussio, Cincinnati Art Galleries, LLC.*

Figure 310. Iris glaze vase decorated in 1908 by Sara Sax with deep purple grapes and green leaves. Base marks: flames mark, the date, shape number 796 B, an incised W for Iris glaze, the artist's cipher, and a wheel-ground X. 9" h. *Courtesy of Mark Mussio, Cincinnati Art Galleries, LLC.*

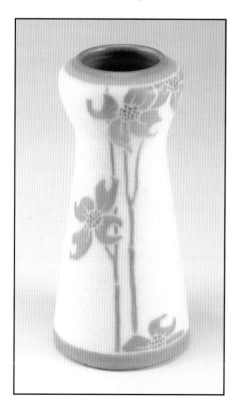

Figure 312. Vellum bulbous vase decorated by Lenore Asbury in 1909 with slip-painted slate gray dogwood blossoms on ivory ground. Base marks: flames mark, the date, and the decorator's initials. 7.5" x 3.5". *Courtesy of David Rago Auctions.*

Figure 313. Iris glaze ovoid vase painted by Elizabeth Lincoln with pink, white, and yellow blossoms on a blue to pink ground, 1909. Base marks: flames mark, the date, shape number 900D, the artist's initials, and W. 6.25" x 3.5". *Courtesy of David Rago Auctions.*

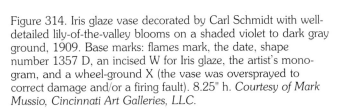

Figure 314. Iris glaze vase decorated by Carl Schmidt with well-detailed lily-of-the-valley blooms on a shaded violet to dark gray ground, 1909. Base marks: flames mark, the date, shape number 1357 D, an incised W for Iris glaze, the artist's mono-gram, and a wheel-ground X (the vase was oversprayed to correct damage and/or a firing fault). 8.25" h. *Courtesy of Mark Mussio, Cincinnati Art Galleries, LLC.*

Rookwood Pottery in 1910

To celebrate Rookwood's thirtieth anniversary, the Pottery introduced Ombroso, the last of the mat glaze lines. Ombroso was an opaque mat glaze in muted grays and browns, often embellished with other colors. When fired, this glaze would separate into several colors with varying effect. The Ombroso glaze was applied to incised or relief decorated wares and would remain available until 1930.

Figure 315. Mat vase carved by William Hentschel in 1915 using a geometric theme and then covered with the Ombroso glaze. Base marks: flames mark, the date, shape number 892 C, and the artist's incised initials. 9.25" h. *Courtesy of Mark Mussio, Cincinnati Art Galleries, LLC.*

Mat glazes would remain very popular for Rookwood and would continue to be used in some form until 1960, when the Rookwood plant in Cincinnati closed. Mat glazes were used on a wide variety of the company's mass-produced, unsigned wares, including ashtrays, bookends, bowls, candlesticks and lamps, and small figurines.

From 1883 to 1913, William Watts Taylor had set Rookwood's course, following the trail Maria L. Nichols had first blazed. He had organized the company and ensured that the Rookwood name would be associated with high quality ceramic art. His leadership ended on November 12, 1913, with his death. The company's vice president and director of the Cincinnati Art Museum, Joseph Henry Gest, replaced Taylor in January 1914.

Figure 316. A thick, dark rose mat glaze covers this vase made in 1912. Base marks: flames mark, the date, shape number 989D, and a wheel-ground X (there is a grinding chip at the base or several pin point size burst glaze bubbles). 8" h. *Courtesy of Mark Mussio, Cincinnati Art Galleries, LLC.*

In 1914, Rookwood added bookends to their product line, beginning with the Reader. Over the next five years, twelve book-end shapes were offered. Selling well, eighty-six numbered book-end shapes and one special shape were created by Rookwood over the years. Worth noting on both the bookends and paperweights is the inclusion of an additional hole in the base of many of these objects. This opening allowed extra weight to be added, usually in the form of sand. Once the sand was in place, the fill hole was covered with soft plaster. This extra weight was useful for both bookends required to hold up weighty tomes and top-heavy fig-ures. Bookends were economical items for Rookwood. Mold pro-duced and simply glazed with no hand decoration, they were inex-pensive to make and sold at lower prices, further expanding Rookwood's market.

Figure 317. Pair of porcelain Buddha bookends designed by William McDonald, made in 1918, and coated in a tan mat glaze. Base marks on each: flames mark, the date, shape number 2362, the cast designer's monogram, a sideways P for porcelain body, and a wheel-ground X (because of firing separations). 7.25" h. each. *Courtesy of Mark Mussio, Cincinnati Art Galleries, LLC.*

Figure 318. Paperweight featuring two geese in white glaze, shape 1855. While this paperweight was produced in 1928, the photos provide a good view of the fill hole covered with soft plaster in the base. 4.25" h. *Courtesy of Seekers Antiques.*

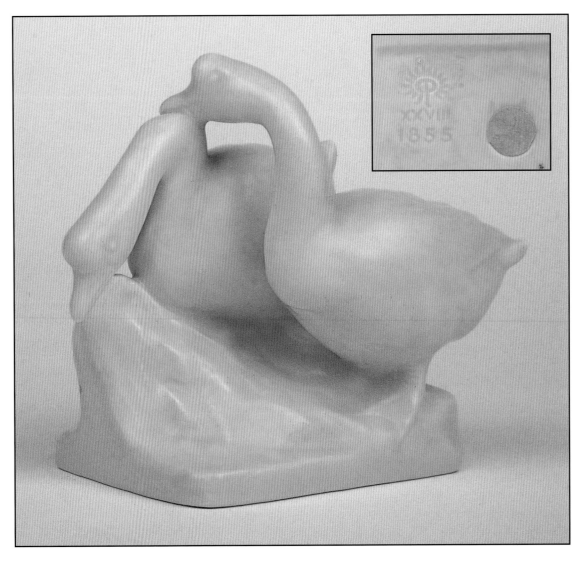

For the Pottery's thirty-fifth anniversary in 1915, Rookwood introduced Soft Porcelain (marked with an impressed "P" among the other marks on the base). Soft Porcelain had a hard, white, vitreous body that had been inspired by the Chinese soft-paste porcelain. Soft Porcelain was used for vases, flower arranging bowls, flower frogs, and paperweights. This body allowed Rookwood to use bright, vibrant colors the company had long sought to produce. By the 1920s, Soft Porcelain would be renamed Jewel Porcelain since consumers began to misconstrue "soft" as indicating this body was weak.

Rookwood continued to forge ahead through World War I without interruption. However, the war itself changed the culture. After the war, the Arts and Crafts Movement was replaced with machine age modernism. The handcrafted, unique, signed art Rookwood had made its name and reputation on was now coming to be considered a quaint, romantic thing of the past. The company would have to change.

Rookwood's 1910s Objects

The following is a sampling of the various wares produced by Rookwood throughout the 1910s, organized by year and, within each year, by artist.

Figure 319. Soft Porcelain bulbous vase painted by Arthur Conant with an Oriental night landscape of flying bluebirds and small white rabbits around blooming trees by a mountain, 1918. Base marks: flames mark, the date, shape number 1278F, P for porcelain, and the artist's cipher. 7.25" x 3.75". *Courtesy of David Rago Auctions.*

Figure 320. Iris glaze vase decorated by Lenore Asbury in 1910 with blue French thistle flowers, leaves, and stalks on a green-to-blue shaded ground. Base marks: flames mark, the date, shape number 925 C, an incised W for Iris glaze, and the artist's incised initials. 9.25" h. *Courtesy of Mark Mussio, Cincinnati Art Galleries, LLC.*

Figure 321. Iris glaze ovoid vase painted by Edward Diers with purple sweetpeas, 1910. Base marks: flames mark, the date, shape number 900D,the artist's initials, and W. 6.5" x 3.75". *Courtesy of David Rago Auctions.*

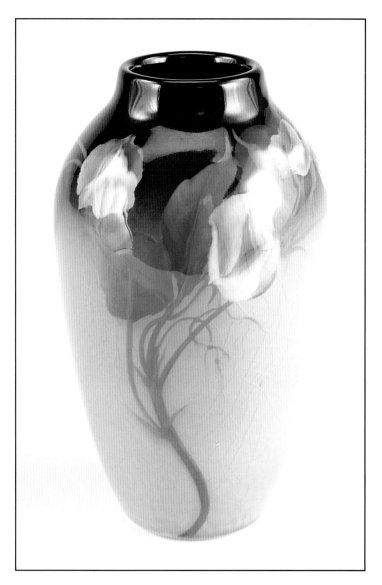

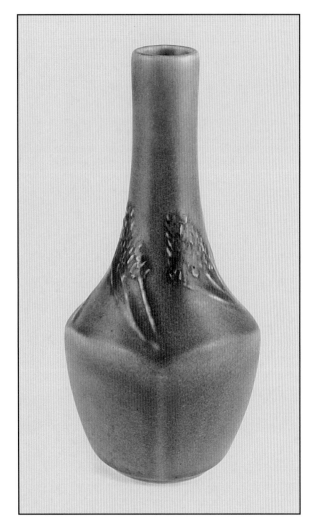

Figure 322. Carved Mat bottle-shaped vase decorated in 1910 by William Hentschel with clusters of blue blossoms on a purple and blue-green ground. Base marks: flames mark, the date, shape number 1697, and the artist's initials. 8.25" x 4". *Courtesy of David Rago Auctions.*

Figure 323. Carved Mat vase decorated in 1910 by William Hentschel with green leaves on green and indigo ground. Base marks: flames mark, the date, shape number 679V, and the artist's initials. 7.25" x 5". *Courtesy of David Rago Auctions.*

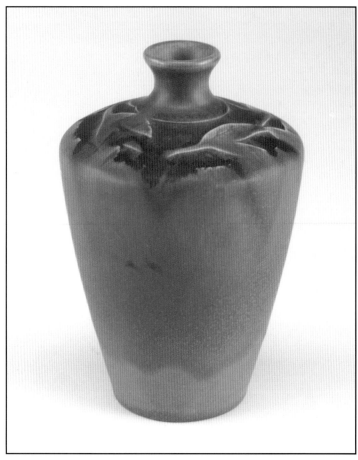

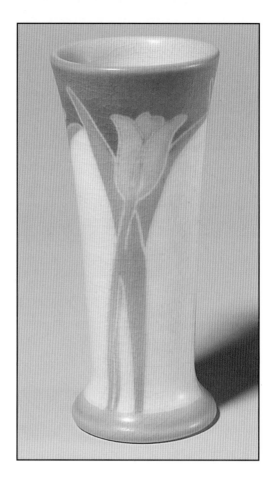

Figure 324. Vellum vase decorated by Elizabeth Lincoln in 1910, featuring stylized pink tulips and green leaves on a gray and cream ground. Base marks: flames mark, the date, shape number 1357 E, a V for Vellum glaze, and the artist's incised initials. 7.25" h. *Courtesy of Mark Mussio, Cincinnati Art Galleries, LLC.*

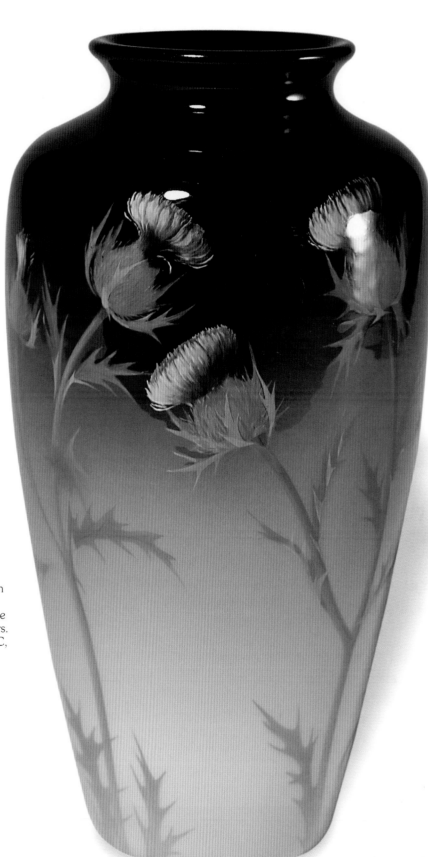

Figure 325. Iris glaze vase with blue thistles decorated in 1910 by Carl Schmidt, featuring detailed flowers and stems that encircle the vase. The shading at the top of the vase is nearly black, adding strong contrast to the flowers. Base marks: flames mark, the date, shape number 614 C, an incised W for white (Iris) glaze, and the impressed artist's monogram. 12.25" h. *Courtesy of Mark Mussio, Cincinnati Art Galleries, LLC.*

Figure 326. Iris glaze scenic vase with lotus blossom motif decorated in 1910 by Kataro Shirayamadani. Flowers and leaves rise out of clear water in which also grow thin grasses. Base marks: flames mark, the date, shape number 951 B, an incised W for white (Iris) glaze, and the incised artist's cipher. 12" h. *Courtesy of Mark Mussio, Cincinnati Art Galleries, LLC.*

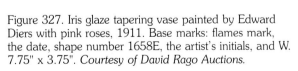

Figure 327. Iris glaze tapering vase painted by Edward Diers with pink roses, 1911. Base marks: flames mark, the date, shape number 1658E, the artist's initials, and W. 7.75" x 3.75". *Courtesy of David Rago Auctions.*

Figure 328. Carved Mat squat bowl decorated by William Hentschel with fish and sea plants in green on a brown-green butterfat ground, 1911. Base marks: flames mark, the date, shape number 438, and the artist's initials. 5.5" x 9.5". *Courtesy of David Rago Auctions.*

Figure 330. Vellum bulbous vase painted with swans in flight on a blue and white ground by Elizabeth Lincoln, 1911. Base marks: flames mark, the date, shape number 942D, an impressed V for Vellum, and the artist's initials. 6" x 4.5". *Courtesy of David Rago Auctions.*

Figure 329. Iris glaze vase decorated with white roses on a pink-to-green ground by Elizabeth Lincoln, 1911. 6" x 5.5". *Courtesy of David Rago Auctions.*

Figure 331. Large mat glaze production vase made at Rookwood in 1911 with three embossed panels, each adorned with a ram's head at the top and Greek keys at the bottom. Base marks: flames mark, the date, and shape number 1658 D. 14.25" h. *Courtesy of Mark Mussio, Cincinnati Art Galleries, LLC.*

Figure 332. Production vase embossed with four-square design under a good raspberry-to-green Mat glaze, 1911. Base marks: flames mark and the date. 8" h. *Courtesy of David Rago Auctions.*

Figure 333. Carved Mat tankard by William Hentschel, with cornflower in blue-green on a raspberry ground, 1912. Base marks: flames mark, the date, 10, and the artist's mark. 11.75" x 6.5". *Courtesy of David Rago Auctions.*

Figure 334. Impressionistic Vellum plaque painted by Edward T. Hurley in 1912, featuring pine trees surrounded by a thick blanket of undisturbed snow, with snow-capped mountains in the background, beneath a peach-to-blue sky. Front marks: the artist's cipher in the lower right hand corner and again on the obverse; back marks: flames mark, the date, and an impressed V for Vellum. 10.25" x 8.25". *Courtesy of Mark Mussio, Cincinnati Art Galleries, LLC.*

Figure 335. Vellum ovoid vase painted in 1912 by Elizabeth Lincoln with grey mistletoe on a mauve and mint ground. Base marks: flames mark, the date, shape number 942E, V, and the artist's initials. 4.75" x 3.75". *Courtesy of David Rago Auctions.*

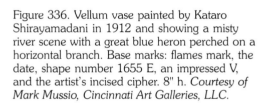

Figure 336. Vellum vase painted by Kataro Shirayamadani in 1912 and showing a misty river scene with a great blue heron perched on a horizontal branch. Base marks: flames mark, the date, shape number 1655 E, an impressed V, and the artist's incised cipher. 8" h. *Courtesy of Mark Mussio, Cincinnati Art Galleries, LLC.*

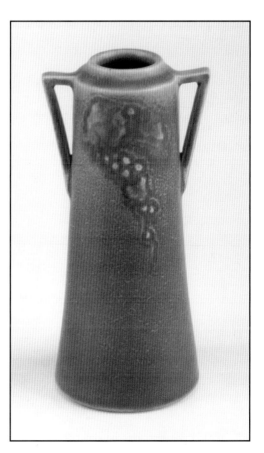

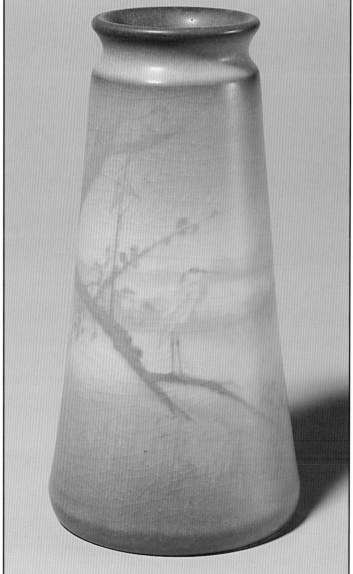

Figure 337. Carved Mat small tapering two-handled vase decorated by Charles S. Todd with grapes and leaves on green and brown butterfat ground, 1912. Base marks: flames mark, the date, shape number 2018, and the artist's initials. 6.75" x 3". *Courtesy of David Rago Auctions.*

Figure 338. Rook inkwell glazed in 1912 in a variegated mat brown Ombroso finish. Base marks: flames mark, the date, and shape number 998. The lid to the inkwell is missing. 7" x 12". *Courtesy of Mark Mussio, Cincinnati Art Galleries, LLC.*

Figure 339. Production vase dating to 1912 with incised stylized leaves under a green-to-pink Vellum glaze. Base marks: flames mark and date. 9.5". *Courtesy of David Rago Auctions.*

Figure 340. Production urn impressed with a geometric pattern under a rich puce and green butterfat glaze, 1912. Base marks: flames mark and date. 18" h. *Courtesy of David Rago Auctions.*

Figure 341. Two production pieces: a flower basket table decoration in polychrome and a rare triangular candlestick with seahorses covered in a mat brown-green glaze, 1912. Both are marked. 6.5"; 4". *Courtesy of David Rago Auctions.*

Figure 342. Production sugar bowl and creamer and sugar bowl embossed with four-square design under shaded blue glaze, 1912. Base marks: flames marks and date. 3" and 2.5". *Courtesy of David Rago Auctions.*

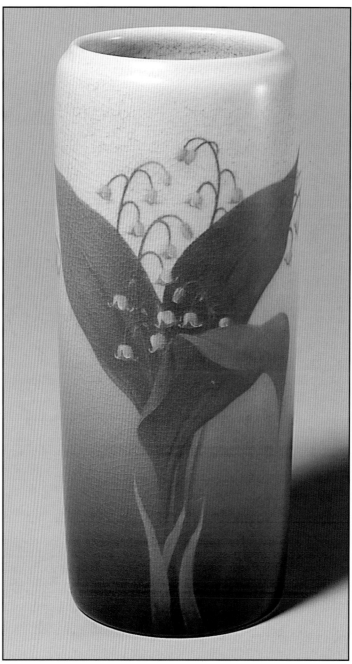

Figure 343. Vellum glaze cylinder vase decorated in 1913 by Carl Schmidt with white lilies of the valley with green stems and leaves. Base marks: flames mark, the date, shape number 952 D, an impressed V for Vellum body, an incised V for Vellum glaze, and the artist's impressed monogram. 9.25" h. *Courtesy of Mark Mussio, Cincinnati Art Galleries, LLC.*

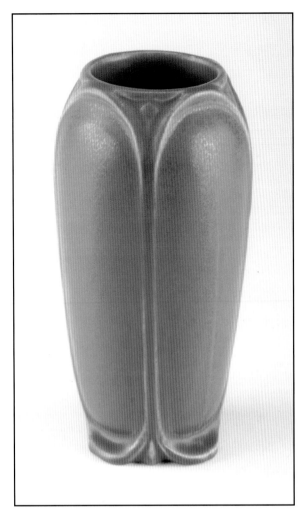

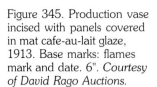

Figure 345. Production vase incised with panels covered in mat cafe-au-lait glaze, 1913. Base marks: flames mark and date. 6". *Courtesy of David Rago Auctions.*

Figure 344. Production paneled vase with buds covered in feathered mat brown glaze, 1913. Base marks: flames mark and date. 9.25" h. *Courtesy of David Rago Auctions.*

Figure 346. Early production potpourri jar, 1913, in feathered pink-to-mat green, complete with inner and outer lids. Base marks: flames mark and date. 6" x 4.75". *Courtesy of David Rago Auctions.*

Figure 347. Early production squat bowl embossed with gingko leaves and fruit under purple and green mat glaze, 1913. Base marks: flames mark, the date, and shape number 1680. 2.25" x 6.5". *Courtesy of David Rago Auctions.*

Figure 348. Tonalistic Scenic Vellum vase displaying trees, hills, and a lake in shades of green, gray and blue, painted in 1914 by Lorinda Epply. Base marks: flames mark, the date, shape number 941 D, an impressed V for Vellum body, an incised V for Vellum glaze, and the artist's incised mark. 8.5" h. *Courtesy of Mark Mussio, Cincinnati Art Galleries, LLC.*

Figure 349. Carved Mat vase decorated by William Hentschel in 1914 with stylized roses under blue, grey, yellow, red, and green Flambé mat glaze. Base marks: flames mark, the date, shape number 614C, and the artist's initials. 13" x 6.5". *Courtesy of David Rago Auctions.*

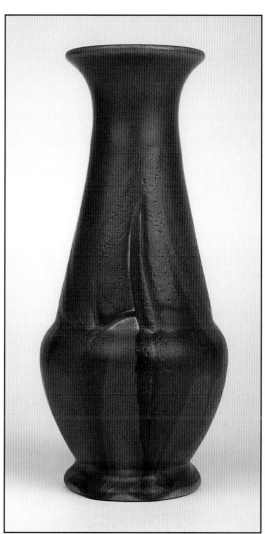

Figure 350. Vase adorned with brown and black glaze with a touch of yellow, executed by William Hentschel, 1914. Base marks: flames mark, the date, and the artist's hand-painted initials. 8.5" h. *Courtesy of Clarence Meyer.*

Figure 351. Carved Mat footed vessel with two square handles decorated by William Hentschel with a stylized pattern in pink, red, and brown, 1914. Base marks: flames mark, the date, and the artist's initials. 3" x 6.75". *Courtesy of David Rago Auctions.*

Figure 352. Carved Mat flaring vessel by William Hentschel with a band of stylized plants in amber on a red and green Flambé ground, 1914. Base marks: flames mark, the date, artist signed, and an X second mark for firing lines. 3" x 5.5". *Courtesy of David Rago Auctions.*

Figure 353. Vellum glaze plaque rendering of the shoreline of Lake Louise, painted in 1914 by Sara Sax and enclosed in an original quarter sawn oak frame. It is signed "Sax" in the lower left hand corner. Base marks: flames mark, the date, and a V on the back. Also on the base is an original Rookwood typewritten label, which reads, "Lake Louise S. Sax." 9.25" x 12.25". *Courtesy of Mark Mussio, Cincinnati Art Galleries, LLC.*

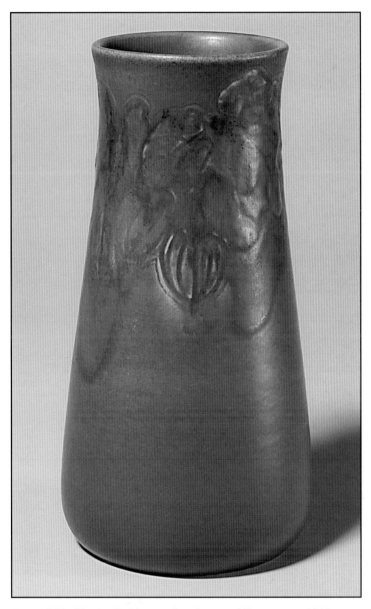

Figure 354. Charles Todd incised and painted this vase in 1914. Using muted shades of green, blue, and maroon, he encircled the upper portion of the vase with gourds and vines upon a mat brown ground. Base marks: flames mark, the date, shape number 1023C, and the artist's incised initials. 10.75" h. *Courtesy of Mark Mussio, Cincinnati Art Galleries, LLC.*

Figure 355. Carved Mat baluster vase by Charles S. Todd with peacock feathers in celadon and brown on flowing mat brown ground, 1914. 9" x 4.5". *Courtesy of David Rago Auctions.*

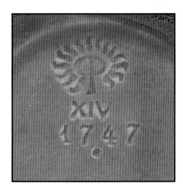

Figure 356. Production vase with molded decoration, 1914. Base marks: flames mark, the date, and shape number 1747. 6.5" h. *Courtesy of Bob Shores and Dale Jones.*

Figure 357. Vellum vase painted by an unknown artist with poppies, 1914. Base marks: flames mark, the date, shape number 2040, E, and V. 7.5" x 3.25". *Courtesy of David Rago Auctions.*

Figure 358. Scenic Vellum vase decorated in 1915 by Sallie Coyne, featuring trees on a rolling landscape with a blue lake in the background beneath a pink and blue sky. Base marks: flames mark, the date, shape number 2102, an impressed V for Vellum, and the artist's monogram. 6.5" h. *Courtesy of Mark Mussio, Cincinnati Art Galleries, LLC.*

Figure 359. Vellum glaze vase decorated by Sallie Coyne in 1915 with red grapes and green leaves descending from the shoulder. Base marks: flames mark, the date, shape number 614 D, an impressed V for Vellum, and the artist's monogram. 11" h. *Courtesy of Mark Mussio, Cincinnati Art Galleries, LLC.*

Figure 360. Large Vellum glaze scenic vase painted in 1915 by Carl Schmidt, with eleven white swans reflected in fairly calm waters with delicate green and mauve highlights. Bright sunlight illuminates the swans, casting shadows of their own necks onto their backs. Base marks: flames mark, the date, shape number 907 C, an impressed V, an incised V for Vellum glaze, and the artist's impressed monogram. 14.75" h. *Courtesy of Mark Mussio, Cincinnati Art Galleries, LLC.*

Figure 361. Carved Mat vase with flat shoulder decorated by Charles S. Todd with stylized floral panels in red and green on cobalt ground, 1915. Base marks: flames mark, the date, and the artist's initials. 9.5" h. *Courtesy of David Rago Auctions.*

Figure 362. Narrow mouth, broad based production vase from 1915 with vertical lines in green glaze. Base marks: flames mark, the date, and shape number 1748. 7" h. *Courtesy of Bob Shores and Dale Jones.*

Figure 363. Small bud vase cast in 1915 and covered with Nacreous glaze. This glaze proved unpopular with the public and was quickly discontinued. Base marks: flames mark, the date, shape number 1831, and an upright P. 4" h. *Courtesy of Mark Mussio, Cincinnati Art Galleries, LLC.*

Figure 364. Production low bowl impressed with peacock feathers under a fine mat green-to-rose glaze, 1915. 8" in diameter. *Courtesy of David Rago Auctions.*

Figure 365. Production squat two-handled vase with a band of Celtic knots under plum-to-turquoise butterfat glaze, 1915. 4" x 5.5". *Courtesy of David Rago Auctions.*

Figure 366. Restful, nocturnal Scenic Vellum vase decorated by Lenore Asbury in 1916. Base marks: flames mark, the date, shape number 942C, an impressed V for Vellum, and the artist's initials. 7.25" h. *Courtesy of Mark Mussio, Cincinnati Art Galleries, LLC.*

Figure 367. Vellum glaze plaque decorated by Margaret McDonald in 1916, featuring a deep blue lake along a tree-lined shore under a brilliant blue sky. Front mark: decorator's monogram in the lower right hand corner. Back marks: flames mark, the date, and an impressed V for Vellum glaze. The frame appears original and a typewritten label reads "The Lake, M.H. McDonald," while a newer brass plate reads "Margaret Helen McDonald, 1893-1964." 5" x 9.25". *Courtesy of Mark Mussio, Cincinnati Art Galleries, LLC.*

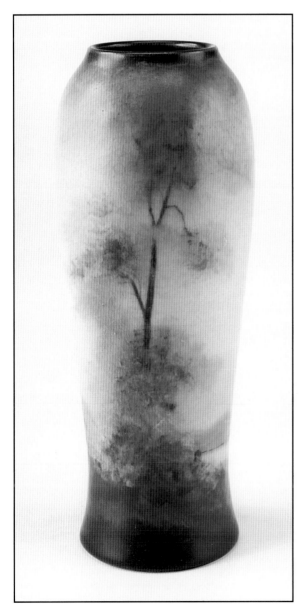

Far left:
Figure 368. Scenic Vellum vase painted by Kate Van Horne with tall trees by a mountain lake, in blues and purples, 1916. Base marks: flames mark, the date, shape number 2040E, V, and the artist's initials. 7.75" x 2.75". *Courtesy of David Rago Auctions.*

Left:
Figure 369. Production vase cast in 1916 and covered with a striated brown mat glaze. Base marks: flames mark, the date, shape number 233, and an impressed V for Vellum body. 8.25" h. *Courtesy of Bob Shores and Dale Jones.*

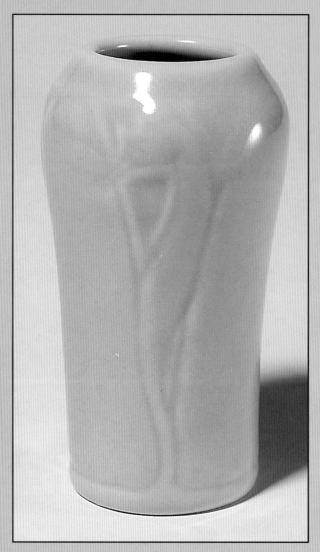

Figure 370. Porcelain production vase cast in 1916 and covered with a deep cobalt glaze. Base marks: flames mark, the date, shape number 2157, and a sideways P indicating a porcelain body. 8.25" h. *Courtesy of Mark Mussio, Cincinnati Art Galleries, LLC.*

Figure 371. Porcelain vase dated 1916 with molded decoration of seahorses encircling the vase. Base marks: flames mark, the date, shape number 2124, and a sideways P for porcelain body. 5" h. *Courtesy of Mark Mussio, Cincinnati Art Galleries, LLC.*

Figure 372. Rare Decorated Porcelain vase in three basic colors decorated in 1917 by Arthur Conant, featuring a pink bird diving toward the flower strewn ground in cobalt and pink against a slate gray ground. The vase's base is encircled with a repeating border of swirls and fish. Base marks: flames mark, the date, shape number 2271, a sideways P for porcelain body, and the artist's incised monogram. 14" h. *Courtesy of Mark Mussio, Cincinnati Art Galleries, LLC.*

Figure 373. Vellum Glaze vase with pretty blue hollyhock decoration, painted by Kate Curry in 1917. Base marks: flames mark, the date, shape number 900 C, the artist's monogram, and a wheel-ground X. *Courtesy of Mark Mussio, Cincinnati Art Galleries, LLC.*

Figure 374. Vellum glaze vase decorated with purple poppies in a band around the shoulder by Elizabeth McDermott in 1917. Base marks: flames mark, the date, shape number 913 D, and the artist's impressed monogram. 8" h. *Courtesy of Mark Mussio, Cincinnati Art Galleries, LLC.*

Figure 375. Unusual Vellum glaze low vase decorated in 1917 by Sara Sax with nine butterflies in a band around the shoulder and alternating vertical bands of black, purple, and green extending down slightly from the rim to meet the butterflies. Base marks: flames mark, the date, shape number 703, an impressed V, an incised V for Vellum glaze, and the artist's impressed monogram. 5.5" h. *Courtesy of Mark Mussio, Cincinnati Art Galleries, LLC.*

Figure 376. Vellum glaze plaque, titled *A Pond in the Meadow*, decorated in an Arts & Crafts manner with an almost tonalist color scheme by Sara Sax in 1917. Silhouettes of trees in black contrast with the soft gray, cream, and rose hues used by the artist. Front mark: Signed "Sax" in black slip on the front. Back marks: flames mark, the date, and an impressed V. An original typewritten label on the back lists the title and artist. 7" x 9.25". *Courtesy of Mark Mussio, Cincinnati Art Galleries, LLC.*

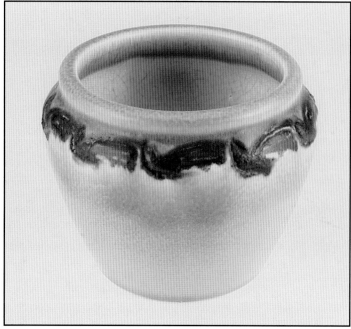

Figure 378. Carved Mat vase by Charles S. Todd with a wreath of stylized blossoms in red, blue, and green on a yellow butterfat ground, 1917. Base marks: flames mark, the date, shape number 964, and the artist's initials. 3.75" x 5". *Courtesy of David Rago Auctions.*

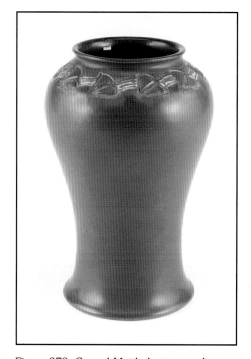

Figure 377. Scenic Vellum vase decorated by Carl Schmidt in 1917, featuring detailed trees and rolling hills, behind which a river flows with blue hills in the far background, all under a dawning sky. Base marks: flames mark, the date, shape number 2102, an impressed V for Vellum Glaze, and the artist's impressed monogram. 6.5" h.

Figure 379. Carved Mat baluster vase by Charles S. Todd with a wreath of stylized leaves in blue, orange, and yellow on cobalt ground, 1917. Base marks: flames mark, the date, shape number 945, and the artist's initials. 9.5" x 6.5". *Courtesy of David Rago Auctions.*

Figure 380. Carved Mat floral vase decorated by Charles S. Todd in 1917 with a carved abstract floral pattern around the top of the vase and a rich mat brown glaze. Base marks: flames mark, the date, shape 1951 D, and the decorator's incised initials. 8.5" h. *Courtesy of Mark Mussio, Cincinnati Art Galleries, LLC.*

Figure 382. Jewel Porcelain bulbous vase painted by Katherine Van Horne with a band and wreath of stylized blossoms and berries in indigo on a pink ground, 1917. Base marks: flames mark, the date, shape number 162D, P, and the artist's initials. 5.25" x 3.75". *Courtesy of David Rago Auctions.*

Figure 381. Scenic Vellum plaque painted in 1917 by Kate Van Horn, titled *Grey Day*. It is mounted in the original frame. Base marks: flames mark, the date, V, the artist's initials, and a title label. Plaque: 9.25" x 5". *Courtesy of David Rago Auctions.*

Figure 383. Chalice-shaped Decorated Porcelain vase painted by Harriet Wilcox in 1917, using a lily pads and lotus flowers theme covered with a blue-tinted glaze. Base marks: flames mark, the date, shape number 2298E, a sideways P for porcelain body, and the artist's incised initials. 4.25" h. *Courtesy of Mark Mussio, Cincinnati Art Galleries, LLC.*

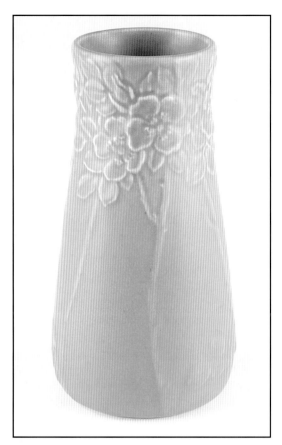

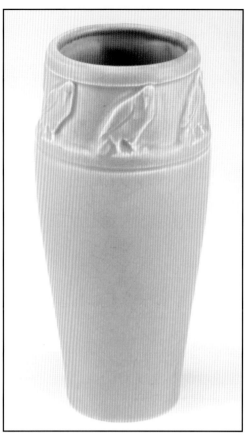

Figure 384. Production vase embossed with branches of roses under green-to-pink butterfat mat glaze, 1917. Base marks: flames mark and date. 10.25" h. *Courtesy of David Rago Auctions.*

Figure 385. Production vase embossed with a band of rooks under green-to-pink glaze, 1917. Base marks: flames mark and date. 7.5" h. *Courtesy of David Rago Auctions.*

Figure 386. Production shell and dolphin flower frog (with six holes) in light green, 1917. Base marks: flames mark, the date, shape number 2251, and P for porcelain. 5" l. *Courtesy of Bob Shores and Dale Jones.*

Figure 387. Decorated Porcelain vase decorated in 1918 by Arthur Conant with red flowering bushes, blue mountains in the background, and what appear to be small boats in white capped water. 5" h. *Courtesy of Mark Mussio, Cincinnati Art Galleries, LLC.*

Figure 388. Vellum squat vase painted by Elizabeth Lincoln in 1918 with stylized pink poppies on a blue-grey ground. Base marks: flames mark, the date, 16, and the artist's initials. 4.75" x 7". *Courtesy of David Rago Auctions.*

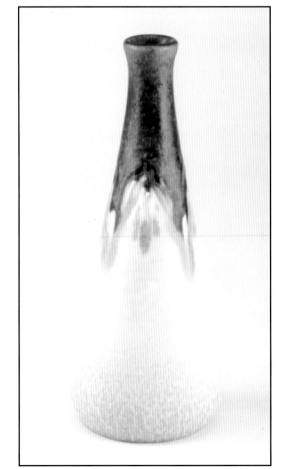

Figure 389. Carved Mat tear-shaped vase by Elizabeth Lincoln with abstracted flowers in indigo, green, butter yellow, and pink butterfat glaze, 1918. Base marks: flames mark, the date, and the artist's initials. 8.5" h. *Courtesy of David Rago Auctions.*

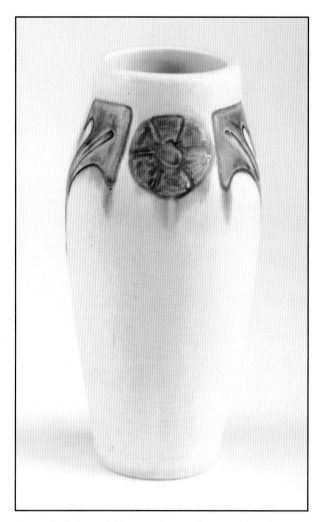

Figure 390. Carved Mat ovoid vase decorated by Elizabeth Lincoln in 1918 with stylized red blossoms and brown leaves on ivory ground. Base marks: flames mark, the date, shape number 30F, and the artist's initials. 6.75" x 3". *Courtesy of David Rago Auctions.*

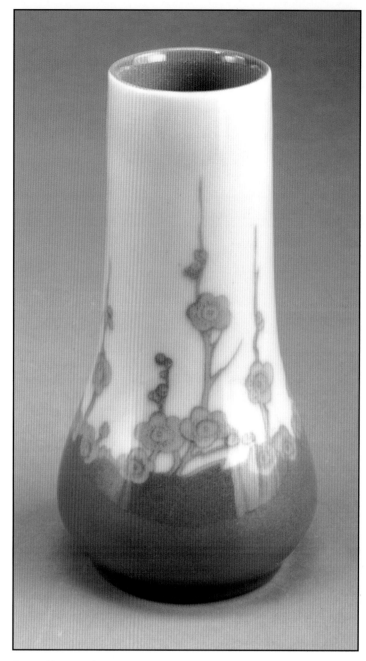

Figure 391. Jewel Porcelain bulbous vase painted by Elizabeth McDermott in 1918 with pink and blue cherry blossoms on buff and purple ground. Base marks: flames mark, the date, shape number 1278F, and the artist's initials. 7.25" x 3.75". *Courtesy of David Rago Auctions.*

Figure 392. Porcelain mat blue production bowl cast in 1918, featuring a dark blue glaze superimposed over a lighter shade. Base marks: flames mark, the date, shape number 1390, and a sideways P for porcelain body. 3" h. *Courtesy of Mark Mussio, Cincinnati Art Galleries, LLC.*

Figure 393. Impressive Decorated Porcelain vase decorated by Arthur Conant in 1919 with a peacock and a peahen perched in a lavishly flowering tree. Base marks: flames mark, the date, shape number 2273, and the artist's incised monogram. 17" h. *Courtesy of Mark Mussio, Cincinnati Art Galleries, LLC.*

Figure 394. Vellum vase decorated by Sallie Coyne and produced in 1919, featuring a broad shoulder sectioned into four panels containing red asters with yellow centers. The outlining of the sections is in green and dark gray and the bottom of the vessel is mat gray. Base marks: flames mark, the date, shape number 1091D, an impressed V, and the decorator's signature. 6.5" h. *Courtesy of Mark Mussio, Cincinnati Art Galleries, LLC.*

Figure 395. Scenic Vellum plaque, titled *Mirror Lake*, painted by Edward Diers with tall trees reflected in a mountain lake, 1919. It is mounted in the original frame. Base marks: flames mark, the date, and the artist's initials. Plaque: 8.75" x 10.75". *Courtesy of David Rago Auctions.*

Figure 396. Imposing Vellum glaze vase from 1919 decorated by Elizabeth Lincoln, featuring carved and painted decor of stylized, deep pink mums on a dark blue and pink background. Base marks: flames mark, the date, shape number 800 A, an impressed V for Vellum, and the decorator's initials. 14" h. *Courtesy of Mark Mussio, Cincinnati Art Galleries, LLC.*

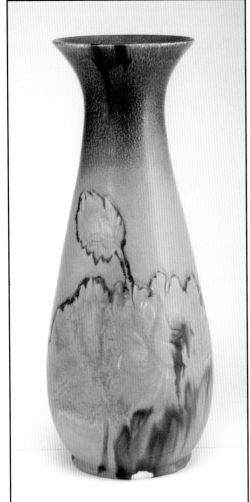

Figure 397. Massive Carved Mat floor vase decorated by Elizabeth Lincoln in 1919, featuring fleshy pink poppies and green foliage on an indigo-to-pink butterfat ground. Base marks: flames mark, the date, shape number 264A, V, and the artist's initials. 22.5" x 9". *Courtesy of David Rago Auctions.*

Figure 398. Jewel Porcelain bud vase painted by Charles J. McLaughlin in 1919 with pink apple blossoms on an ivory and indigo ground. Base marks: flames mark, the date, shape number 2308, and the artist's initials. 6.5" x 3.25". *Courtesy of David Rago Auctions.*

Figure 399. Scenic Vellum plaque decorated by Frederick Rothenbusch in 1919, featuring a tree-lined lane along a placid river with fields and hills visible in the background. This is an attractive landscape done by one of Rookwood's finest scenic artists. Front mark: artist's initials in the plaque's lower right hand corner. Back marks: flames mark and the date. 8.5" x 11". *Courtesy of Mark Mussio, Cincinnati Art Galleries, LLC.*

Figure 400. Large, impressive Vellum glaze scenic vase decorated in 1919 by Carl Schmidt, portraying a peaceful twilight setting with the rosy evening sky reflected in a lake, surrounded by tall trees that reflect in the water as you follow the scene around the vase. Base marks: flames mark, the date, shape number 614 B, an incised V for Vellum glaze, and the artist's impressed monogram. 15" h. *Courtesy of Mark Mussio, Cincinnati Art Galleries, LLC.*

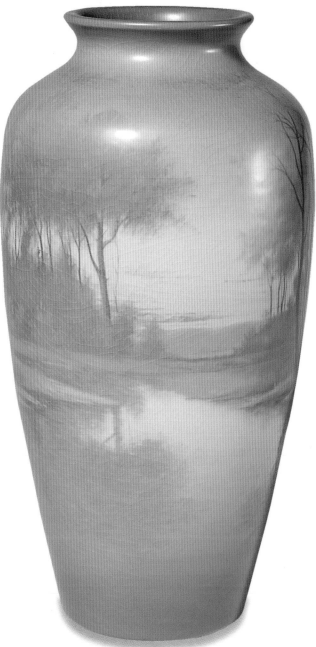

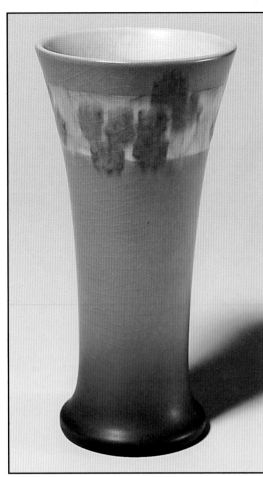

Figure 401. Vellum glaze vase decorated by Carrie Steinle in 1919 with a band of dark blue berries in a band around the upper portion of the vase. Base marks: flames mark, the date, shape number 1357 D, a V for Vellum, and the decorator's incised mark. 9" h. *Courtesy of Mark Mussio, Cincinnati Art Galleries, LLC.*

Figure 402. Painted Mat vase decorated with an abstract floral theme by Charles Todd in 1919. Base marks: flames mark, the date, shape number 270, and the designer's incised initials. 11.75" h. *Courtesy of Mark Mussio, Cincinnati Art Galleries, LLC.*

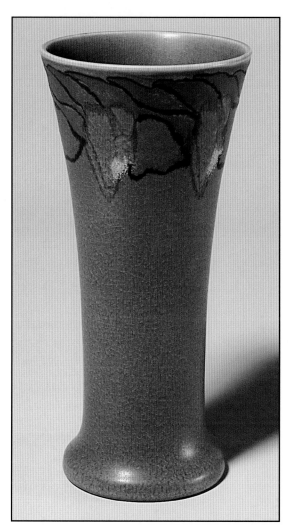

Figure 403. Lightly carved and painted mat glaze vase executed by Charles S. Todd in 1919 with a band of rose and yellow flowers encircling the top part of the vase along with green leaves, outlined in black. Base marks: flames mark, the date, shape number 1357 D, and the artist's incised initials. 9" h. *Courtesy of Mark Mussio, Cincinnati Art Galleries, LLC.*

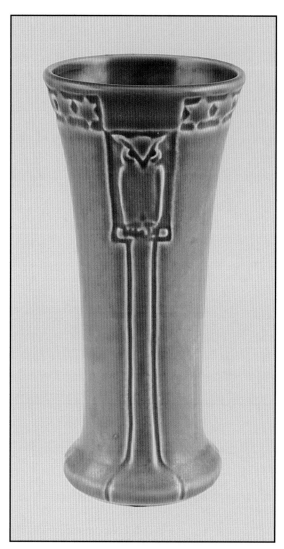

Figure 404. Production flaring vase embossed with stars and owls under a cafe-au-lait glaze, 1919. Base marks: flames mark and date. 8.5" h. *Courtesy of David Rago Auctions.*

Figure 405. Production vase embossed with a band of rooks under indigo glaze, 1919. Base marks: flames mark and date. 7.5" h. *Courtesy of David Rago Auctions.*

Figure 406. Production flaring vase embossed with bamboo stalks under a fine beige and blue mat crystalline glaze, 1919. Base marks: flames mark and date. 6.25" h. *Courtesy of David Rago Auctions.*

Figure 407. Stylish production vase dated to 1919 glazed in a raspberry high glaze covered with a cobalt overspray, allowing the underglaze to show through, and making for a very stylish effect. Base marks: flames mark, the date, and shape number 991. 4.75" h. *Courtesy of Mark Mussio, Cincinnati Art Galleries, LLC.*

Figure 408. Production bud vase cast in 1919 and covered with a striking mottled green and blue high glaze. Base marks: flames mark, the date, and shape number 357F. 6.25" h. *Courtesy of Mark Mussio, Cincinnati Art Galleries, LLC.*

Rookwood Pottery in the 1920s

In 1920, Rookwood had 200 employees, kept fifteen kilns in operation, and had more than 500 glazes at its command. The company celebrated its fortieth anniversary in 1920 with a reintroduction of the Tiger Eye glaze line. Differing from the previous glaze line of the same name, this Tiger Eye had a green tint to it and is referred to either as Golden or Green Tiger Eye to differentiate the earlier and later lines. Throughout this decade and the 1930s, Rookwood turned away from Japanese design for inspiration and toward China.

In 1920, Rookwood was entering its last decade of real success. Only ten decorators would be hired in the 1920s, and not one would remain with the company for long. The 1920s would also see a certain confusion among the firm's art pottery; these items were not named by the company, as had been the general rule in earlier decades. Kenneth Trapp speculated on the reasoning behind this move in 1992, "It may be Rookwood chose not to name each of the many artistic wares because such practice seemed unnecessary: the buyer bought 'Rookwood,' itself the most important name. Also, possibly, particular glazes and decorative treatments were not made in large enough numbers to warrant naming." (Trapp 1992, 35) Regardless of the paucity of names, these art pottery items were decorated with wide ranging motifs, some harkening back to early patterns while others emulated the decade's modern styles.

There were named lines during the 1920s, however—ten in all. The names referred to various attributes, including body type, glaze, or decoration. The ten lines were Black Opal; Butterfat; Coromandel; Empire Green and Gold-Chartreuse Tiger Eye; Flambé; French Red; Jewel Porcelain (Soft Porcelain renamed); Mat Moderne; Oxblood; and Wax Mat.

Figure 409. In 1920, Rookwood was entering its last decade of real success. "Bust of Unknown Woman," cast in 1929, depicts the head and shoulders of a serene young woman and is covered with an ivory mat glaze. Base marks: flames mark, the date, and shape number 2026. 7.5" h. *Courtesy of Mark Mussio, Cincinnati Art Galleries, LLC.*

Figure 410. Black Opal vase decorated with lotus flowers and lily pads by Harriet Wilcox in 1924. Base marks: flames mark, the date, shape number 1781, and the artist's incised initials. 6" h. *Courtesy of Mark Mussio, Cincinnati Art Galleries, LLC.*

Figure 411. Jewel Porcelain trumpet vase painted by Sara Sax with stylized branches of blossoms in vermillion and green on a purple butterfat ground, against a dramatic black butterfat interior, 1926. Base marks: flames mark, the date, shape number 2735, and the artist's cipher. 8.5" x 6". *Courtesy of David Rago Auctions.*

Figure 412. Reaching ahead into the 1930s, here are several examples of lines introduced in the 1920s. Coromandel glaze flaring vase cast at Rookwood in 1932 and accented with amber drips and blue near the top. Atypically, it is lined in a striated tan mat glaze. Base marks: flames mark, the date, and shape number 6305. 5" h. *Courtesy of Mark Mussio, Cincinnati Art Galleries, LLC.*

Figure 413. Porcelain ovoid vase in deep Chinese purple Flambé glaze, 1938. Base marks: flames mark and date. 12.25" h. *Courtesy of David Rago Auctions.*

Figure 414. Jewel Porcelain vase by Sara Sax delicately painted with white and red cherry blossoms on an eggplant ground. Base marks: flames mark, the date, shape number 2191, and the artist's cipher. 5" x 4". *Courtesy of David Rago Auctions.*

Figure 415. Unusual Oxblood vase produced circa 1930, unusual not only for the Oxblood glaze but also because the vase is accented with blue-green, not the white that is more common. Base marks: only a portion of the flames mark and date may be seen, as glaze obscures much of the base. 5" h. *Courtesy of Mark Mussio, Cincinnati Art Galleries, LLC.*

Figure 416. Fine, large Wax Mat baluster vase incised and painted in 1926 by Louise Abel with fleshy vermillion magnolias on a rich gold and orange butterfat ground. Base marks: flames mark, the date, shape numbers 424B, and the artist's cipher. 14.25" x 7". *Courtesy of David Rago Auctions.*

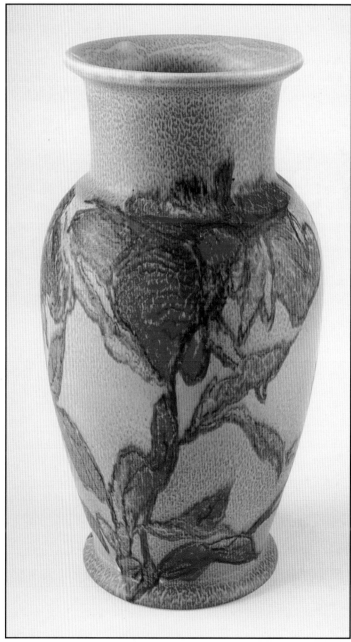

During the 1920s, there was a definite turn to modernism in both decoration and body shape. Heavy mat glazes, vibrant colors, and Asian body forms were employed, creating lively ware with a decidedly different look from the Victorian and turn of the twentieth century wares the company had used to establish its reputation. Slipping in among these modern decorative motifs were Egyptian designs, capturing the fascination for ancient Egypt that erupted throughout the Western world when Howard Carter opened King Tutankhamen's tomb in 1922.

Figure 419. Uncommon flower frog, a nude female fairy sitting among a cluster of mushrooms, designed by Ernest Bruce Haswell and glazed in yellow mat glaze in 1921. Base marks: flames mark, the date, and shape number 2281. 6.25" h. *Courtesy of Mark Mussio, Cincinnati Art Galleries, LLC.*

Figure 417. Squat production vase with molded seagull decoration potted during the 1920s. 2.5" h. x 5" d. *Courtesy of Bob Shores and Dale Jones.*

Figure 418. Elegant cup and saucer, probably made during the 1920s, with dark green edged with black. Base marks: the Rookwood dinnerware mark and a wheel-ground X. 2.5" h. *Courtesy of Mark Mussio, Cincinnati Art Galleries, LLC.*

Figure 420. A pair of Sphinx bookends, designed by Louise Abel, and covered with a runny mat blue glaze tinged with green, and dated 1920. Base marks: flames mark, the date, and shape number 2503. This is an excellent example of a hard-to-find set of bookends. 7" h. *Courtesy of Mark Mussio, Cincinnati Art Galleries, LLC.*

By 1927, Rookwood was also producing two or three paperweights a year. Then came the stock market crash of October 1929. During the 1930s, paperweights would become a more significant production item as the Depression robbed the public of its ability to buy luxurious wares.

Figure 421. Elephant paperweight, designed by William McDonald and cast in 1926, glazed in a good crystalline mat blue. Base marks: flames mark, the date, shape number 2797, and the designer's initials on the side of the plinth. A paper showroom label is affixed to the bottom. 3.25" h. *Courtesy of Mark Mussio, Cincinnati Art Galleries, LLC.*

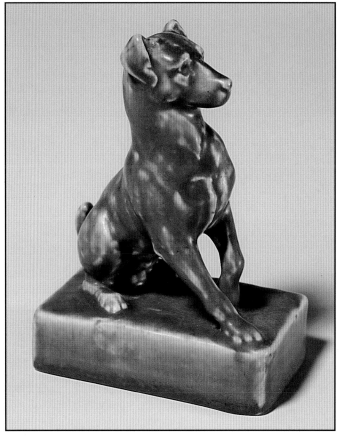

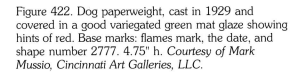

Figure 422. Dog paperweight, cast in 1929 and covered in a good variegated green mat glaze showing hints of red. Base marks: flames mark, the date, and shape number 2777. 4.75" h. *Courtesy of Mark Mussio, Cincinnati Art Galleries, LLC.*

Figure 423. "Double Goose" paperweight cast in 1929 and covered with the Ivory Mat glaze. Base marks: flames mark, the date, and shape number 1855. 4.25" h. *Courtesy of Mark Mussio, Cincinnati Art Galleries, LLC.*

Rookwood's 1920s Art Pottery Objects

The following is a sampling of the various wares produced by Rookwood throughout the 1920s, organized by year and, within each year, by artist.

Figure 424. Scenic Vellum vase painted by Lenore Asbury in 1920, adorned with a twilight scene of trees by a lake. Base marks: flames mark, the date, shape number 950 D, an impressed V for Vellum, and the artist's initials. 9.5" h. *Courtesy of Mark Mussio, Cincinnati Art Galleries, LLC.*

Figure 425. Low vase decorated by Lenore Asbury in 1920 with dandelions around the rim. Base marks: flames mark, the date, shape number 1375 V, and the incised decorator's initials. 6" x 9". *Courtesy of Bob Shores and Dale Jones.*

Figure 426. Large Turquoise Blue vase with intricate Islamic designs executed in 1920 by William Hentschel. Displayed among the abundant flowers are small exotic birds and lion-like creatures set off with repeating bands. Base marks: flames mark, the date, shape number 2367, and the artist's incised monogram. 15.5" h. *Courtesy of Mark Mussio, Cincinnati Art Galleries, LLC.*

Figure 427. Jewel Porcelain tall vase decorated by William Hentschel in 1920 with an overall pattern of stylized blue flowers on brown leaves against a canary yellow ground. Base marks: flames mark, the date, shape number 1664D, and the artist's initials. 10.75" x 4.75". *Courtesy of David Rago Auctions.*

Figure 428. Decorated Mat vase decorated by Elizabeth Lincoln with both incised and painted pinecones and needles upon a deep maroon ground in 1920. Base marks: flames mark, the date, shape number 1781, and the artist's incised initials. 6.5" h. *Courtesy of Mark Mussio, Cincinnati Art Galleries, LLC.*

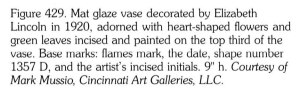

Figure 429. Mat glaze vase decorated by Elizabeth Lincoln in 1920, adorned with heart-shaped flowers and green leaves incised and painted on the top third of the vase. Base marks: flames mark, the date, shape number 1357 D, and the artist's incised initials. 9" h. *Courtesy of Mark Mussio, Cincinnati Art Galleries, LLC.*

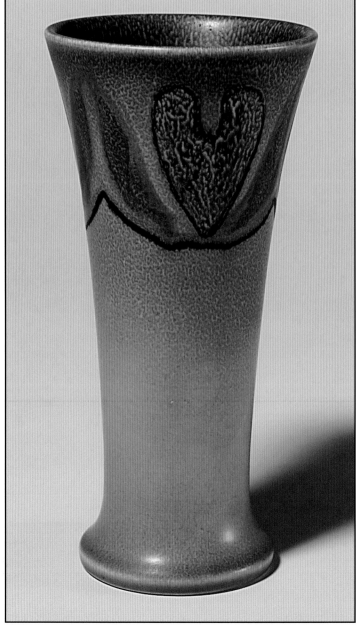

Figure 430. Large Vellum glaze scenic plaque painted by Fred Rothenbusch in 1920 with a summer evening setting of tall trees beside a small stream. Front marks: the artist's monogram appears in the lower right hand corner. Back marks: impressed marks on the back include the flames mark and date. 13.75" x 11". *Courtesy of Mark Mussio, Cincinnati Art Galleries, LLC.*

Figure 431. Sizable Vellum glaze scenic vase decorated in 1920 by Fred Rothenbusch with trees and a tranquil lake with blue hills in the distance. Back marks: flames mark, the date, shape number 614 B, an impressed V, and the artist's impressed monogram. 15.25" h. *Courtesy of Mark Mussio, Cincinnati Art Galleries, LLC.*

Figure 434. Tall Decorated Mat glaze vase decorated by Elizabeth Lincoln in 1921, using heavy slip to create abstract flowers, leaves, and stems, in hues of green, blue, and orange, on a deep maroon ground. Base marks: flames mark, the date, shape number 614C, and the artist's incised signature. 12.5" h. *Courtesy of Mark Mussio, Cincinnati Art Galleries, LLC.*

Figure 432. Very stylized vase decorated in 1921 by William Hentschel, who completely covered the surface of the vessel with floral and other designs in a Moresque fashion, entirely in blue on the white ground. Base marks: flames mark, the date, shape number 1091D, and the artist's incised monogram. 6.25" h. *Courtesy of Mark Mussio, Cincinnati Art Galleries, LLC.*

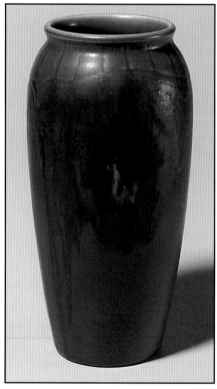

Figure 435. Decorated Mat vase decorated by Elizabeth Lincoln in 1921, with a lightly incised and painted abstract floral motif, featuring red flowers and green leaves offset by the dark blue background. Base marks: flames mark, the date, shape number 892C, and the decorator's incised initials. 9" h. *Courtesy of Mark Mussio, Cincinnati Art Galleries, LLC.*

Figure 433. Large two-handled mat glaze vase with several incised and painted peacock feathers decorated in 1921 by Elizabeth Lincoln. Base marks: flames mark, the date, shape number 339 B, and the incised artist's initials. 14" h. *Courtesy of Mark Mussio, Cincinnati Art Galleries, LLC.*

Figure 436. Tall Scenic Vellum vase decorated in 1921 by Fred Rothenbusch, featuring a scene of trees around a placid lake with blue hills and a peach sky in the background. Base marks: flames mark, the date, shape number 907D, an impressed V for Vellum, and the artist's incised initials. 12" h. *Courtesy of Mark Mussio, Cincinnati Art Galleries, LLC.*

Figure 437. Vellum vase painted by Vera Tischler with blue cornflowers and green arabesques on cobalt ground, 1921. Base marks: flames mark and date. 8" h. *Courtesy of David Rago Auctions.*

Figure 438. Unusual Carved Mat tall cylindrical vase decorated by Charles S. Todd in 1921 with vines of red flowers against a blue brick wall, and ochre ground. Base marks: flames mark, the date, shape number 589D, and the artist's initials. 12" x 3.5". *Courtesy of David Rago Auctions.*

Figure 439. Decorated Mat vase displaying dark blue, yellow, black, and vibrant green abstract floral decoration on a dark pink ground by Charles S. Todd in 1921. Base marks: flames mark, the date, shape number 607C, and the artist's incised initials. 5.25" h. *Courtesy of Mark Mussio, Cincinnati Art Galleries, LLC.*

Figure 440. Scenic Vellum vase featuring stylized blooming trees, a pink to yellow sky, and chocolate ground and tree trunks rendered by Lenore Asbury in 1922. Base marks: flames mark, the date, shape number 977, an impressed V for Vellum, and the artist's incised signature. 11" h. *Courtesy of Mark Mussio, Cincinnati Art Galleries, LLC.*

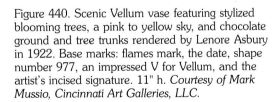

Figure 442. Wax Mat baluster vase painted by Elizabeth Lincoln with bluebells on blue and purple butterfat ground, 1922. Base marks: flames mark, the date, and the artist's initials. 7.5" h. *Courtesy of David Rago Auctions.*

Figure 441. Decorated Porcelain lamp base decorated by William Hentschel in 1922 with an abstract floral motif. Base marks: flames mark, the date, shape number 2649, and the artist's initials in black slip. 8.25" h. *Courtesy of Mark Mussio, Cincinnati Art Galleries, LLC.*

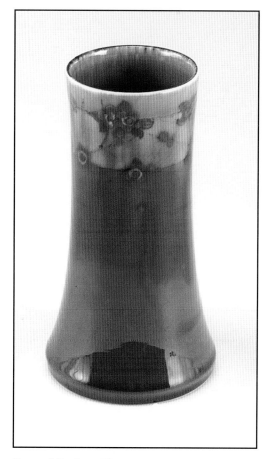

Figure 443. Sung Plum corseted vase painted by Vera Tischler with pink cherry blossoms on a grey, mauve, and blue ground, 1922. Base marks: flames mark, the date, and the artist's initials. 6" x 3.5". *Courtesy of David Rago Auctions.*

Figure 444. Large and impressive hand thrown Vellum glaze vase with red hollyhocks, blue foxglove, and blue asters painted in 1923 by Lenore Asbury. Base marks: flames mark, the date, shape number 614 B, an incised V for Vellum glaze, and the incised initials of the artist. 14.5" h. *Courtesy of Mark Mussio, Cincinnati Art Galleries, LLC.*

Figure 446. Large mat glaze two handled vase with cascading red flowers on a blue-green ground decorated in 1923 by Elizabeth Lincoln. Base marks: flames mark, the date, shape number 339 B, and the artist's initials in blue slip. 14" h. *Courtesy of Mark Mussio, Cincinnati Art Galleries, LLC.*

Figure 445. Scenic Vellum plaque painted by Edward Diers in 1923, featuring detailed trees along a lake shore beneath clouds, all of which are mirrored in the water. Back marks: flames mark and the date. An old label attached to the frame reads, "Reflection, E. Diers." 8.5" x 5". *Courtesy of Mark Mussio, Cincinnati Art Galleries, LLC.*

Figure 447. Mat glaze vase decorated by Elizabeth Lincoln in 1923 with berries and leaves on a mottle pink background and accented with black. Base marks: flames mark, the date, shape number 2105, and the artist's initials in black slip. 5" h. *Courtesy of Mark Mussio, Cincinnati Art Galleries, LLC.*

Figure 448. Vellum Glaze vase decorated in 1923 by Margaret Helen McDonald with white wild roses with leaves and branches upon a dark blue to lighter blue to ivory surface. Base marks: flames mark, the date, shape number 839B, an impressed V for Vellum Glaze, and the impressed artist's mark. 9.25" h. *Courtesy of Mark Mussio, Cincinnati Art Galleries, LLC.*

Figure 449. Small porcelain bowl decorated in 1923 by Fred Rothenbusch with red flowers and green vines upon a blue ground and then covered with a dark blue glaze. Base marks: flames mark, the date, shape number 955, a P for porcelain body, the incised initials "DB" (possibly for Dark Blue glaze), and the decorator's monogram. 3.5" h. *Courtesy of Mark Mussio, Cincinnati Art Galleries, LLC.*

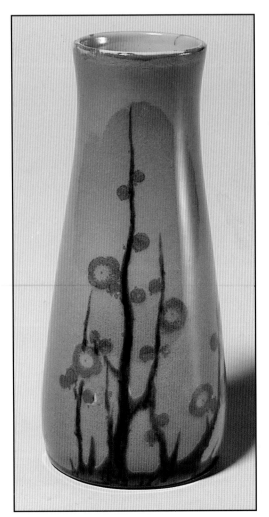

Figure 450. Decorated Porcelain vase decorated in 1923 by Kataro Shirayamadani with stylized blue flowers with yellow centers and stems on an uncrazed mauve to blue background and lined with lime green. Base marks: flames mark, the date, and shape number 950F. 6" h. *Courtesy of Mark Mussio, Cincinnati Art Galleries, LLC.*

Figure 451. Decorated Porcelain vase with stylized blue and mauve blossoms painted by Lenore Asbury in 1924. Base marks: flames mark, the date, shape number 2719, and the artist's incised initials. 6.5" h. *Courtesy of Mark Mussio, Cincinnati Art Galleries, LLC.*

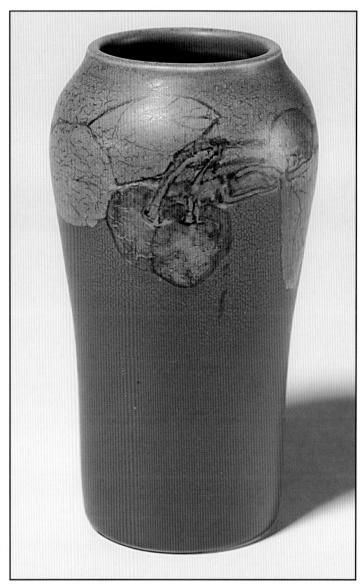

Figure 453. Mat glaze vase with large red cherries amid leaves and branches over a deep red background painted by Sallie Coyne in 1924. Base marks: flames mark, the date, shape number 935 E, and the artist's initials in black slip. 7" h. *Courtesy of Mark Mussio, Cincinnati Art Galleries, LLC.*

Figure 452. Scenic Vellum vase painted by Sallie Coyne in 1924 with trees by a river in blues, greens, and apricot. Base marks: flames mark, the date, shape number 1661D, V, and the artist's initials. 10.75" x 5". *Courtesy of David Rago Auctions.*

Figure 454. Decorated Porcelain vase, painted by Edward Diers in 1924, featuring cascading wisteria flowers and vines on a body covered in a lightly blue-tinted glaze. Base marks: flames mark, the date, shape number 614 D, and the artist's incised signature. 10.75" h. *Courtesy of Mark Mussio, Cincinnati Art Galleries, LLC.*

Figure 455. Vase decorated by Edward Diers in 1924, featuring white wild roses encircling the vase on a blue ground. Base marks: flames mark, the date, shape number 63, an impressed V for Vellum, a wheel-ground X, and the artist's initials. The glaze failed to adhere to the rim of the vase, accounting for the X. 4.25" h. *Courtesy of Mark Mussio, Cincinnati Art Galleries, LLC.*

Figure 456. Squat vase thrown by Anton Lang at the Pottery in 1924 and covered with the Nubian Black glaze on the exterior and a deep green on the interior. Anton Lang's signature boldly adorns the shoulder of the vase. Base marks: flames mark and the date. *Courtesy of Mark Mussio, Cincinnati Art Galleries, LLC.*

Figure 457. Black Opal vase decorated by Sara Sax in 1924 with stylized red peonies, aligned geometrically on a striated gray ground, and Moresque styling to decorate the foot. Base marks: flames mark, the date, shape number 2787, and the artist's initials in black slip. *Courtesy of Mark Mussio, Cincinnati Art Galleries, LLC.*

Figure 458. Vellum glaze harbor scene painted in 1924 by Carl Schmidt, featuring sailing ships, individual sailors clearly visible, and high thin clouds. Base marks: flames mark, the date, the partially obscured shape 2040C, an incised V for Vellum glaze, and the decorator's monogram. 12" h. *Courtesy of Mark Mussio, Cincinnati Art Galleries, LLC.*

Figure 459. Decorated Mat vase decorated in 1925 by Elizabeth Lincoln with Virginia creeper. Base marks: flames mark, the date, shape number 838 A, and the artist's initials in black slip. 15.25" h. *Courtesy of Mark Mussio, Cincinnati Art Galleries, LLC.*

Figure 460. Decorated Mat vase with trailing flowers decorated in 1925 by Elizabeth Lincoln. Base marks: flames mark, the date, shape number 2898, and the artist's initials in black slip. 11.25" h. *Courtesy of Mark Mussio, Cincinnati Art Galleries, LLC.*

Figure 461. Wax Mat bulbous vase painted in 1925 by Elizabeth Lincoln with branches of cherry blossoms in black against a shaded red ground. Base marks: flames mark, the date, shape number 538V, and the artist's initials. 7.5" x 3.5". *Courtesy of David Rago Auctions.*

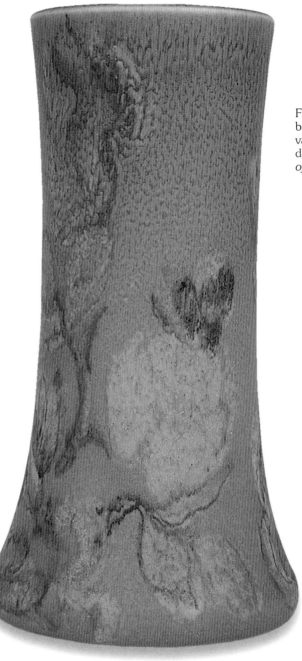

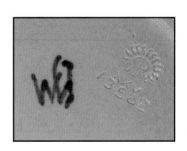

Figure 462. Wax Mat vase decorated in 1925 by Elizabeth McDermott with a floral motif encompassing the vase and a single butterfly. Base marks: flames mark, the date, and the artist's hand signed initials. 7" h. *Courtesy of Clarence Meyer.*

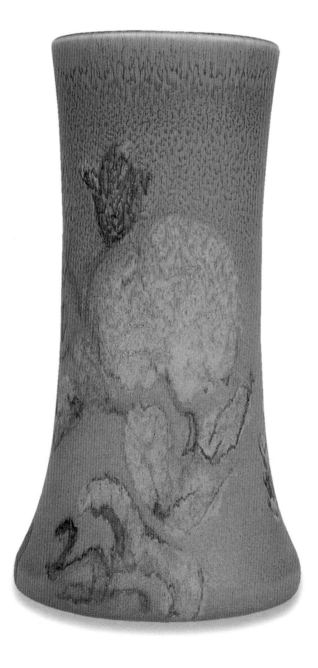

Figure 463. Jewel Porcelain vase with a squat base and flaring neck painted by Kataro Shirayamadani in 1925 with purple and orange cornflowers on a plum ground. Base marks: flames mark, the date, shape number 2719, and the artist's cipher. 6.5" x 4". *Courtesy of David Rago Auctions.*

Figure 465. Large Scenic Vellum plaque by Edward Diers, titled *Waterfalls,* 1926. It is mounted in the original frame. Plaque: 9" x 12". *Courtesy of David Rago Auctions.*

Figure 464. Vellum bowl decorated in 1925 by Harriet Wilcox with an array of pink cornflowers and stems around the shoulder of the vase. The background is blue and the interior is lined in the same pink used for the flowers. According to Cincinnati Art Galleries, "There is some haziness to the decoration and it is unknown if this was purposeful." Base marks: flames mark, the date, shape number 1110, an incised V for Vellum, and the artist's incised signature. 3.75" h. *Courtesy of Mark Mussio, Cincinnati Art Galleries, LLC.*

Figure 466. Vellum Glaze vase painted by Edward Diers in 1926 with encircling pink wild roses with green leaves on a blue to pink ground. Base marks: flames mark, the date, shape number 513, a V for Vellum glaze, and the decorator's initials. 5.5" h. *Courtesy of Mark Mussio, Cincinnati Art Galleries, LLC.*

Figure 467. Wax Mat closed-in bowl painted in 1926 by Elizabeth Lincoln with red chrysanthemums on a red ground. Base marks: flames mark, the date, shape number 214B, and the artist's initials. 3.5" x 6.5". *Courtesy of David Rago Auctions.*

Figure 469. Wax Mat center bowl decorated in 1926 by Margaret H. McDonald with plum and yellow blossoms on purple and green ground. Base marks: flames mark, the date, shape number 2574D, and the artist's initials. 3" x 10.5". *Courtesy of David Rago Auctions.*

Figure 468. Ovoid vase with floral decoration painted by Margaret Helen McDonald in 1926. Base marks: flames mark, the date, shape number 913 F, and the artist's initials. 5.5" h. *Courtesy of Bob Shores and Dale Jones.*

Figure 470. Vellum vase painted by Carl Schmidt in 1926 with irises on shaded pink and blue ground. Base marks: flames mark, the date, shape number 2544, V, and the artist's cipher. 8.25" x 4". *Courtesy of David Rago Auctions.*

Figure 471. Decorated Porcelain vase embellished by Kataro Shirayamadani in 1926 by trailing white and yellow anemone with green vines around the upper portion of the vase while the lower part is shaded mauve over striated green. Base marks: flames mark, the date, shape number 654D, and the decorator's incised Japanese signature. 4.5" h. *Courtesy of Mark Mussio, Cincinnati Art Galleries, LLC.*

Figure 472. Jewel Porcelain flaring vase painted by Harriet Wilcox in 1926 with white clematis on a plum ground. Base marks: flames mark, the date, shape number 2789, and the artist's initials. 11" x 6.75". *Courtesy of David Rago Auctions.*

Figure 473. Vellum glaze vase with blue and white crocuses painted in 1927 by Edward Diers. Base marks: flames mark, the date, shape number 925 E, an incised V for Vellum glaze, and the artist's incised monogram. 7.25" h. *Courtesy of Mark Mussio, Cincinnati Art Galleries, LLC.*

Figure 474. Flower holder designed by Kataro Shirayamadani and hand painted in 1927 by Lorinda Epply (including the flower, the buds, the leaves, and the base) in a very fashionable manner. Base marks: flames mark, the date, shape number 2979, and Ms. Epply's signature in black slip. 2.75" h. *Courtesy of Mark Mussio, Cincinnati Art Galleries, LLC.*

Figure 475. Three-piece temple jar (outer and inner lids and base) produced in 1927 and decorated by Edward T. Hurley with colorful parrots and foliage around the circumference of the large jar over a vivid yellow ground. Base marks: flames mark, the date, shape number 2448, and the artist's initials in black slip. 14.5" h. *Courtesy of Mark Mussio, Cincinnati Art Galleries, LLC.*

Figure 476. Decorated Mat vase with red roses painted in 1927 by Katherine Jones. Base marks: flames mark, the date, shape number 2785, and the artist's monogram in black slip. 13.25" h. *Courtesy of Mark Mussio, Cincinnati Art Galleries, LLC.*

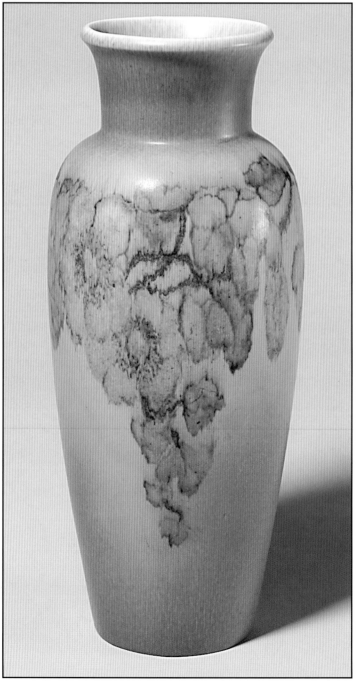

Figure 477. Wax Mat ovoid vase painted in 1927 by Elizabeth Lincoln with fleshy red chrysanthemums on a green ground. Base marks: flames mark, the date, shape number 2790, and the artist's initials. 12" x 5.5". *Courtesy of David Rago Auctions.*

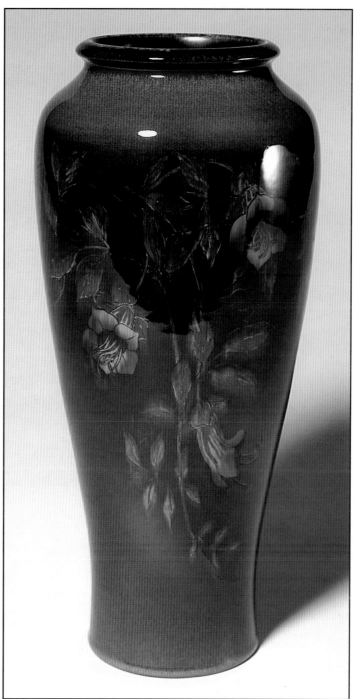

Figure 479. Black Opal vase decorated in 1927 by Harriet Wilcox with trumpet creepers; the flowers and leaves encircle the vase with one cascade of flowers extending nearly to the base. Base marks: flames mark, the date, shape number 2551, and the artist's initials in black slip. 14" h. *Courtesy of Mark Mussio, Cincinnati Art Galleries, LLC.*

Figure 478. Black Opal squat vessel painted by Sara Sax in 1927 with stylized blossoms in white, yellow, and pink on a cobalt ground. Base marks: flames mark, the date, shape number 1929, and the artist's cipher. 4.75" x 6.75". *Courtesy of David Rago Auctions.*

Figure 480. Black Opal vase painted in 1927 by Harriet Wilcox with white roses encircling the base and the interior lined with a mottled, iridescent brown glaze. Base marks: flames mark, the date, shape number 2719, and the artist's initials painted in black slip. 6.25" h. *Courtesy of Mark Mussio, Cincinnati Art Galleries, LLC.*

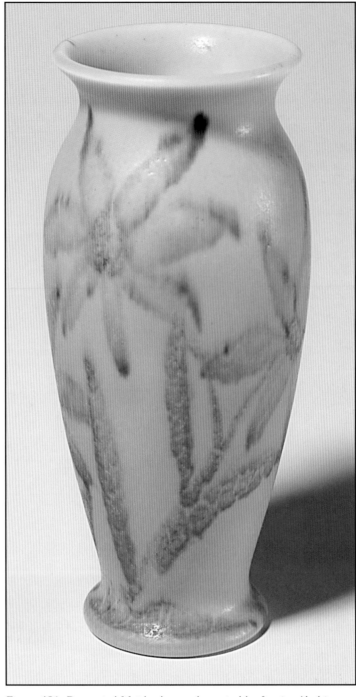

Figure 481. Decorated Mat bud vase decorated by Louise Abel in 1928, featuring stylized blue daisies, with ochre centers and green leaves, on a green ground. Base marks: flames mark, the date, shape number 2721, and the artist's monogram in blue slip. 6.25" h. *Courtesy of Mark Mussio, Cincinnati Art Galleries, LLC.*

Figure 482. Vellum vase painted by Lenore Asbury in 1928 with Art Deco flowers gracing the shoulder. Base marks: flames mark, the date, shape number 2191, an incised V for Vellum glaze, and the artist's incised initials. 5.25" h. *Courtesy of Mark Mussio, Cincinnati Art Galleries, LLC.*

Figure 483. Vellum vase decorated in 1928 by Edward Diers, featuring a cascade of pink flowers and large green leaves, on a pink and black background, encompassing the upper portion of the vase and separated from the lower portion by a green line. Base marks: flames mark, the date, shape number 77C, a V for Vellum glaze, and the artist's incised mark. 5.5" h. *Courtesy of Mark Mussio, Cincinnati Art Galleries, LLC.*

Figure 484. Decorated Porcelain vase painted in 1928 by Lorinda Epply with hydrangea. Cincinnati Art Galleries state, "The interior is lined with an early version of Rookwood's Anniversary glaze which drips down the rim slightly." Base marks: flames mark, the date, shape number 2246 C, and the artist's monogram in black slip. 14" h. *Courtesy of Mark Mussio, Cincinnati Art Galleries, LLC.*

Figure 485. Jewel Porcelain bulbous vase painted in the classical style by Lorinda Epply in 1928 with a band of pink and indigo blossoms on ivory and indigo ground. Base marks: flames mark, the date, shape number 975D, P, and the artist's initials. 6.25" x 4.5". *Courtesy of David Rago Auctions.*

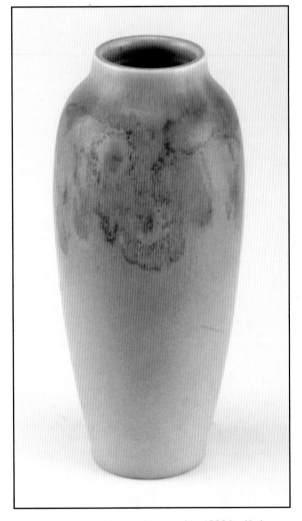

Figure 486. Wax Mat vase decorated in 1928 by Katherine Jones with pink roses and green leaves on a pink ground. Base marks: flames mark and date. 7.5" x 3.5". *Courtesy of David Rago Auctions.*

Figure 487. Wax Mat vase painted in 1928 by Margaret H. McDonald with pink leaves on a turquoise butterfat ground. Base marks: flames mark, the date, shape number 2182, and the artist's initials. 5.25" x 4". *Courtesy of David Rago Auctions.*

Figure 488. Painted Mat vase decorated in 1928 by John Wesley Pullman with red roses and green leaves covered with an unusual, stippled mat rust-brown glaze. The interior of the vase has been lined with the same color, to which was introduced deep blue. Base marks: flames mark, the date, shape number 402, and the artist's signature painted in blue slip. 6.25" h. *Courtesy of Mark Mussio, Cincinnati Art Galleries, LLC.*

Figure 489. High glaze scenic vase decorated by Fred Rothenbusch in 1928 with a landscape with trees and a stream with hills in the background. Base marks: flames mark, the date, shape number 1917B, the artist's monogram, and the incised initials "SV." 10" h. *Courtesy of Mark Mussio, Cincinnati Art Galleries, LLC.*

Figure 490. Mat glaze two-handled vase decorated in 1929 by Sallie Coyne with pink morning glories. Base marks: flames mark, the date, shape number 6111, and the artist's monogram in blue slip. 9" h. *Courtesy of Mark Mussio, Cincinnati Art Galleries, LLC.*

Figure 491. Decorated Porcelain twin-handled vase decorated in 1929 by Lorinda Epply with Art Deco flowers and berries. The vase is lined with an iridescent blue-black glaze. Base marks: flames mark, the date, shape number 6115, and the artist's monogram in black slip. 10.25" h. *Courtesy of Mark Mussio, Cincinnati Art Galleries, LLC.*

Figure 493. Scenic Vellum ovoid vase painted by Edward T. Hurley in 1929 with a landscape of trees at dusk. Base marks: flames mark, the date, shape number 925C, and the artist's initials. 10.25" x 5". *Courtesy of David Rago Auctions.*

Figure 492. Bulbous vase painted in the squeeze bag technique by William Hentschel in 1929 with an Art Deco pattern and brown sprigs on rich brown ground. 5.25" x 5.25". *Courtesy of David Rago Auctions.*

Figure 494. Three-part potpourri jar decorated by Edward T. Hurley in 1929 with white daisies in a band around the shoulder. The jar has a reticulated outer lid and an inner lid. Base marks: flames mark, the date, shape number 1321 E, an impressed V, an incised V for Vellum glaze, and the artist's incised initials. 4" h. *Courtesy of Mark Mussio, Cincinnati Art Galleries, LLC.*

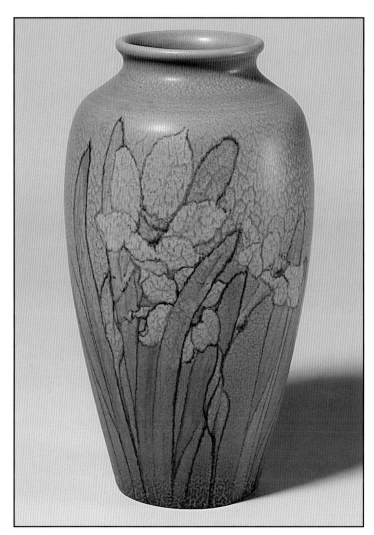

Figure 497. Jewel Porcelain bulbous vase painted in 1929 by Kataro Shirayamadani with large orange and red chrysanthemums. Base marks: flames mark, the date, shape number 927D, and the artist's Japanese signature. 9" x 6.25". *Courtesy of David Rago Auctions.*

Figure 495. Decorated Mat vase painted by Margaret McDonald in 1929, featuring blooming irises on a stippled brown ground. Base marks: flames mark, the date, shape number 614 D, and the artist's monogram in black slip. The vase was presented as a gift originally and was marked in black paint with "Bankers Life Company, R.L. Twombley, 1912-1932." 10.5" h. *Courtesy of Mark Mussio, Cincinnati Art Galleries, LLC.*

Figure 496. Jewel Porcelain ovoid vase decorated in 1929 by Kataro Shirayamadani with red wild roses and green leaves on a brick, sky blue, and black shaded ground. Base marks: flames mark, the date, shape number 356E, and the artist's cipher. 6.75" x 3.5". *Courtesy of David Rago Auctions.*

Figure 498. Mat glaze vase with floral decoration painted by an unknown artist (the piece has no artist's mark on the base) in 1929. 7.25" h. *Courtesy of Clarence Meyer.*

Rookwood's 1920s Artware Production Objects

Now that the numbers of molded artware pieces have climbed, it will be useful to view them separately from the hand-painted, artist signed art pottery wares.

Figure 500. Two production vases embossed with Moorish flowers, one covered in cafe-au-lait butterfat glaze (1920), the other in Mat mustard (1925). Both are marked. 7.75" and 5.25" h. *Courtesy of David Rago Auctions.*

Figure 499. Production vase from 1920 featuring embossed foxglove decoration under a crystalline deep purple-gray mat glaze. Base marks: flames mark, the date, and part of the shape number 2167 (both the date and most of the shape number are obscured by glaze). 8.25" h. *Courtesy of Mark Mussio, Cincinnati Art Galleries, LLC.*

Figure 501. Production ovoid vase from 1920 with stylized dogwood blossoms, covered in pink glaze. Base marks: flames mark and date. 9" h. *Courtesy of David Rago Auctions.*

Figure 502. A pair of candleholders covered with a mat blue crystalline glaze in 1920. Base marks: flames mark, the date, and shape number 822 D. 6.5" h. each. *Courtesy of Mark Mussio, Cincinnati Art Galleries, LLC.*

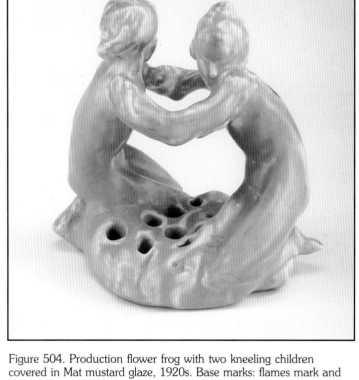

Figure 504. Production flower frog with two kneeling children covered in Mat mustard glaze, 1920s. Base marks: flames mark and date. 6.25" x 6.25". *Courtesy of David Rago Auctions.*

Figure 503. Production four-piece console set with a low bowl, figural flower frog with a young girl and a frog, and a pair of candlesticks in Mat ivory glaze with a green interior, dating from the 1920s. Base marks: flames marks and dates. Bowl: 3" x 13"; frog: 5.75"; candlesticks: 5" h. *Courtesy of David Rago Auctions.*

Figure 505. Mat glaze production vase decorated with deep relief patterns of flowers and swirls, designed by William Hentschel and glazed in a rich purple in 1921 (the glaze's first year of production). Base marks: flames mark, the date, and shape number 2556. 8.25" h. *Courtesy of Mark Mussio, Cincinnati Art Galleries, LLC.*

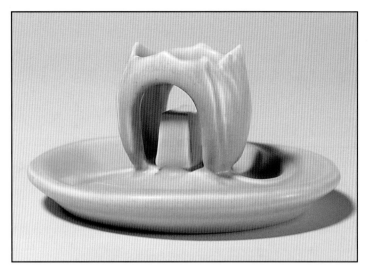

Figure 506. Match holder in an Arts and Crafts form designed by Kataro Shirayamadani in the form of a tulip and cast in 1921. It was covered with a yellow mat glaze. Base marks: flames mark, the date, and shape number 1695. *Courtesy of Mark Mussio, Cincinnati Art Galleries, LLC.*

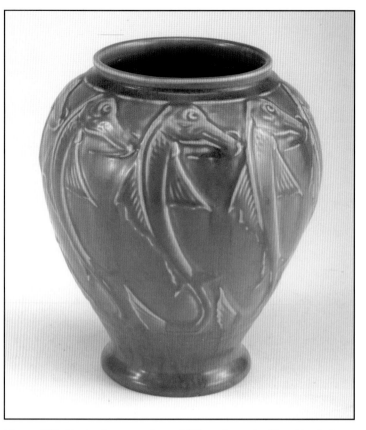

Figure 508. Production vase from 1921 embossed with whimsical seahorses under a frothy mat green glaze. Base marks: flames mark, the date, and shape number 2220. 8" x 7". *Courtesy of David Rago Auctions.*

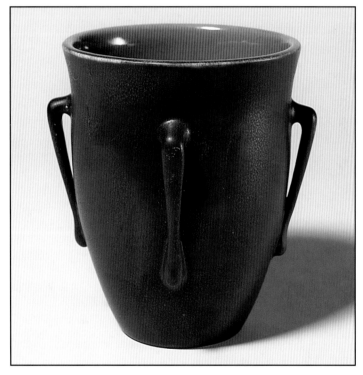

Figure 507. Four-handled production vase cast in 1921. The exterior of the piece has been glazed in mat black; the interior is glazed in a deep, glossy dark pumpkin. Base marks: flames mark, the date, and shape number 2196. 8.25" h. *Courtesy of Mark Mussio, Cincinnati Art Galleries, LLC.*

Figure 509. Production vase with a bulge in the neck, black glaze at the rim, and reddish brown elsewhere, dating from 1921. Base marks: flames mark, the date, and shape number 2546 C. 10.75" h. *Courtesy of Bob Shores and Dale Jones.*

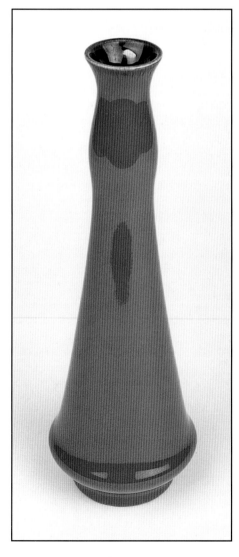

Figure 510. Production barrel-shaped vase covered in a rich mottled purple glossy glaze, 1921. Base marks: a couple of shallow scratches, flames mark, and the date. 8" h. *Courtesy of David Rago Auctions.*

Figure 511. Production vase with molded shoulder decoration dating from 1921. Base marks: flames mark, the date, shape number 2155. 2.25" x 5". *Courtesy of Clarence Meyer.*

Figure 512. Unusual tile featuring a long-eared squirrel nibbling a nut. Dated to 1921, the tile is covered with a light blue mat glaze. Base marks: flames mark, the date, and shape number 2053. 3.25" x 4.75". *Courtesy of Mark Mussio, Cincinnati Art Galleries, LLC.*

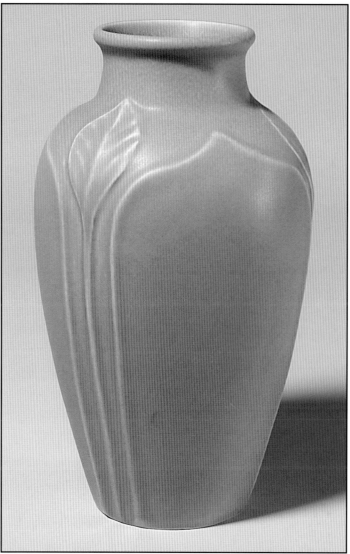

Figure 513. Production vase decorated with a leaf-and-stem motif interspersed with panels and covered with a pink mat glaze, oversprayed with pale green, in 1922. Base marks: flames mark, the date, and shape number 2379. 10" h. *Courtesy of Mark Mussio, Cincinnati Art Galleries, LLC.*

Figure 514. Urn-shaped production vase with handles dating from 1922. 4.25" h. *Courtesy of Clarence Meyer.*

Figure 515. Production bowl dating from 1922 with three buttresses and a molded quatrefoil design covered with a variegated brown mat glaze. Base marks: flames mark, the date, and shape number 1807. 2.25" h. *Courtesy of Mark Mussio, Cincinnati Art Galleries, LLC.*

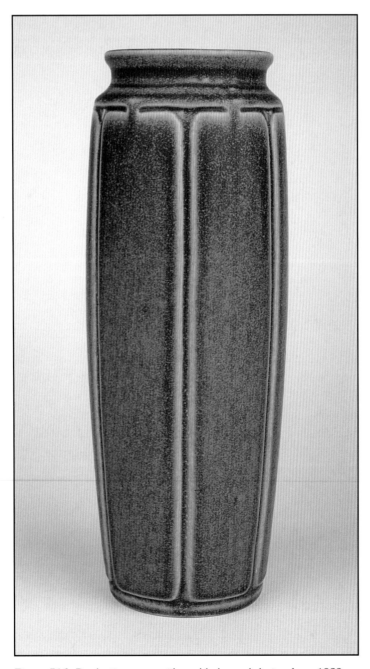

Figure 516. Production vase with molded panel design from 1923. Base marks: flames mark, the date, and shape number 2420. 9" h. *Courtesy of Bob Shores and Dale Jones.*

Figure 517. Production baluster vase covered in a mat black butterfat glaze with crackled turquoise interior, 1923. Base marks: flames mark and date. 11" h. *Courtesy of David Rago Auctions.*

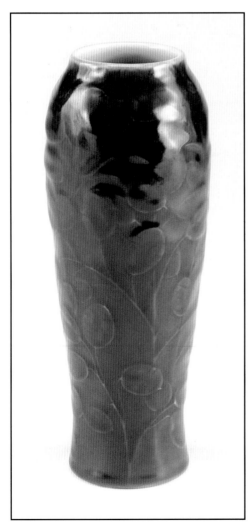

Figure 518. Production vase with honesty branches under a semi-mat indigo glaze, dating to 1923. Base marks: flames mark and date. 9.5" h. *Courtesy of David Rago Auctions.*

Figure 519. Production baluster vase covered in crackled curdling blue glaze, dating from 1923. Base marks: flames mark and date. 9.5" h. *Courtesy of David Rago Auctions.*

Figure 520. Production vase with buttresses and dogwood blossoms under an unusual purple crystalline mat glaze, 1923. 7.75" h. *Courtesy of David Rago Auctions.*

Figure 521. Production narrow vase embossed with a band of seahorses under blue glaze, 1923. 6.75" h. *Courtesy of David Rago Auctions.*

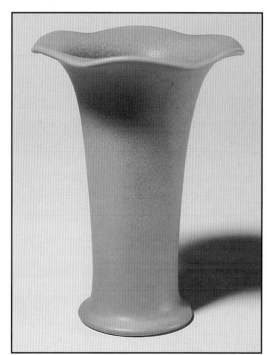

Figure 522. Production vase in mat blue-green glaze, 1924. A second mark was applied for two small glaze misses. Base marks: flames mark, date, and the X. 10.75" h. *Courtesy of David Rago Auctions.*

Figure 523. Production trumpet-shaped vase covered in pink and eggplant crystalline glaze, 1924. Base marks: flames mark and date. 7.5" h. *Courtesy of David Rago Auctions.*

Figure 524. Production vase with a flaring rim cast in 1924 and covered with a mat pink and with a green overspray glaze. Base marks: flames mark, the date, and shape number 2736. 7" h. *Courtesy of Mark Mussio, Cincinnati Art Galleries, LLC.*

Figure 525. Production vase from 1925 with a narrow base flaring to a wide top adorned with molded decoration at the shoulder. Base marks: flames mark, the date, and shape number 2863. 6" h. *Courtesy of Bob Shores and Dale Jones.*

Figure 526. Small production vase from 1925 covered in pink glaze with a strip of molded rectangles just below shoulder. Base marks: flames mark, the date, and shape number 2284. 5" h. *Courtesy of Bob Shores and Dale Jones.*

Figure 527. Two production pieces covered in teal blue mat glaze: an urn with a faceted base and curled handles dating to 1925, and a spherical vase embossed with flowers dating to 1931. Base marks: both have the flames mark and date. *Courtesy of David Rago Auctions.*

Figure 528. Flower holder designed by Kataro Shirayamadani featuring a frog sitting atop a mound with flowers. Cast in 1925, the figure was covered in a jet black high glaze, which has been applied so that highlights of the clay show through. Base marks: flames mark, the date, and shape number 2712. 3.5" h. *Courtesy of Mark Mussio, Cincinnati Art Galleries, LLC.*

Figure 529. Production trivet cast in 1925, adorned with a green cockatoo with yellow beak and talons. Base marks: flames mark, the date, and shape number 2043. 5.5". *Courtesy of Mark Mussio, Cincinnati Art Galleries, LLC.*

Figure 530. Production vase from 1926 with handles, greenish-brown to reddish brown glaze from top to bottom. Base marks: flames mark, the date, and shape number 607C. 5" h., 5" across the handles. *Courtesy of Bob Shores and Dale Jones.*

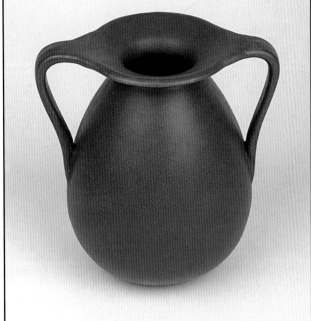

Figure 531. Production tyg decorated with a geometric design under a cobalt glaze, 1926. Base marks: flames mark and date. 5.75" h. *Courtesy of David Rago Auctions.*

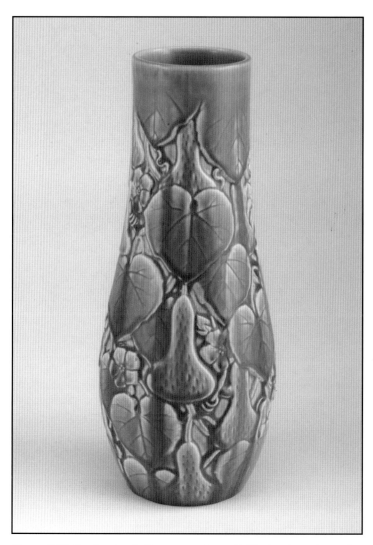

Figure 534. Short, blue glazed production vase with handles, dating from 1927. Base marks: flames mark, the date, and shape number 63. 4.25" h. *Courtesy of Bob Shores and Dale Jones.*

Figure 532. Production bulbous vase from 1927, deeply embossed with squash blossoms and leaves under blue glaze. Base marks: flames mark and date. 13.75" x 5.75". *Courtesy of David Rago Auctions.*

Figure 533. Two production bulbous squat vases, each embossed with stylized floral designs, one in mat pink, the other in mat blue, dating from 1927 and 1928. Base marks: flames mark and date. 4". *Courtesy of David Rago Auctions.*

Figure 535. Production vase cast in 1927, with a mat pink glaze covering the architectural-style molded decoration. Base marks: flames mark, the date, and shape number 2907. *Courtesy of Mark Mussio, Cincinnati Art Galleries, LLC.*

Figure 536. Trivet tile with an indigo rook against an Oriental trellis, dating from 1927. Base marks: flames mark and date. 5.75" square. *Courtesy of David Rago Auctions.*

Figure 537. Impressively large production vase from 1928 covered with a turquoise high glaze. Base marks: flames mark, the date, and shape number 2370. 21.25" h. *Courtesy of Mark Mussio, Cincinnati Art Galleries, LLC.*

Figure 538. Production vase with a stylized curvilinear design under a mat blue glaze, dating from 1928. Base marks: flames mark and date. 10" x 8.5". *Courtesy of David Rago Auctions.*

Figure 539. Mat production vase dating from 1928, the upper half being covered with an intricate floral design and glazed with a blue crystalline finish. Base marks: flames mark, the date, and shape number 6029. 6.25" h. *Courtesy of Mark Mussio, Cincinnati Art Galleries, LLC.*

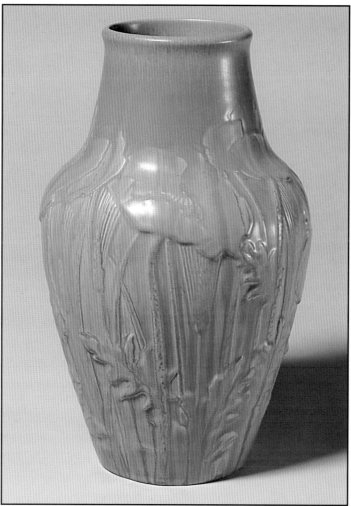

Figure 540. Large production vase cast in 1929, a Kataro Shirayamadani design bursting with poppies all around the body and glazed with mat shades of lavender and green. Base marks: flames mark, the date, and shape number 6006. 11.75" h. *Courtesy of Mark Mussio, Cincinnati Art Galleries, LLC.*

Figure 541. Production vase cast in 1929 with molded shoulder and rim decoration. Base marks: flames mark and date. 5.25" h. *Courtesy of Bob Shores and Dale Jones.*

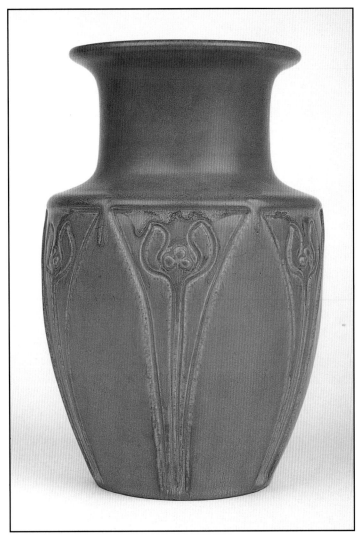

Figure 542. Production vase cast in 1929 and glazed in green with gold accents around the molded flower decoration. Base marks: flames mark, the date, and shape number 2413. 7.25" h. *Courtesy of Bob Shores and Dale Jones.*

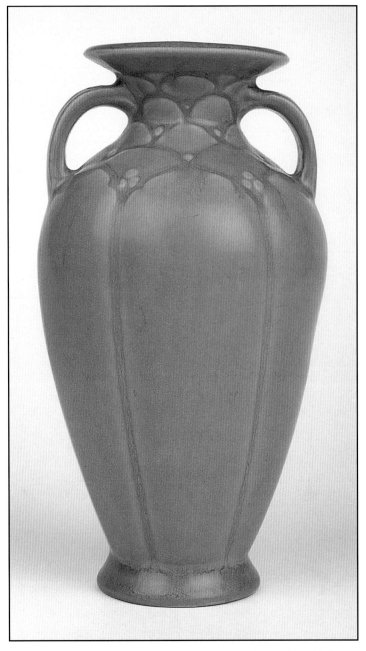

Figure 543. Production vase with handles in green glaze with molded decoration around the neck, 1929. Base marks: flames mark, the date, and shape number 2675. 6.5" h. *Courtesy of Bob Shores and Dale Jones.*

Figure 544. Floral set cast in 1929, consisting of a large bowl (2.5" x 12") and a 6" flower holder in the forms of a nude nymphet and a frog deep in contemplation of each other. Base marks: flames mark, the date, and shape numbers 2527 and 2925. *Courtesy of Mark Mussio, Cincinnati Art Galleries, LLC.*

Figure 545. Tea tile from 1929 featuring a midnight blue rook on a white and blue geometric background and mounted in a 3" oak Arts & Crafts frame. Base marks: flames mark, the date, and shape number 1794. 5.5" square. *Courtesy of Mark Mussio, Cincinnati Art Galleries, LLC.*

Figure 546. Ivory mat dog designed by William McDonald and cast in 1929. Base marks: flames mark, the date, and shape 2777. 4.75" h. *Courtesy of Mark Mussio, Cincinnati Art Galleries, LLC.*

Bookends

Figure 547. A pair of Rook bookends cast in 1920 and covered with a variegated mat green glaze. Base marks: flames mark, the date, and shape number 2275. 4.75" h. *Courtesy of Mark Mussio, Cincinnati Art Galleries, LLC.*

Figure 548. A pair of "Little Boy" bookends dated from 1922, covered with a dark mat blue glaze and designed by William McDonald. Base marks: flames mark, the date, and shape number 2447. 5.25" h. each. *Courtesy of Mark Mussio, Cincinnati Art Galleries, LLC.*

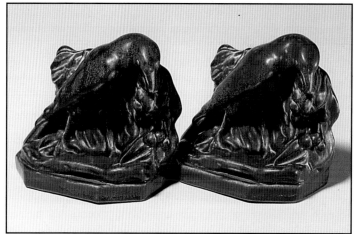

Figure 549. Rook bookends cast in 1922 and covered with a mat blue crystalline glaze. Cincinnati Art Galleries states, "The detail of the bookends is excellent and the glaze is extraordinary." Base marks: flames mark, the date, and shape number 2275. 5" h. *Courtesy of Mark Mussio, Cincinnati Art Galleries, LLC.*

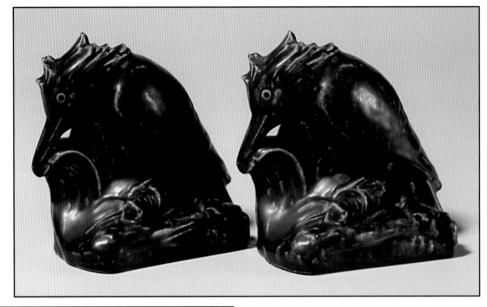

Figure 550. Two Kingfisher bookends, one dated 1923, the other 1924, each covered with a rich, dark blue mat glaze. Base marks: flames mark, the date, shape number 2657, the mold signature of designer William McDonald, and a sticker from the Marshall Field Co., Chicago's twelve story department store that convinced Rookwood's management to offer their wares in upscale department stores. 5.5" h. *Courtesy of Mark Mussio, Cincinnati Art Galleries, LLC.*

Figure 551. A crouching frog bookend in mat mustard glaze, dating from 1923. Also in the image are a pair of tall faceted production candlesticks covered in mat rose glaze, dating from 1924. All are marked. 4.5" and 7.5". *Courtesy of David Rago Auctions.*

Figure 552. A pair of production bookends by William P. McDonald shaped as owls perched on books, and covered in mat green and brown crystalline glaze, 1924. Base marks: flames mark, the date, shape number 2656, and the designer's initials. 6.75" x 4.25". *Courtesy of David Rago Auctions.*

Figure 553. An unusual pair of double penguin bookends in metallic grey and beige, dating to 1924. Base marks: flames marks and date. 5.5" h. *Courtesy of David Rago Auctions.*

Figure 554. A pair of Rook bookends produced in 1924 and covered in a blue-green "frogskin" glaze. Base marks: flames mark, the date, and shape number 2275. 5" h. *Courtesy of Mark Mussio, Cincinnati Art Galleries, LLC.*

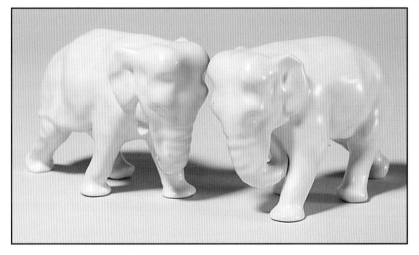

Figure 555. Very unusual (as they do not stand on bases) elephant bookends produced in 1925 and covered in an ivory mat glaze. Base marks: flames mark, the date, and shape number 2444 D. 4" h. *Courtesy of Mark Mussio, Cincinnati Art Galleries, LLC.*

Figure 556. A set of "Blue Jay" bookends produced in 1926 and covered with a crystalline green mat glaze that closely resembles weathered bronze. Base marks: flames mark, the date, and shape number 2829. *Courtesy of Mark Mussio, Cincinnati Art Galleries, LLC.*

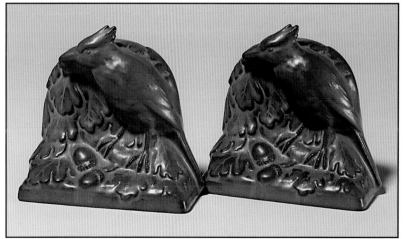

Figure 557. A pair of production elephant bookends designed by William P. McDonald, their trunks up in the air, covered in mat green glaze, 1929. Base marks: flames mark, the date, and the artist's stamp. 7.25" x 5.5". *Courtesy of David Rago Auctions.*

Figure 558. A pair of Lion bookends designed by Louise Abel in mat rust glaze, produced in 1929. Base marks: flames mark, the date, shape number 6019, and the designer's impressed monogram. 6.25" h. *Courtesy of Mark Mussio, Cincinnati Art Galleries, LLC.*

Figure 559. Single lion bookend-figure cast in 1929, designed by Louise Abel and covered with a striated, mat green glaze. Base marks: flames mark, the date, shape number 6019, and the designer's mold mark. 6.75" h. *Courtesy of Mark Mussio, Cincinnati Art Galleries, LLC.*

Figure 560. A pair of Polar Bear bookends standing on a snow-covered plinth, glazed in ivory mat in 1929 and designed by Kataro Shirayamadani. Base marks: flames mark, the date, and shape number 2678. 4.5" x 6.5". *Courtesy of Mark Mussio, Cincinnati Art Galleries, LLC.*

Rookwood Pottery in the 1930s and Beyond

In 1930, Rookwood celebrated its fiftieth anniversary with the firing of the "jubilee kiln." This special kiln held 1,200 items sporting a special commemorative mark comprised of a "50" enclosed in a black kiln outline. These modern wares represented the work of twenty-three artists. There was not a great deal to celebrate after that.

Figure 561. "Test shape" vase dating from 1930, covered with the Oxblood glaze. Base marks: flames mark, the date, and shape number 2587 F. 4.25" h. *Courtesy of Mark Mussio, Cincinnati Art Galleries, LLC.*

Top right:
Figure 562. Decorated Mat Glaze vase graced with abstract flowers around the vase, decorated by Sallie Coyne in 1930. Base marks: flames mark, the date, shape number 6101, a fan-shaped Fiftieth Anniversary mark, and the decorator's cipher in blue slip. 4.75". *Courtesy of Mark Mussio, Cincinnati Art Galleries, LLC.*

Right:
Figure 563. Decorated Mat vase from 1930 with Art Deco designs in tan and brown, with hints of blue and green, on a lighter tan background, decorated by Janet Harris. The interior is lined in blue. Base marks: flames mark, the date, shape number 6184 C, an esoteric mark connoting the pottery's Fiftieth Anniversary, and the decorator's initials painted in brown slip. 5" h. *Courtesy of Mark Mussio, Cincinnati Art Galleries, LLC.*

Figure 564. Decorated Mat vase with red coreopsis and green leaves on a yellow background, painted by Elizabeth Lincoln in 1930. Base marks: flames mark, the date, shape 80 C, a fan-shaped mark denoting the Fiftieth Anniversary of the pottery, and the artist's initials in blue slip. 7" h. *Courtesy of Mark Mussio, Cincinnati Art Galleries, LLC.*

Figure 565. Double Vellum vase adorned with exotic flowers and vines, decorated in 1930 by Margaret McDonald. Base marks: flames mark, the date, shape 907 E, and a fan-shaped mark denoting the Fiftieth Anniversary. 9.25" h. *Courtesy of Mark Mussio, Cincinnati Art Galleries, LLC.*

Figure 566. Mat glaze four-footed vase decorated by Margaret McDonald in 1930 with brown and blue abstract designs on a yellow ground. Base marks: flames mark, the date, shape number 6036, a fan-shaped mark denoting the Fiftieth Anniversary, and the artist's initials in blue slip. 6" h. *Courtesy of Mark Mussio, Cincinnati Art Galleries, LLC.*

In 1930, decorator Harriet E. Wilcox left on her own accord. William P. McDonald died in 1931, ending a forty-seven year career with Rookwood. Then, with too great an inventory and too few sales, Rookwood closed for a very short time in October 1931. Eight decorators were let go or retired, seven of whom had been with the company since its earliest decades.

In the 1930s and 1940s, Rookwood introduced small figurines in the forms of people, animals, birds, and fish. Fanciful figures were becoming quite popular in a nation suffering from first economic depression and then the threat of global warfare.

Figure 568. Monkey figure designed by Louise Abel, cast in 1935 and covered with a striated brown high glaze with blue accents. Base marks: flames mark, the date, shape number 6501, and the cast designer's monogram. According to Cincinnati Art Galleries, "The Shape Record lists this as a bookend, but it has neither the form nor the heft to serve well in such a capacity." 6" h. *Courtesy of Mark Mussio, Cincinnati Art Galleries, LLC.*

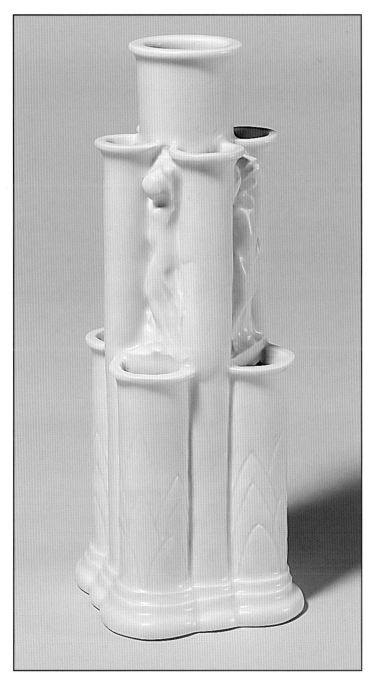

Figure 567. A very unusual tall vase designed by William McDonald and covered in an ivory mat glaze in 1930. The vase is constructed in three levels, the lowest displaying a geometric design and allowing four openings for flowers; the second also allows for the placement of flowers in four positions and is graced with four semi-nude female figures, while the third level is a single opening. Base marks: flames mark, the date, shape number 6163, and an esoteric mark, perhaps to signal Rookwood's Fiftieth Anniversary. 9.25" h. *Courtesy of Mark Mussio, Cincinnati Art Galleries, LLC.*

Figure 569. Alert, poised, and graceful feline figure designed by Louise Abel, dating from 1946, and coated with a tan high glaze. Base marks: flames mark, the date, shape number 6182, the impressed designer's monogram, an incised 39, and a quarter inch long ground line. 6.75" h. *Courtesy of Mark Mussio, Cincinnati Art Galleries, LLC.*

Figure 570. Large rook figural designed by William McDonald and cast in 1944, coated in apple green high glaze. Base marks: flames mark and date. 10" x 9". *Courtesy of David Rago Auctions.*

Faced with mounting loses, Joseph Henry Gest resigned as president in 1934. He was replaced by John Wareham, who was unable to halt the decline. The company's longstanding reputation as a manufacturer of luxury art, so carefully cultivated by William Taylor, would not serve Rookwood well now. Few Americans were inclined to purchase art pottery. While decorators Lorinda Epply, William Ernst Hentschel, Margaret McDonald, Edward T. Hurley, Jens Jensen, and Kataro Shirayamadani remained on staff, the production of artist-signed pottery was limited at best. Hand-decorated wares were largely replaced with molded forms with interesting glazes, quickly and inexpensively produced. Rookwood's advertising reflected this shift in emphasis, addressing glazes and forms in some detail while virtually ignoring decoration altogether.

Figure 571. Jewel Porcelain baluster vase painted in 1931 by Lorinda Epply with mauve poppies on ivory ground. Base marks: flames mark, the date, shape number 6195C, and the artist's initials. 9.25" x 6". *Courtesy of David Rago Auctions.*

Figure 572. Mat Glaze vase decorated by William Hentschel in 1931 with leaves and seeds, using a squeeze bag technique, in a design influenced by the Art Deco movement. Base marks: flames mark, the date, shape number 6180 F, and the decorator's incised initials. 4.5" h. *Courtesy of Mark Mussio, Cincinnati Art Galleries, LLC.*

Figure 575. Utilizing a squeeze bag technique, Jens Jensen applied red high glaze irises and leaves upon a mat red background in 1943. Base marks: flames mark, the date, shape number 6197 F, and the artist's incised mark. 4.5" h. *Courtesy of Mark Mussio, Cincinnati Art Galleries, LLC.*

Figure 573. Yellow glazed vase decorated by Margaret McDonald with flowers, leaves, and bands. Base marks: flames mark, the date, S (at times an impressed S was used to denote an item thrown to demonstrate the technique), and the artist's initials. 7.5" h. *Courtesy of Clarence Meyer.*

Figure 574. Vellum vase decorated by Edward T. Hurley in 1938 using colorful red and white apple blossoms around the upper third of the vase. Base marks: flames mark, the date, shape number 6199 D, and the artist's incised initials. 4.75" h. *Courtesy of Mark Mussio, Cincinnati Art Galleries, LLC.*

Figure 576. Ovoid Double Vellum vase decorated with both red and white dogwood blossoms painted in 1944 by Kataro Shirayamadani. Base marks: flames mark, the date, shape number 6199 C, and the artist's incised initials. 6" h. *Courtesy of Mark Mussio, Cincinnati Art Galleries, LLC.*

The State of the Pottery Industry, 1930s-1940s

During the 1930s, pottery manufacturers were increasingly frustrated by foreign competition in their home market. They felt the American public remained biased toward overseas goods, not just for price considerations, but also out of that persistent, deep-seated belief that domestic products were inferior. That was an image American potters had been battling since 1876. It was felt that American merchants held the same bias.

In 1937, Frederick H. Rhead, by then the art director for the Homer Laughlin China Company, reported on the state of affairs overseas. What Rhead observed was no comfort to the American potting industry. At the Paris Exposition, Rhead observed, "… the ceramic and other craft works, particularly those shown by Italy, Sweden, and Denmark, are very fine." From there, he moved on to Florence and Milan, Italy, and toured two pottery works, "… the former producing very beautiful porcelain and artwares and the latter, equipped with tunnel kilns and an elaborate system of conveyors concentrating on mass production approaching that of any American factory." (*Ceramic Industry* September 1937) Many in the American industry saw World War II as an opportunity to make inroads into the domestic market while the foreign trade was cut off.

Figure 577. Impressive large Decorated Porcelain vase with Art Deco lotus decoration created with several types of glazes and decorating styles by William Hentschel in 1930. One large white blossom is the central focus, applied in front of a medium blue pad, painted on in heavy slip. Smaller leaves are interspersed and a series of vertical white lines, applied by slip trailing, cover a 6" section of the vase. The interior is done in Rookwood's Anniversary glaze, a mottled gray-brown, some of which drips down large sections of the surface and is intentionally used in other areas. Base marks: flames mark, the date, shape number 2462, a fan-shaped esoteric mark, and the artist's incised initials of the artist. 13.25" h. Cincinnati Art Galleries states, "Hentschel was producing some amazing Art Deco pieces in 1930 and it is truly a shame that the Depression interrupted him and Rookwood so abruptly." *Courtesy of Mark Mussio, Cincinnati Art Galleries, LLC.*

The Second World War also created a number of challenges for American potters. The availability of raw materials was unpredictable; workers were scarce. Some companies took to hiring high school boys part time after school to handle general maintenance and janitorial work around the pottery plants. The Selective Service and munitions factories took many of the available workers. While women had been working in Ohio potteries since the nineteenth century, predominantly in decorating departments like Rookwood's, pottery factories took additional steps to accommodate greater numbers of women in their work force. Fuel shortages were always a worry. Transportation for wares produced was limited and far from reliable.

During the war years, pottery companies were forced to cut back on production. They culled out the slow selling wares, offering lines reduced to their best sellers of years past, at times featuring different glazes or decorations. Little in the way of new shapes and decorative treatments were produced during the war, particularly as most plants were now turning at least part of their production over to war materials commissioned by the national government.

Of the artware industry, the *Bulletin of the American Ceramic Society* reported:

> The combined production of art and garden pottery achieved a total of 5.7 million dollars in 1939. Although no exact data are available, the 1943 volume undoubtedly was much larger owing to greater demand, cessation of imports, and relative freedom from materials shortages. In California, there has been a marked increase in the number of whiteware plants in recent years, almost all of which are engaged in the production of artware and ceramic novelties of various types. The California producers, though small operators in many cases, are producing artware of first quality, both ceramically and artistically. They have done much to educate the public to the merits of American-made ceramic ware and have gained for domestic producers a large part of the artware market formerly monopolized by European producers. Based on shipments of raw materials to the artware industry, it is estimated that the 1943 output of art and garden pottery totaled 14.3 million dollars, a great increase over the 1939 figure. Postwar sales will vary directly with the national income and should remain at the level of at least 10 million dollars in the immediate postwar period, even allowing for some resumption of imports. (Newcomb 1945, 49)

During the war, hardware stores had trouble stocking their shelves with metal products due to wartime restrictions. To fill the space, store managers turned to artware, along with china, glass, and mirrors.

Figure 578. Rare "Proud Fisherman" statue created by Jean Reich and produced in limited numbers in 1942. Cincinnati Art Galleries reports, "We have only seen two others and each is done with different colors and glazes. All have some bisque components and in this case, the hands, face and plinth are unglazed. The fisherman's hat and pants are done in cobalt blue, his shirt and shoes in tan and his suspenders in purple. The huge gar he is holding is done in Aventurine glaze." Base marks: flames mark, the date, shape number 6808, and the artist's name "J. Reich." 8.5" h. *Courtesy of Mark Mussio, Cincinnati Art Galleries, LLC.*

During the late 1930s, the board of directors would try in vain to find a buyer with the financial resources necessary to revitalize the ailing firm. Failing in the attempt, Rookwood Pottery filed for bankruptcy on April 16, 1941.

Rookwood Pottery was then purchased in September 1941 by Walter E. Schott, his wife Margaret, and several associates. They planned to hire back decorators and reintroduce decorated wares, but at prices affordable to much of the buying public. John Wareham was retained to manage the operation.

Unfortunately, the new owners of Rookwood had exquisitely bad timing. Within weeks of the company's reopening, the United States was plunged into the Second World War. However, despite shortages in material and personnel, Rookwood soldiered on through the war. In January 1942, the company presented a new glaze, Marine, to the public.

However, by late 1942, the Schott group had enough of pottery manufacturing and transferred Rookwood Pottery as a gift to the St. Thomas Institute (Institutum Divi Thomae), part of Cincinnati's Roman Catholic Archdiocese. In turn, the Institute sold Rookwood's commercial rights to Sperti, Inc. Reorganization ensued, with Wareham again remaining in charge of company management.

Rookwood managed to reestablish a small decorating department as part of this latest reorganization. Decorators in 1943 included, Lorinda Epply, Edward T. Hurley, Elizabeth B. Jensen, Jens Jensen, Margaret H. McDonald, Wilhelmine Rhem, and Kataro Shirayamadani.

Figure 579. A pair of Double Vellum vases with differing floral decorations created in 1943 by Kataro Shirayamadani. According to Cincinnati Art Galleries, "The vases were purchased from a gift shop in Auburn, Alabama, in the 1940s for a Mother's Day gift and have been in the same family since then." Base marks: flames mark, the date, shape number 6827, and the vase with the blue ground has the artist's incised initials. 6.5" h. *Courtesy of Mark Mussio, Cincinnati Art Galleries, LLC.*

Three new glaze colors and a line of decorative ware were offered to the public in 1943. The glazes were Aurora Orange, Lagoon Green, and Wine Madder; the decorative ceramics would eventually receive the name Designed Crystal.

Looking toward the war's end and a brighter future under new ownership, Rookwood established a "junior decorating department," led by Lois Furukawa, a member of the staff only since 1942. The junior decorators were ten to twelve young women learning a decorator's skills. Those who showed promise were to become full decorators for the company's future.

This new decorating department and the training of new decorators would not last long, however. In 1948, Kataro Shirayamadani died after an accident at the plant. In time, the decorating department closed. From this point forward, Rookwood's wares would be largely mass-produced artware.

Figure 581. Leaf-form vase hand-colored by a Junior Decorator in 1945. Base marks: flames mark, the date, shape number 6818, the decorator's initials "MP," and the number 423 painted in blue slip. 6" h. *Courtesy of Mark Mussio, Cincinnati Art Galleries, LLC.*

Figure 580. Designed Crystal vase decorated by Jens Jensen in 1945, adorned with green and brown buds, leaves, and stems on a cream high glaze background and lined in blue-green. Base marks: flames mark, the date, shape number 6866, and the decorator's monogram painted on in brown slip. 9" h. *Courtesy of Mark Mussio, Cincinnati Art Galleries, LLC.*

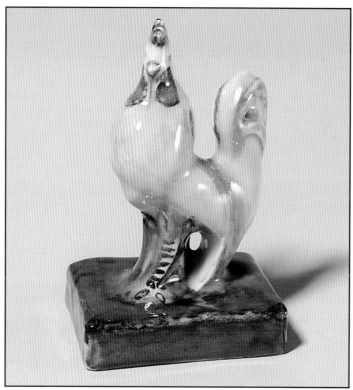

Figure 582. Rooster paperweight decorated by a Junior Decorator in 1946 in shades of brown, yellow, white, and red. Base marks: flames mark, the date, shape number 6030, and "EK-113" painted on in brown slip. 4.75" h. *Courtesy of Mark Mussio, Cincinnati Art Galleries, LLC.*

Once the war ended and restrictions were removed on materials available to Rookwood Pottery, the company strove to expand operations by improving older glaze lines. New glaze lines were also added, including Bengal Brown, Rambo, and Vista Blue.

Figure 583. Elegant, large lamp vase cast in 1951 and covered with a highly textured Bengal Brown glaze. Base marks: flames mark, the date, shape number 7083, and a factory hole for an electrical cord. 11.5" h. *Courtesy of Mark Mussio, Cincinnati Art Galleries, LLC.*

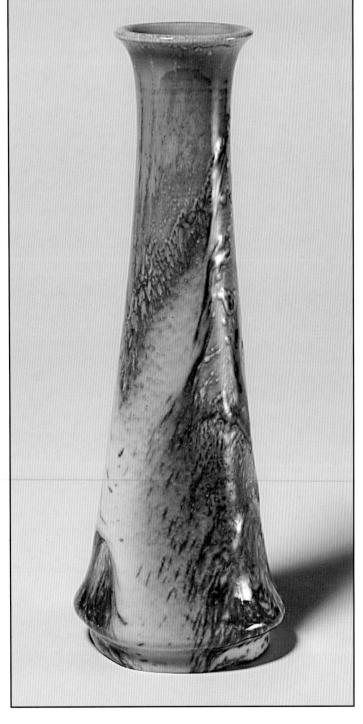

Figure 584. A Special shape tapering vase made in 1954 and decorated by Earl Menzel, coated with an ochre high glaze over which was dripped a thick Vista Blue glaze. Base marks: flames mark, an S for Special shape, the date, and the decorator's full signature. 10.5" h. *Courtesy of Mark Mussio, Cincinnati Art Galleries, LLC.*

Despite their best efforts, Rookwood management could not engage the public's interest. In the early 1950s, Cirrus, the company's last glaze line under current management, was released.

Figure 585. Cirrus Glaze vase decorated in 1954 by Loretta Holtkamp, using the squeeze bag technique, with a glossy white sailing ship upon the flat black ground. Base marks: flames mark, the date, shape number 6514 E, and the decorator's incised initials. 3.5" h. *Courtesy of Mark Mussio, Cincinnati Art Galleries, LLC.*

In the mid-1950s, Rookwood Pottery was up for sale again. William MacConnell and James M. Smith purchased the venerable firm but quickly found they did not have a profitable venture. In 1959, MacConnell and Smith sold the plant to Cincinnati's Herschede Hall Clock Company.

Figure 586. Circular advertising medallion made for the Herschede Clock Company, who owned and operated the Rookwood Pottery from 1959 until its closure, in 1963, displaying images of three types of clock and the name "Herschede" in cursive script. The medallion was covered in a pumpkin high glaze. Base marks: the Rookwood logo, the date, and shape number 7206. 5.75" in diameter. *Courtesy of Mark Mussio, Cincinnati Art Galleries, LLC.*

Herschede moved Rookwood Pottery to Starkville, Mississippi, in 1960, seeking lower labor costs and significant tax breaks. In Mississippi, Rookwood would release artware in at least eleven glaze lines, including Cerulean Blue, Clair de Lune, Cocoa Brown, Commercial Ware Vellum, Emerald Green Mat, Gray, Moonglow, Mustard Seed, Orange, Rust, and Tiger Eye Green. Despite management's best efforts, Rookwood Pottery no longer enticed consumers in profitable numbers and closed for the last time in 1967.

Figure 587. Seated Polar Bear figure designed by Louise Abel, cast in 1965, and glazed in glossy gray. Cincinnati Art Galleries reports, "Listed as a bookend in the Shape Catalogue, he has no flat sides nor is he sufficiently tall to be used in that manner." Base marks: the Rookwood logo, the date, and shape number 6484. *Courtesy of Mark Mussio, Cincinnati Art Galleries, LLC.*

Figure 588. Classically styled urn dated to 1965 and covered with the Mustard Seed glaze, which was used solely at Rookwood's Starkville location. Base marks: the Rookwood logo, the date, shape number 7058, and "ROOKWOOD POTTERY STARKVILLE MISS." in block letters. 10.75" h. *Courtesy of Mark Mussio, Cincinnati Art Galleries, LLC.*

Rookwood's 1930s and 1940s Art Pottery Objects

The following is a sampling of the various wares produced by Rookwood throughout the 1930s through the 1940s, organized by year and, within each year, by artist.

Figure 589. Vase decorated in 1930 by Jens Jensen with a profusion of stylized irises in orange, pink, and blue, on a striated black mat ground, highlighted by silver and green accents. Base marks: flames mark, the date, shape number 6181C, an esoteric mark seen only on 1930 pieces and probably connotative of Rookwood's Fiftieth Anniversary, and the artist's monogram painted on in black slip. 8.5" h. *Courtesy of Mark Mussio, Cincinnati Art Galleries, LLC.*

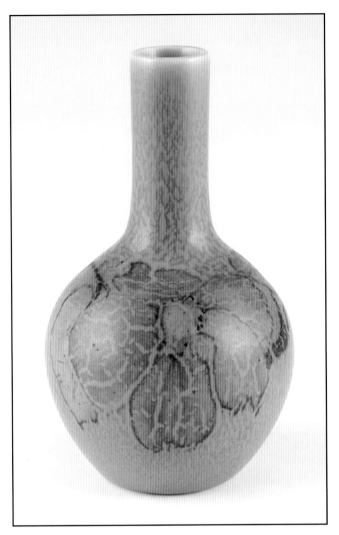

Figure 590. Wax Mat bottle-shaped bud vase painted by Katherine Jones in 1930 with large red flowers on pink and purple butterfat ground. Base marks: flames mark and date. 5.5" h. *Courtesy of David Rago Auctions.*

Figure 591. Wax Mat barrel-shaped vase painted in 1930 by Elizabeth Lincoln with purple berries on green and red leaves over a pink butterfat ground. Base marks: flames mark, the date, shape number 6180, the artist's initials, and a Kiln. 6" x 5.25". *Courtesy of David Rago Auctions.*

Figure 592. Mat glaze vase painted in 1930 by Margaret McDonald with large magnolia flowers, leaves, and branches on a blue ground, all of which has been covered with a textured red glaze effect. Base marks: flames mark, the date, shape number 900C, and the artist's cipher, along with a fan-shaped esoteric mark seen only on 1930-31 items, perhaps to designate Rookwood's Fiftieth Anniversary. 8.25" h. *Courtesy of Mark Mussio, Cincinnati Art Galleries, LLC.*

Figure 593. Wax Mat footed flaring vase decorated in 1930 by Margaret H. McDonald with branches of blossoms in mint green and yellow. Base marks: flames mark, the date, shape number 6207F, and the artist's initials. 5.25" x 3.5". *Courtesy of David Rago Auctions.*

Figure 594. Vellum glaze vase decorated in 1930 by Fred Rothenbusch with colorful nasturtium decoration. Base marks: flames mark, the date, shape number 1781, a fan shaped esoteric mark, an incised V for Vellum glaze, and the incised artist's monogram. 6.25" h. *Courtesy of Mark Mussio, Cincinnati Art Galleries, LLC.*

Figure 595. Unusual Jewel Porcelain Art Deco four-sided vase painted in 1931 by Louise Abel with an abstract design in indigo, pink, and grey on ivory. Base marks: flames mark and date. 7.5" x 6". *Courtesy of David Rago Auctions.*

Figure 597. Wax Mat bulbous vase painted by Sallie Coyne in 1931 with pink poppies on light green ground. Base marks: flames mark, the date, and the artist's initials. 5.75" h. *Courtesy of David Rago Auctions.*

Figure 596. Crystalline mat vase, decorated in 1931 in an Art Deco style by Elizabeth Barrett, using a squeeze bag to create dark brown dots of increasing size in rows down the necked vase. Base marks: flames mark, the date, shape number 6146, the artist's monogram, and an esoteric mark. 5.5" h. *Courtesy of Mark Mussio, Cincinnati Art Galleries, LLC.*

Figure 598. Glaze effect vase by Edward T. Hurley, dated to 1931, with a very unusual treatment of vibrant colors dripped over each other. The colors range from maroon to black to orange topped with a rich, variegated blue. Base marks: flames mark, the date, shape number 614 C, a fan-shaped esoteric mark, a wheel-ground X, and the artist's initials in black slip. 12.5" h. *Courtesy of Mark Mussio, Cincinnati Art Galleries, LLC.*

Figure 599. Jewel Porcelain ovoid vase decorated in 1931 by Jens Jensen with large pink flowers on blue ground in butterfat glaze. Base marks: flames mark, the date, shape number 6184C, and the artist's cipher. 9.5" x 6.5". *Courtesy of David Rago Auctions.*

Figure 600. Mat glaze vase painted by Jens Jensen in 1931 with three sprays of red cherries on a pale blue ground. Base marks: flames mark, the date, shape number 130, a fan-shaped esoteric mark, and the artist's monogram in black slip. *Courtesy of Mark Mussio, Cincinnati Art Galleries, LLC.*

Figure 601. Mat glaze vase with Virginia creeper decoration created in 1931 by Elizabeth
Lincoln. Leaves and vines encircle the vase and a band of stylized leaves encircle the shoulder.
Base marks: flames mark, the date, shape number 904 B, a fan-shaped esoteric mark, and the
artist's initials in blue slip. 13.75" h. *Courtesy of Mark Mussio, Cincinnati Art Galleries, LLC.*

Figure 602. Vase decorated in 1931 by Elizabeth Lincoln with leaves and flowers descending from the shoulder to the center of the vase. Base marks: flames mark, the date, shape number 6194F, a curved six bar mark that could be the Fiftieth Anniversary mark, and the artist's mark. *Courtesy of Bob Shores and Dale Jones.*

Figure 603. Handled vase decorated in 1931 by Elizabeth Lincoln, adorned with flowers and leaves descending from the shoulder. Base marks: flames mark, the date, shape number 2425, and the artist's hand-signed initials. 7.5" h. *Courtesy of Clarence Meyer.*

Figure 604. Decorated Porcelain vase decorated by David Seyler in 1931 with the outline of a nude woman glancing at a flower, glazed in a dusty rose. Base marks: flames mark, the date, shape number 6301, and the artist's unique monogram in slip. 9.5" h. Cincinnati Art Galleries reports, "Seyler was about 14 when he did this piece and his work at Rookwood is quite rare." *Courtesy of Mark Mussio, Cincinnati Art Galleries, LLC.*

Figure 605. Decorated Porcelain lidded scent jar with stylized lotus blossoms on blue waters, the work of Kataro Shirayamadani in 1931, and glazed in Turquoise Blue. The interior is lined in Nubian Black glaze, which is allowed to drip down the exterior rim slightly. The jar is equipped with inner and outer lids. Base marks: flames mark, the date, shape number 2451, and the artist's incised cipher. 9.75" h. *Courtesy of Mark Mussio, Cincinnati Art Galleries, LLC.*

Figure 606. Decorated Mat vase painted by Sallie Coyne in 1932, adorned with lotus flowers, buds, and leaves. Base marks: flames mark, the date, shape number 2785, and the decorator's initials in pink slip. There is also a notation on the vase's base indicating it was a presentation gift to R.L. Twombley by the Bankers Life Co. for twenty years of service. 13.25" h. *Courtesy of Mark Mussio, Cincinnati Art Galleries, LLC.*

Figure 607. Jewel Porcelain ovoid vase painted in 1932 by Jens Jensen with Art Deco flowers in brown, pink, and indigo butterfat glaze on ivory ground. Base marks: flames mark, the date, S, and the artist's cipher. 7.75" x 3.75". *Courtesy of David Rago Auctions.*

Figure 608. Wax Mat bulbous vase painted by Edward T. Hurley in 1933 with orange roses and green foliage on an ivory ground. Base marks: flames mark, the date, S, and the artist's initials. 6.25" x 4". *Courtesy of David Rago Auctions.*

Figure 609. Decorated Porcelain vase decorated in 1933 by Jens Jensen, featuring four fish swimming across the vessel's uncrazed surface. The vase is lined with Rookwood's Anniversary Glaze. Base marks: flames mark, the date, an impressed S for Special shape, Jensen's monogram in brown slip, and a wheel-ground X (probably due to a small area on one of the fish where the glaze did not "take" as it should have). 6" h. *Courtesy of Mark Mussio, Cincinnati Art Galleries, LLC.*

Figure 610. Jewel Porcelain vase painted in 1936 by Margaret H. McDonald with branches of oak leaves and acorns on a butterfat ground. Base marks: flames mark, the date, shape number 621, and the artist's initials. 10" x 6.25". *Courtesy of David Rago Auctions.*

Figure 612. Decorated Porcelain scenic vase decorated in 1939 by Margaret McDonald in shades of blue, gray and white. Base marks: flames mark, the date, shape number 932 C, P for porcelain body, and the artist's monogram in blue slip. 11.25" h. *Courtesy of Mark Mussio, Cincinnati Art Galleries, LLC.*

Figure 611. Mat glaze unusual scenic vase decorated on a Special form in 1936 by Margaret McDonald with brown cattails growing in a lake and blue sky in the background. Base marks: flames mark, the date, an S for Special shape, and the decorator's initials in brown slip. 7" h. *Courtesy of Mark Mussio, Cincinnati Art Galleries, LLC.*

Figure 613. Decorated Porcelain lamp vase decorated in 1942 by Jens Jensen with an overall decoration of dogwood blossoms and stems. The top rim, throat, and foot are glazed in a thick, mottled blue. Base marks: flames mark, the date, shape number S 2139, and the artist's monogram in brown slip. 12" high. *Courtesy of Mark Mussio, Cincinnati Art Galleries, LLC.*

Figure 615. A pair of Design Crystal vases decorated in 1944 by Edward T. Hurley featuring magenta tulips with green leaves and stems on a white ground, the interior lined with cobalt blue, which extends slightly over the rim. Base marks: flames mark, the date, shape number 2194, and the artist's monogram. 9.5" h. *Courtesy of Mark Mussio, Cincinnati Art Galleries, LLC.*

Figure 614. Footed vase form decorated in 1944 by Elizabeth Barrett with a bright floral motif. Using very heavy slip, Barrett fashioned large yellow magnolias with brown leaves while lining the interior with a mottled gray glaze. Base marks: flames mark, the date, shape number 6185 D, and the artist's incised monogram. 8.25" h. *Courtesy of Mark Mussio, Cincinnati Art Galleries, LLC.*

Figure 616. Tall Jewel Porcelain baluster vase painted and incised in 1944 by Jens Jensen with green and blue birds, fish, and oversized leaves on a white and amber ground under a crackled overglaze. Drilled hole to bottom. Base marks: flames mark, the date, shape number 614B, and the artist's cipher. 15.5" x 7.5". *Courtesy of David Rago Auctions.*

Figure 617. Decorated Porcelain vase decorated in 1944 by Jens Jensen with the entire surface covered with fish and flora. Base marks: flames mark, the date, shape number 6864, and the artist's monogram in black slip. 7.5" h. *Courtesy of Mark Mussio, Cincinnati Art Galleries, LLC.*

Figure 618. Vase attributed to Elizabeth Barrett in 1944 using squeeze bag decoration to create a bird perched on a branch among leaves, executed in brown slip onto a mat blue ground. Base marks: flames mark, the date, and shape number 356 E. As Cincinnati Art Galleries states, "No signature can be located, but it is attributed to Elizabeth Barrett, based on the date, her fondness for these colors, her frequent use of this method of decoration, and the style of the artwork." 6.5" h. *Courtesy of Mark Mussio, Cincinnati Art Galleries, LLC.*

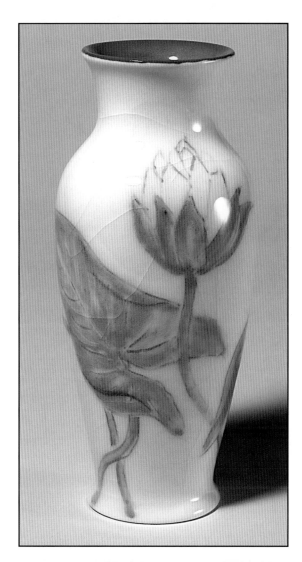

Figure 620. Design Crystal vase decorated in 1945 by Kataro Shirayamadani using a pink flowers and buds and green leaves theme on a blue to peach ground. Base marks: flames mark, the date, shape number 2193, an incised 6793, and the artist's incised initials, along with a wheel-ground X, probably for small grinding chips. 4.5" h. *Courtesy of Mark Mussio, Cincinnati Art Galleries, LLC.*

Figure 619. Design Crystal vase decorated by Jens Jensen in 1945 with green and brown buds, leaves, and stems on a cream high glaze background and lined in blue-green. Base marks: flames mark, the date, shape number 6866, and the decorator's monogram painted on in brown slip. 9" h. *Courtesy of Mark Mussio, Cincinnati Art Galleries, LLC.*

Figure 621. Scenic Vellum plaque, titled *Hurley's Hidden Mountain Pool*, painted by Edward T. Hurley in 1946 with a blue lake nestled in the mountains, fed by melting snows. The plaque is mounted in a probably original gilded frame. Base marks: stamped flames mark, the date, and the artist's initials. Plaque: 10" x 12". *Courtesy of David Rago Auctions.*

Figure 622. High glaze vase decorated by Jens Jensen in 1946 with magnolia blooms and foliage. Base marks: flames mark, the date, shape number 2194, the artist's signature, and the number 8565 painted in brown slip. 9.25" h. *Courtesy of Mark Mussio, Cincinnati Art Galleries, LLC.*

Figure 623. Decorated Porcelain vase decorated in 1946 by Kataro Shirayamadani with hyacinths. Base marks: flames mark, the date, shape number 2194, the incised number "6615," and the incised artist's initials. 9.25" h. *Courtesy of Mark Mussio, Cincinnati Art Galleries, LLC.*

Rookwood's 1930s and 1940s Artware Production Objects

Figure 624. Large production vase cast in 1930 with a purple glaze over which was stippled a rich dark blue high glaze. Base marks: flames mark, the date, shape number 2523, and an esoteric mark, perhaps connotative of Rookwood's Fiftieth Anniversary. 17" h. *Courtesy of Mark Mussio, Cincinnati Art Galleries, LLC.*

Figure 625. A pair of production ovoid vases from 1930 with embossed peacock feathers under a green-to-pink Mat finish. Base marks: flames mark and date. 6" x 3". *Courtesy of David Rago Auctions.*

Figure 626. Production five-sided vase embossed in 1930 with rooks under a brown glaze. Base marks: flames mark and date. 4.5". *Courtesy of David Rago Auctions.*

Figure 628. Small Coromandel glaze vase cast in 1930. Base marks: flames mark, the date, shape number 587 F, and the Anniversary mark in the form of radiating bars. 4" h. *Courtesy of Mark Mussio, Cincinnati Art Galleries, LLC.*

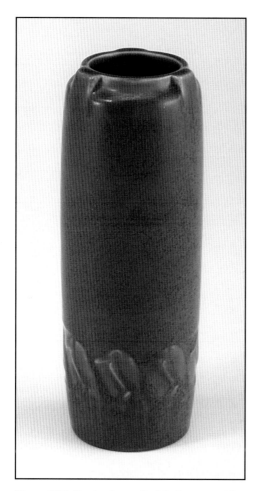

Figure 627. Production cylindrical vase cast in 1930 with three buttresses and a band of embossed rooks under indigo glaze. Base marks: flames mark and date. 6.5" h. *Courtesy of David Rago Auctions.*

Figure 629. Production fan vase covered in a fine blue and green butterfat glaze, cast in 1930. Base marks: flames mark and date. 6.75" h. *Courtesy of David Rago Auctions.*

Figure 630. Production bulbous vase from 1930 embossed with gadroons and swirls under mat pink and green mottled ground. Base marks: flames mark and date. 5" h. *Courtesy of David Rago Auctions.*

Figure 631. Coromandel glaze vase estimated to be from the early 1930s, the rich glaze partially obscuring the date and shape number and a bit of the Rookwood mark. 3" h. *Courtesy of Mark Mussio, Cincinnati Art Galleries, LLC.*

Figure 632. Production vase cast in 1931 and embossed with mistletoe under a blue and green butterfat ground. Base marks: flames mark and date. 7.5" h. *Courtesy of David Rago Auctions.*

Figure 633. Water lily bowl and flower frog produced in 1931 with the interior of the bowl glazed in lavender mat with an ivory mat exterior and an intricate flower holder glazed in lavender mat. Base marks: flames mark, the date, and shape numbers 2875 and 2979 respectively, along with a Fiftieth Anniversary marking. 3.25" h. *Courtesy of Mark Mussio, Cincinnati Art Galleries, LLC.*

Figure 634. A pair of production vases made in 1931 and glazed with a medium blue mat with hints of red around the upper portion. Base marks: flames mark, the date, shape number 2874, and a fan-shaped esoteric Fiftieth Anniversary mark. 3.75" h. each. *Courtesy of Mark Mussio, Cincinnati Art Galleries, LLC.*

Figure 635. Production vase cast in 1931, decorated with gazelles and covered with mat blue glaze with red overspray. Base marks: flames mark, the date, shape number 6214, and an esoteric mark, probably denoting the Pottery's Fiftieth Anniversary. 4.5" h. *Courtesy of Mark Mussio, Cincinnati Art Galleries, LLC.*

Figure 636. Colorful Glaze Effect vase, dated 1932, coated in a taupe glaze, with hints of blue, dripped over a lush Coromandel glaze. Base marks: flames mark, the date, and shape number 6308. 8" h. *Courtesy of Mark Mussio, Cincinnati Art Galleries, LLC.*

Figure 637. Production vase cast in 1933 featuring a strong Art Deco shape accented with Ivory Mat exterior and Nubian Black interior glazes. Base marks: flames mark, the date, and an impressed S for special shape. 5.25" h. *Courtesy of Mark Mussio, Cincinnati Art Galleries, LLC.*

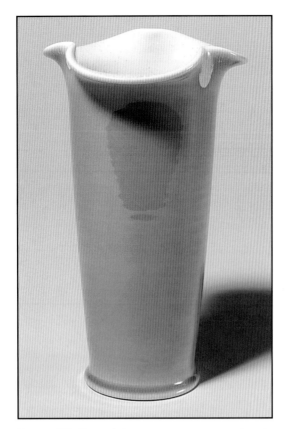

Figure 638. Special shape tapering vase produced in 1933, the exterior glazed in glossy butterscotch while the interior is coated in milky white that drips slightly over the exterior. Base marks: flames mark, the date, an S for Special shape, and a wheel-ground X. 9" h. *Courtesy of Mark Mussio, Cincinnati Art Galleries, LLC.*

Figure 640. Production ovoid vase produced in 1934 with embossed berries and leaves under a bright yellow mat glaze. Base marks: flames mark and date. 4.75" h. *Courtesy of David Rago Auctions.*

Figure 639. Production vase made in 1934, glazed with a glossy turquoise. Base marks: flames mark, the date, and shape number 270. 11.5" h. *Courtesy of Mark Mussio, Cincinnati Art Galleries, LLC.*

Figure 641. Two production pieces from 1936: a satyr and turtle flower frog in mat green glaze and an ovoid blue vase, 1936. Base marks: flames mark and date. 7" h. and 5.5" h. *Courtesy of David Rago Auctions.*

Figure 642. Tall production vase made in 1937 with an intricate design of flowers, leaves, and stems, covered with Coromandel glaze. Base marks: flames mark, the date, and shape number 6045, in addition to a circular drilling guide that was never used. 11.5" h. *Courtesy of Mark Mussio, Cincinnati Art Galleries, LLC.*

Figure 643. Coromandel bulbous vase from 1937 embossed with stylized decoration under a rich, metallic gold, and deep brown glaze. Base marks: shape number 2857. 4" x 6". *Courtesy of David Rago Auctions.*

Figure 644. Porcelain production vase embossed in 1937 with honesty branches under a celadon glaze. Base marks: flames mark and date. 7" h. *Courtesy of David Rago Auctions.*

Figure 645. Coromandel lamp vase dated to 1937 and coated in a rich red glaze accented with gold encircling the neck and descending inside the vase. Base marks: flames mark, the date, and shape number 6311. A wheel-ground X is present due to two glaze bulges. 7.25" h. *Courtesy of Mark Mussio, Cincinnati Art Galleries, LLC.*

Figure 646. Production fluted covered box dated to 1937, commemorating the Western and Southern Legion, glazed in mat mint green. Base marks: flames mark and date. 3.5" h. *Courtesy of David Rago Auctions.*

Figure 647. Production vase dated to 1940 with embossed panels of fish and birds under a flowing green mat glaze. Base marks: flames mark and date. 8.5" x 6". *Courtesy of David Rago Auctions.*

Figure 648. Production lamp decorated in 1945 with a molded stylized floral and leaf design, coated in a celadon green glaze, and finished with the original base hardware. Base marks: flames mark and date. Overall: 27" h. Vase: 12" h. *Courtesy of Bob Shores and Dale Jones.*

Figure 650. Production vase from 1949 with a yellow interior glaze, green exterior glaze, and molded leaf decoration. Base marks: flames mark, the date, and shape number 6955. 8.25" h. x 10" rim diameter. *Courtesy of Bob Shores and Dale Jones.*

Figure 649. Late production barrel-shaped porcelain vase in Oxblood glaze, 1948. Base marks: flames mark and date. 4.75" h. *Courtesy of David Rago Auctions.*

Figure 651. Drip-glaze production vase made in 1949, coated with high glaze blue descending over a violet gray glaze. Base marks: flames mark, the date, and shape number 6204 C. 7" h. *Courtesy of Mark Mussio, Cincinnati Art Galleries, LLC.*

Figure 652. Two production porcelain pieces: a faceted covered nut jar with a peanut finial from 1949 and a four-sided vase with daisies from 1951, both covered in glossy green glaze. Base marks: both with flames marks and dates. 5.5" and 5.25" h. *Courtesy of David Rago Auctions.*

Bookends

Figure 654. Rare "Double Fish" bookend dated from 1931, glazed in a mat green. Cincinnati Art Galleries reports, "This is one of the rarer bookends that Rookwood produced." Base marks: flames mark, the date, the elliptical anniversary mark, and shape number 6259. 6" h. *Courtesy of Mark Mussio, Cincinnati Art Galleries, LLC.*

Figure 653. Rook tray covered with a Nubian Black glaze, most likely made in the late 1940s. Base marks: the Rookwood symbol and shape number 1139. 4.25" h. *Courtesy of Mark Mussio, Cincinnati Art Galleries, LLC.*

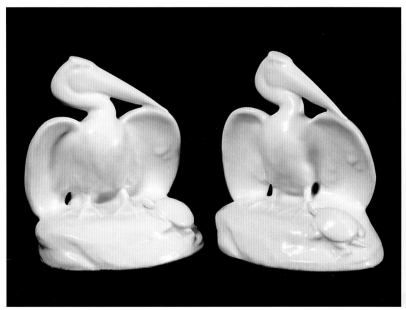

Figure 655. A set of rare pelican bookends made in 1934 and glazed in white mat. A small turtle shares the plinth with the pelican. Base marks: flames mark, the date, and shape number 2614. 6.5" h. *Courtesy of Mark Mussio, Cincinnati Art Galleries, LLC.*

Figure 656. A pair of penguin bookends cast in 1934 and glazed in traditional penguin colors of black and white. Base marks: flames mark, the date, shape number 2659, and a showroom label. 5.5" h. *Courtesy of Mark Mussio, Cincinnati Art Galleries, LLC.*

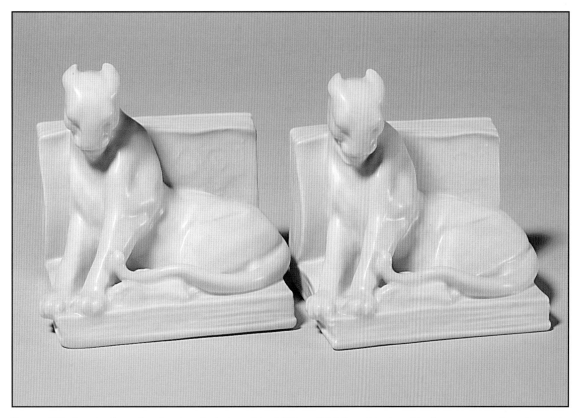

Figure 657. A pair of panther bookends designed by William P. McDonald, glazed in Ivory mat, and produced in 1936. Base marks: flames mark, the date, shape number 2564, and the designer's initials. *Courtesy of Mark Mussio, Cincinnati Art Galleries, LLC.*

Figure 658. A pair of "Scarlett" bookends from 1936, each figure with brown hair, wearing a lilac colored dress, and sitting upon an eggplant shaded chair. Base marks: flames mark, the date, and shape number 6252. 6.5" h. *Courtesy of Mark Mussio, Cincinnati Art Galleries, LLC.*

Figure 659. A pair of bookends cast in 1937, featuring a nude girl seated on a rock watching a frog, and coated in an ivory mat glaze. Base marks: flames mark, the date, and shape number 6521. 4.5" h. *Courtesy of Mark Mussio, Cincinnati Art Galleries, LLC.*

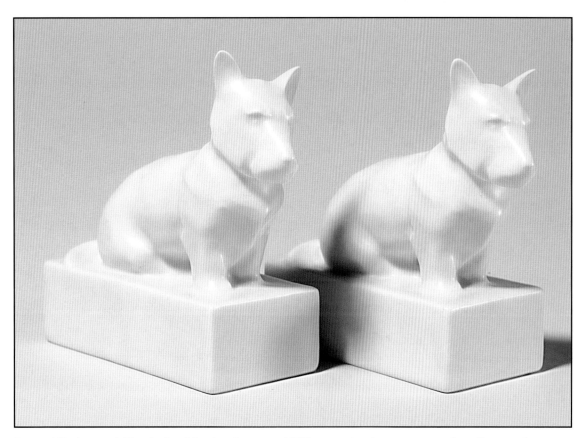

Figure 660. A pair of "Scottie Dog" bookends, cast in 1937, covered with an ivory mat glaze. Base marks: flames mark, the date, and shape number 6449. *Courtesy of Mark Mussio, Cincinnati Art Galleries, LLC.*

Figure 661. A pair of "Scarlet O'Hara" Ivory Mat bookends cast in 1938. Base marks: flames mark, the date, and shape number 6252. 6.5" h. *Courtesy of Mark Mussio, Cincinnati Art Galleries, LLC.*

Figure 662. A pair of rook bookends covered in blue, rose, and green glossy glaze, cast in 1943. Base marks: flames mark and date. 5.5" x 6". *Courtesy of David Rago Auctions.*

Figure 663. A pair of eagle bookends with their wings spread, designed by William McDonald and made in 1945, covered with a green high glaze. Base marks: flames mark, the date, shape number 2653, and the designer's monogram. 6" h. *Courtesy of Mark Mussio, Cincinnati Art Galleries, LLC.*

Figure 664. A pair of St. Francis of Assissi bookends produced in 1945, showing St. Francis dressed in a brown robe comforting a gray wolf and a gray bird. Base marks: flames mark, the date, and shape number 6883. 7.25" h. *Courtesy of Mark Mussio, Cincinnati Art Galleries, LLC.*

Paperweights

Figure 665. Fabeltier paperweight designed by Louise Abel, cast in 1931 and glazed in mat brown. Base marks: flames mark, the date, shape number 6243, and the designer's impressed monogram. 4" h. *Courtesy of Mark Mussio, Cincinnati Art Galleries, LLC.*

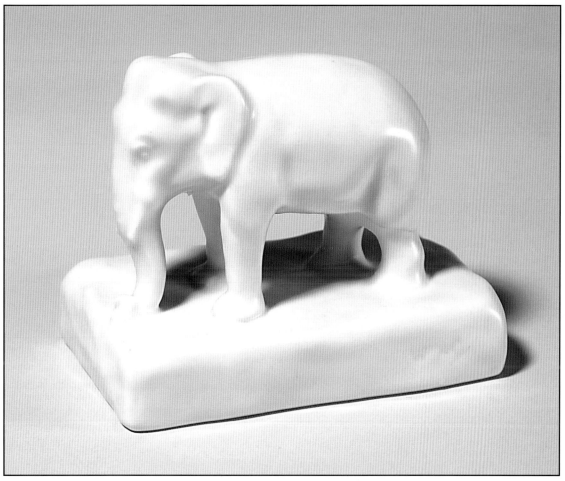

Figure 666. Ivory mat elephant paperweight designed by William McDonald and cast in 1933. Base marks: flames mark, the date, shape number 2797, a wheel-ground "giveaway" mark, and the designer's initials molded into the side of the plinth. 3.25" h. *Courtesy of Mark Mussio, Cincinnati Art Galleries,*

Figure 667. Ivory mat donkey paperweight designed by Louise Abel and produced in 1934. Base marks: flames mark, the date, shape number 6241, and the designer's molded monogram. 6" h. *Courtesy of Mark Mussio, Cincinnati Art Galleries, LLC.*

Figure 669. Mat blue elephant paperweight designed by William P. McDonald and dated to 1934. Base marks: flames mark, the date, shape number 2797, and the designer's initials on the side of the plinth. 3.25" h. *Courtesy of Mark Mussio, Cincinnati Art Galleries, LLC.*

Figure 668. Rare eagle paperweight designed by Louise Abel and covered in gunmetal brown glaze, dating to 1934. Base marks: flames mark and date. 5.5" x 8". *Courtesy of David Rago Auctions.*

Figure 670. Ivory mat sailing ship paperweight cast in 1934. Base marks: flames mark, the date, and shape number 2792. 3.75" h. *Courtesy of Mark Mussio, Cincinnati Art Galleries, LLC.*

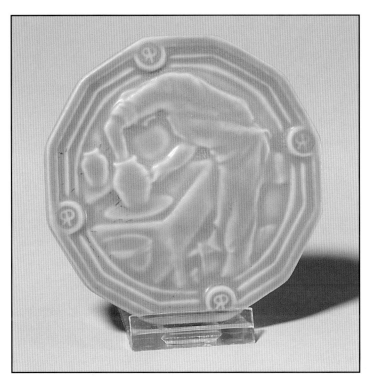

Figure 671. Potter at the Wheel paperweight, an advertising piece cast in 1935 and covered with a green glaze, showing a potter throwing a vase. Base marks: flames mark, the date, and the notation: "Potter at the Wheel, Rookwood, Cincinnati, Ohio." *Courtesy of Mark Mussio, Cincinnati Art Galleries, LLC.*

Figure 673. Bulldog paperweight designed by Louise Abel, cast in 1945 and colored with brown, white, and blue glazes. Base marks: flames mark, the date, shape number 6483, and the designer's cast monogram. 4.5" h. *Courtesy of Mark Mussio, Cincinnati Art Galleries, LLC.*

Figure 672. Frog paperweight, designed by Kataro Shirayamadani and glazed with mat green and brown highlights. While no date is visible, the glaze is most often seen on pieces dating from the early 1940s. Base marks: flames mark, the date, and shape number 6097. 2.75" h. *Courtesy of Mark Mussio, Cincinnati Art Galleries, LLC.*

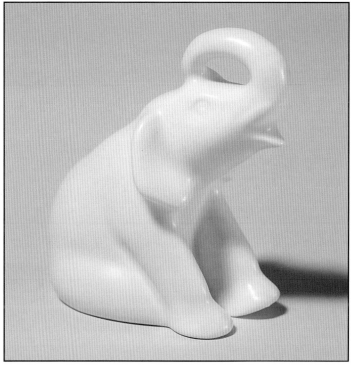

Figure 674. Seated elephant paperweight designed by Kataro Shirayamadani, made in 1946 and covered in an ivory mat glaze. Base marks: flames mark, the date, and shape number 6490. 4" h. *Courtesy of Mark Mussio, Cincinnati Art Galleries, LLC.*

Tiles

Figure 675. Two trivet tiles with Dutch peasant scenes in pastel mat glazes, dating from 1930. Base marks: flames mark and date. 5.75" square each. *Courtesy of David Rago Auctions.*

Rookwood's 1950s and 1960s Objects

Figure 676. Design Crystal lamp vase decorated by Loretta Holtkamp in 1950 with a village scene. Base marks: flames mark, the date, shape number 6292 C, and the artist's monogram in black slip. 7.75" h. *Courtesy of Mark Mussio, Cincinnati Art Galleries, LLC.*

Figure 677. Glaze Effect vase from 1950 decorated by Earl Menzel for Rookwood's 70th Anniversary kiln. Mr. Menzel initially covered the vase, a Special shape, with a medium brown high glaze, over which he dripped a darker brown, an electric blue, and then repeated the lighter brown while the interior was lined with pink. Base marks: flames mark, the date, an S for Special shape, the Menzel "whorl," a 70th Anniversary kiln mark, and the decorator's incised initials. 5.5" h. *Courtesy of Mark Mussio, Cincinnati Art Galleries, LLC.*

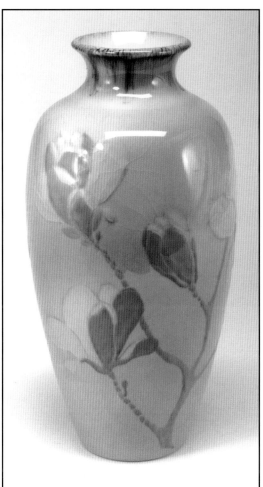

Figure 678. Late porcelain vase painted by Loretta Holtkamp in 1951, with mauve and ivory magnolia blossoms on a pearl-grey ground. Base marks: flames mark, the date, and shape number 2984A. 15.5" x 7.25". *Courtesy of David Rago Auctions.*

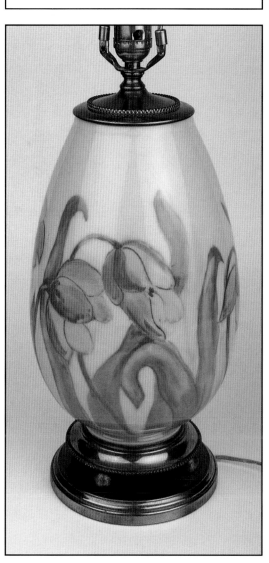

Figure 680. Glaze Effect vase, dated 1951, and glazed by Earl Menzel, who first covered the piece with a brown high glaze, over which he dripped a crystalline blue glaze. The interior of the vessel was glazed in pink, with the blue slightly descending over the rim. Base marks: flames mark, the date, an S for Special Shape, the decorator's partly obscured initials, and his "whorl" mark. 8" h. *Courtesy of Mark Mussio, Cincinnati Art Galleries, LLC.*

Figure 679. Table lamp painted in 1951 by Loretta Holtkamp, with stylized yellow tulips and leaves with high glaze finish. Base marks: flames mark, the date, shape number S2136, and the artist's initials. Overall height: 30" Vase: 12" h. *Courtesy of Bob Shores and Dale Jones.*

Figure 681. Planter with a resting angel figure cast in 1953. Cincinnati Art Galleries states, "What makes this curious is that the shape catalog shows this to be a clock case, of which we have seen an example, but this is a planter, with no aperture where the clock face would fit and being open at the top, for a plant, where no such opening exists with the clock case. This has been covered with a frothy white over dark caramel high glaze." Base marks: flames mark, the date, and shape number 7053. 6" h. x 9.75 w. *Courtesy of Mark Mussio, Cincinnati Art Galleries, LLC.*

Figure 682. Lidded candy dish with a wooden finial and base, cast in 1953. The lid has a molded hole for the finial, and is covered with a glossy black glaze. Base marks: flames mark, the date, and shape number 7108 D. 4.25" h. *Courtesy of Mark Mussio, Cincinnati Art Galleries, LLC.*

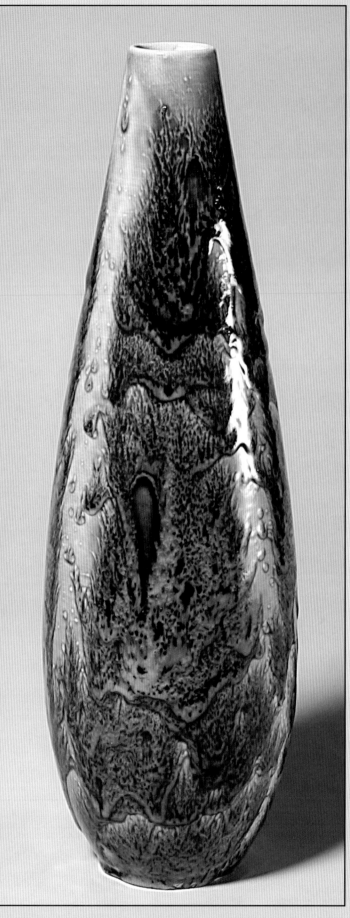

Figure 683. Huge, Special shape, Rookwood vase produced in 1954 and covered with a rich, textured Bengal Brown glaze. Base marks: flames mark, the date, Special shape S 2211 (which bears no resemblance to Rookwood's regular shape 2211), and the impressed "ROOKWOOD CINTI, O" in block letters. 19.25" h. *Courtesy of Mark Mussio, Cincinnati Art Galleries, LLC.*

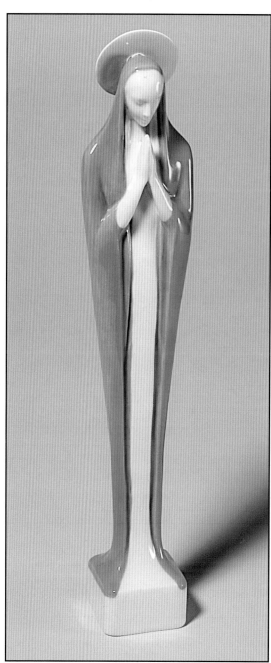

Figure 684. High glaze maroon vase cast in 1958 with a lizard crawling up its neck. Base marks: flames mark, Special shape S 2206, and a diamond-shaped mark with the notation "Rookwood Anniversary 75th." 7.25" h. *Courtesy of Mark Mussio, Cincinnati Art Galleries, LLC.*

Figure 685. Tall Madonna statue cast in 1959 and coated in blue and white high glaze. Base marks: flames mark, the date, shape number 6904, and "ROOKWOOD, CINTI, O" in block letters. 14.75" h. *Courtesy of Mark Mussio, Cincinnati Art Galleries, LLC.*

Bookends

Figure 686. A pair of dark green high glazed "Owl on a Book" bookends made in 1954. Base marks: flames mark, the date, and shape number 2655. 5.5" h. each. *Courtesy of Mark Mussio, Cincinnati Art Galleries, LLC.*

Figure 687. White, high glaze angel bookend made in 1959. Base marks: flames mark, the date, shape number 6897, and the notation "ROOKWOOD CINTI, O" in block letters. 6.75" h. *Courtesy of Mark Mussio, Cincinnati Art Galleries, LLC.*

Paperweights

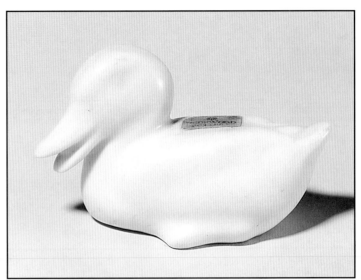

Figure 688. Duck paperweight, designed by Kataro Shirayamadani and cast in 1965. Base marks: flames mark, the date, shape number 6064, and a Rookwood label that the pottery used following its move to Starkville. 2.25" h. *Courtesy of Mark Mussio, Cincinnati Art Galleries, LLC.*

Figure 689. Monkey paperweight designed by Kataro Shirayamadani, cast in 1965, and covered in a pumpkin glaze. Base marks: flames mark, the date, shape number 6084, and a foil label often found on items produced at Starkville. 4" h. *Courtesy of Mark Mussio, Cincinnati Art Galleries, LLC.*

Chapter Three

Artist-Signed Rookwood

Concluding this overview of Rookwood Pottery's production is a selection of the artist-signed, hand-decorated pottery from the company's most productive decades, beginning in the mid-1880s and ending in 1931. These are the wares by the artists that made the Rookwood name famous. These are the wares the company was speaking of when they advertised in the early twentieth century, "Rookwood Is The Best Gift ... because no piece is ever duplicated, and the piece you have is an original painting on pottery—there is no other like it in the world." (Duke University n.d.)

Figure 690. Harriet Wenderoth decorated this Dull Finish lidded box in 1884 with white flowers and fired on gold on a bluish-gray background. Base marks: ROOKWOOD in block letters, the date, shape 43C, an impressed W for white clay body, and the decorator's incised initials. 3.25" h. *Courtesy of Mark Mussio, Cincinnati Art Galleries, LLC.*

Figure 691. Anna Bookprinter may have decorated this Standard glaze chocolate pot with both incised and painted floral decoration in 1885. Base marks: ROOKWOOD in block letters, the date, shape number 81 C, and S for sage green clay. 6" h. *Courtesy of Mark Mussio, Cincinnati Art Galleries, LLC.*

Figure 692. Laura Fry painted this rare and early vase with ruffled rim in 1885. It features white chrysanthemums on a blue-gray textured dead-mat ground. Base marks: stamped ROOKWOOD 1885, and the artist's cipher. 7.25" x 3.5". *Courtesy of David Rago Auctions.*

Figure 693. Albert Valentien decorated this early Standard glaze vase in 1885 with crabs scouring the ocean floor. Base marks: ROOKWOOD in block letters, the date, shape number 77, an impressed S for sage clay, and the artist's incised initials. 5.5" h. *Courtesy of Mark Mussio, Cincinnati Art Galleries, LLC.*

Figure 694. Mary Luella Perkins decorated this Standard glaze vase with yellow wild rose decoration, circa 1888. Base marks: a W for white clay, an incised L for Light Standard glaze, and the decorator's incised name. *Courtesy of Mark Mussio, Cincinnati Art Galleries, LLC.*

Figure 695. Artus Van Briggle decorated this Cameo Glaze triple bud vase, consisting of three tubes decorated with white flowers and pink ribbons, in 1888. Base marks: flames mark, Special shape 684 S, an impressed W for white clay, an incised W for clear glaze, and the artist's incised initials. 5.25" h. *Courtesy of Mark Mussio, Cincinnati Art Galleries, LLC.*

Figure 696. Matthew Daly decorated this Standard glaze pitcher in 1889 with a plums on branch decoration on both sides. Base marks: shape number S843 and the artist's initials. 11" h. to rim. *Courtesy of Seekers Antiques.*

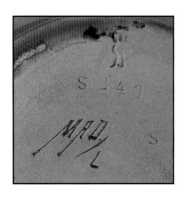

Figure 697. Amelia Sprague's hand-painted floral decoration Standard glaze ewer, dating to 1889. Base marks: flames mark, shape number 33, and the artist's incised initials. 6.75" h. *Courtesy of Bob Shores and Dale Jones.*

Figure 698. Jeanette Swing decorated this Light Standard glaze chocolate pot painted with golden chrysanthemum blossoms in 1889. Base marks: flames mark and the artist's initials. 9" x 6.5". *Courtesy of David Rago Auctions.*

Figure 699. Albert Valentien decorated this 1890 Light Standard glaze low vase with three strap handles with nasturtium. Base marks: flames mark, Special shape number S 899, W for white clay, an incised L for Light Standard glaze, and the artist's incised initials. 5" h. x 10" in diameter. *Courtesy of Mark Mussio, Cincinnati Art Galleries, LLC.*

Figure 700. Sallie Toohey's decorated 1891 Standard glaze vase with spider mums. Base marks: flames mark, shape number 486 E, an impressed S for sage clay, an incised L for Light Standard glaze, and the decorator's incised initials. 7" h. *Courtesy of Mark Mussio, Cincinnati Art Galleries, LLC.*

Figure 701. Edward Abel's decorated 1892 Standard glaze pitcher with cherries. Base marks: flames mark, shape number 18, an impressed W for white clay, an incised L for Light Standard glaze, and the artist's incised initials. 6.25" h. *Courtesy of Mark Mussio, Cincinnati Art Galleries, LLC.*

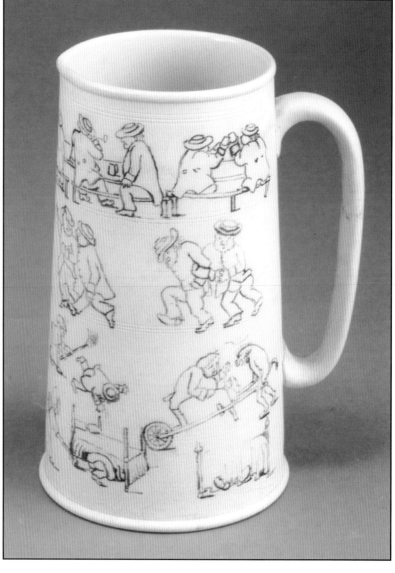

Figure 702. Edward Pope Cranch's 1892 decorated tankard incised with a bar scene. It is signed, "Last work by E.P. Cranch, Nov, 1892." Base marks: flames mark, shape number 286C, and W. 8" x 6". *Courtesy of David Rago Auctions.*

Figure 703. Charles J. Dibowski's decorated 1894 squat Standard glaze vase with long green leaves and red berries. Base marks: flames mark, shape number 687, an impressed W for white clay, and the decorator's incised initials. 3" h. *Courtesy of Mark Mussio, Cincinnati Art Galleries, LLC.*

Figure 704. Bruce Horsfall's 1894 unusual Standard glaze pitcher decorated with the image of a sailor in foul weather gear drinking from a mug with a complex netting hanging behind him. Base marks: flames mark, shape number 758, a W for white clay, and the artist's incised monogram. 5.75" h. *Courtesy of Mark Mussio, Cincinnati Art Galleries, LLC.*

Figure 705. Kate Matchette's 1894 Standard glaze vase with tapering neck decorated with nasturtiums. Base marks: flames mark, shape number 611 and the artist's incised initials. 8.75" h. *Courtesy of Mark Mussio, Cincinnati Art Galleries, LLC.*

Figure 706. William P. McDonald's decorated 1894 rare Standard glaze pillow vase painted with a woman's portrait. Base marks: flames mark, shape number 707B, W, and the artist's initials. 5.5" x 5". *Courtesy of David Rago Auctions.*

Figure 707. Sadie Markland's decorated 1895 Standard glaze vase with hand-painted yellow flowers, green leaves, and floral sprig. Base marks: flames mark, shape number 744C, and the artist's initials. 8" h. *Courtesy of W & D Antiques.*

Figure 708. Edith Regina Felten's flowers decorate the body of this Standard glaze teapot. The lid has an offset square finial. Base mark: flames mark and shape number 770. Edith Felten worked for Rookwood from 1896 to 1908. *Courtesy of Seekers Antiques.*

Figure 709. Sadie Markland decorated this Standard glaze vase in 1896 with ripe, red cherries. Base marks: flames mark, shape number 743 C, an incised L for Light Standard glaze, and the artist's incised initials. 7" h. *Courtesy of Mark Mussio, Cincinnati Art Galleries, LLC.*

Figure 710. Adeliza Drake Sehon's decorated Standard glaze bulbous 1896 vase painted with orange nasturtium. Base marks: flames mark and the X second mark, possibly for two small burst overglaze bubbles. 4.5" h. *Courtesy of David Rago Auctions.*

Figure 711. Sallie Coyne painted this 1897 Standard glaze vase, featuring dogwood blooms. Base marks: flames mark, shape number 779 D, a V-shaped esoteric mark, and the decorator's initials. 7" h. *Courtesy of Mark Mussio, Cincinnati Art Galleries, LLC.*

Figure 712. Rose Fechheimer painted this small lidded jar in 1898 with an embossed, hand-painted flower with leaves on the stem. Base marks: flames mark and the artist's initials. *Courtesy of Bob Shores and Dale Jones.*

Figure 713. Frederick Sturgis Laurence painted this Standard glaze tyg featuring the portrait of a Native American, "Moki," in 1898. Base marks: flames mark, shape number 659 C, the artist's initials, and the incised name of the subject, "Moki." 6" h. *Courtesy of Mark Mussio, Cincinnati Art Galleries, LLC.*

Figure 714. Kataro Shirayamadani decorated this scenic Standard glaze tankard in 1897 with flying geese amid somewhat stylized trees and an unusual ground, comprised of ellipses. Base marks: flames mark, shape number 564B, a diamond-shaped esoteric mark, and the artist's Japanese signature. 11.25" h. *Courtesy of Mark Mussio, Cincinnati Art Galleries, LLC.*

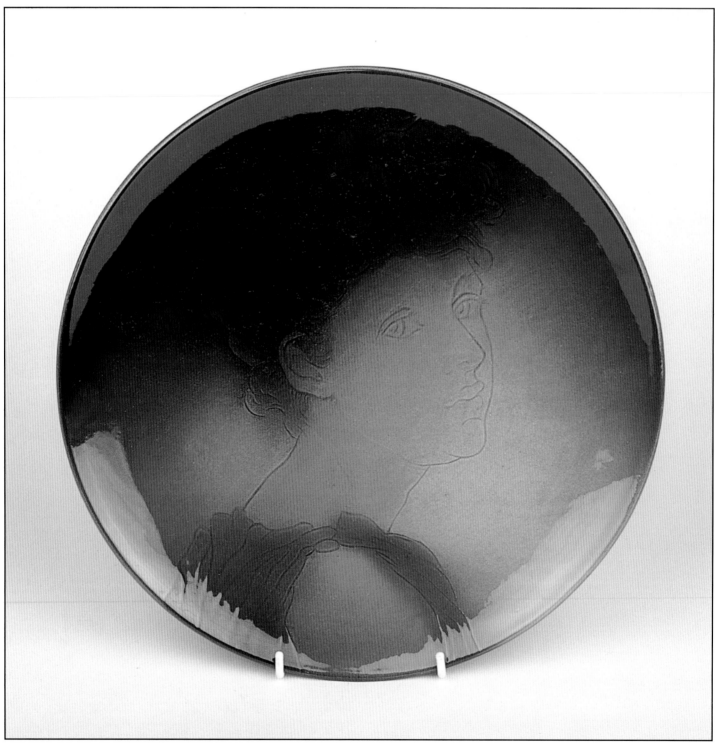

Figure 715. Anna Marie Valentien painted this rare Standard glaze charger in 1898 with the portrait of a young woman with outlined features in brown and yellow-green glazes. Base marks: flames mark, shape number T 1061 B, and red crayon numbers (deaccessioned from the Cincinnati Museum, and catalogued in Stanley Burt's inventory). 12.25" in diameter. *Courtesy of Seekers Antiques.*

Figure 716. Josephine Zettel decorated this Standard glaze vase with yellow wild roses in 1898. Base marks: flames mark, shape number 611D, and the artist's incised initials. 8.25" h. *Courtesy of Mark Mussio, Cincinnati Art Galleries, LLC.*

Figure 717. Howard Altman painted this Standard glaze vase with yellow wisteria hanging loosely from the vine in 1900. Base marks: flames mark, shape number 748D, and the artist's monogram. 6" h. *Courtesy of Mark Mussio, Cincinnati Art Galleries, LLC.*

Figure 718. Constance Baker painted this Standard glaze vase with a cluster of blooms in 1900. Base marks: flames mark and the artist's initials. 7.25" h. *Courtesy of Bob Shores and Dale Jones.*

Figure 719. Sarah "Sallie" Elizabeth Coyne painted a floral motif on this Standard glaze vase in 1900. Base marks: flames mark and the artist's incised initials. 5.25" h. *Courtesy of Bob Shores and Dale Jones.*

Figure 720. Virginia B. Demarest painted the yellow roses on this Standard glaze bottle-shaped vase in 1900. Base marks: flames mark, shape number 743C, and the artist's initials. 7" x 4". *Courtesy of David Rago Auctions.*

Figure 721. Edith Felten painted this well executed portrait of Conquering Deer, a Native American Sioux in native garb, in 1900 on this Standard glaze vase. Base marks: flames mark, shape number 656, the notation "Conquering Deer Sioux," and the artist's incised initials. 5" h. *Courtesy of Mark Mussio, Cincinnati Art Galleries, LLC.*

Figure 722. Mary Nourse painted the daffodils that grace this Standard glaze two-handled vase produced in 1900. Base marks: flames mark, shape number 459C, and the artist's initials. 6.75" h. *Courtesy of Seekers Antiques.*

Figure 723. Grace Young painted this sensitive and lifelike portrait of a Native American male with full headdress, titled *Susie Shot in the Eye Sioux*, on a Standard glaze pillow vase in 1900. Base marks: flames mark, shape number 707 X, the notation *Susie Shot in the Eye Sioux*, and the artist's monogram. 11.5" h. *Courtesy of Mark Mussio, Cincinnati Art Galleries, LLC.*

Figure 725. Grace Young's watercolor on paper of a monk reading in an interior setting. Approximately 8" x 10". *Courtesy of Mark Mussio, Cincinnati Art Galleries, LLC.*

Figure 724. Grace Young worked for Rookwood Pottery from 1886 to 1891, and then again from 1896 to 1903. Here are several examples of her artwork, starting with Grace Young's self portrait oil painting on board with the artist dressed in traditional Japanese fashion. According to Cincinnati Art Galleries, "The painting was inherited by Virginia Cummins, Young's daughter, and then passed on to Virginia's daughter, Mary Hopkins. Typical of all of Young's work, this painting is unsigned ..." 9" x 7". *Courtesy of Mark Mussio, Cincinnati Art Galleries, LLC.*

Figure 726. Grace Young's oil on a wooden panel showing an interior setting with what appears to be a furled American flag beside a spinning wheel, illuminated by sunlight coming through an open window on whose sill sit several potted nasturtiums in full bloom. 11" x 6.75". *Courtesy of Mark Mussio, Cincinnati Art Galleries, LLC.*

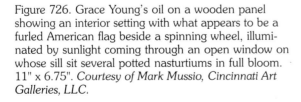

Figure 727. William Klemm painted this Standard glaze candleholder in a Turkish design in 1901 with orange and yellow pansies. Base marks: flames mark, the date, shape number 635, and the artist's incised initials. 3" h. *Courtesy of Mark Mussio, Cincinnati Art Galleries, LLC.*

Figure 728. Lenore Asbury painted this Standard glaze vase in a floral motif in 1902. Base marks: flames mark, the date, shape number 906 C, and the artist's incised initials. 6" h. *Courtesy of Bob Shores and Dale Jones.*

Figure 729. Clara Christina Lindeman decorated this small Standard glaze decorative ewer with painted flowers on stems in gold and muted red in 1902. Base marks: flames mark, the date, shape number 872, and the artist's incised initials. 5" h. *Courtesy of Bob Shores and Dale Jones.*

Figure 730. Marianna D. Mitchell decorated this Standard glaze two-handled vase in 1902 with ripe red cherries dangling from a branch amidst green leaves. Base marks: flames mark, the date, shape number 583F, and the artist's incised initials. 4.75" h. *Courtesy of Mark Mussio, Cincinnati Art Galleries, LLC.*

Figure 731. Olga Geneva Reed decorated this Painted Mat vase with a single red wild rose with green leaves on a deep maroon background in 1902. Base marks: flames mark, the date, shape number 6 Z, and the artist's initials in black slip. 5.25" h. *Courtesy of Mark Mussio, Cincinnati Art Galleries, LLC.*

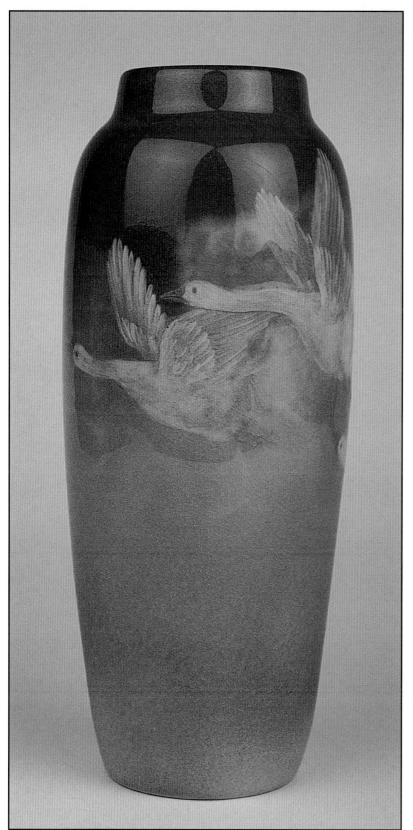

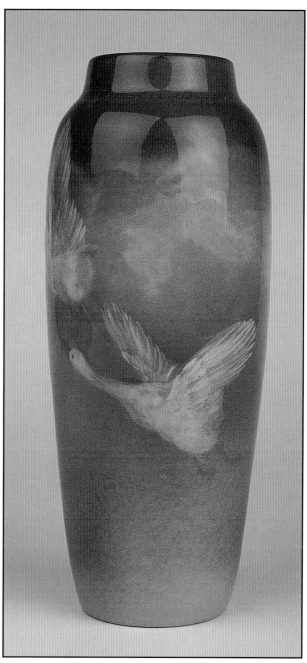

Figure 732. Edward Timothy Hurley painted this
Iris glaze vase with geese in 1903. 9.75" h.
Courtesy of Seekers Antiques.

Figure 733. Sara Sax painted this Iris glaze bulbous vase with yellow jonquil in 1903. Base marks: flames mark, the date, shape number 926C, W, and the artist's cipher. 8.25" x 4.5". *Courtesy of David Rago Auctions.*

Figure 734. Leona Vera Van Briggle painted flowers on this 1903 Standard glaze vase with a pinched neck. Base marks: flames mark, the date, shape number 667, and the artist's incised initials. 6.75" h. *Courtesy of Bob Shores and Dale Jones.*

Figure 735. Caroline F. Bonsall decorated this Standard glaze vase with blue hyacinth flowers in 1904. Base marks: flames mark, the date, shape number 904E, and the artist's signature. 6.5" h. *Courtesy of Mark Mussio, Cincinnati Art Galleries, LLC.*

Figure 736. Laura E. Lindeman decorated this Standard glaze vase with a sprig of mistletoe in shades of green and gold in 1904. Base marks: flames mark, the date, shape number 214 C, and the artist's lightly incised initials. 2.5" x 5". *Courtesy of Bob Shores and Dale Jones.*

Figure 737. Caroline "Carrie" Frances Steinle decorated this Standard glaze vase with wild roses in 1904. Base marks: flames mark, the date, shape number 932 F, and the artist's incised initials. 6" h. *Courtesy of Mark Mussio, Cincinnati Art Galleries, LLC.*

Figure 738. Edith Noonan painted this Vellum ovoid vase with a branch of pink apple blossoms in 1906. Base marks: flames mark and date. 6.5" h. *Courtesy of David Rago Auctions.*

Figure 739. Irene Bishop painted this Iris glaze vase with white lily-of-the-valley flowers and green leaves on a shaded lavender-to-gray ground in 1907. Base marks: flames mark, the date, shape number 912 E, a W for Iris glaze, and the artist's initials. 5.75" h. *Courtesy of Mark Mussio, Cincinnati Art Galleries, LLC.*

Figure 741. Katherine Van Horne painted this late Standard glaze vase with yellow nasturtiums in 1908. Base marks: flames mark, the date, shape number 913 E, and the artist's incised monogram. 5" h. *Courtesy of Mark Mussio, Cincinnati Art Galleries, LLC.*

Figure 740. A strong Arts & Crafts influence is seen in Cecil Duell's decoration—an incised broad, stylized design around the vessel and colored with dark blue against the dark green mat background of this squat vase. The vase was decorated in 1907. Base marks: flames mark, the date, shape number 214A, and the artist's incised initials. 4" h. *Courtesy of Mark Mussio, Cincinnati Art Galleries, LLC.*

Figure 742. Fred Rothenbusch painted this Iris glaze tapering vase in 1909 with white dogwood blossoms. Base marks: flames mark, the date, shape number 1658 D, an incised W for Iris glaze, and the artist's cipher. 9.25" h. *Courtesy of Mark Mussio, Cincinnati Art Galleries, LLC.*

Figure 743. Carl Schmidt decorated this Iris glaze vase with pink roses in 1909. Base marks: flames mark, the date, shape number 1660 C, an incised W for white (Iris) glaze, and the artist's impressed monogram. 10.5" h. *Courtesy of Bob Shores and Dale Jones.*

Figure 744. Kataro Shirayamadani decorated this Vellum glaze vase in 1910 with thirteen fish swimming around the circumference of the vessel. Base marks: flames mark, the date, shape number 1342, an impressed V for Vellum, and the artist's signature in Japanese script. 8.5" h. *Courtesy of Mark Mussio, Cincinnati Art Galleries, LLC.*

Figure 745. Lorinda Epply painted this Scenic Vellum plaque in 1914, depicting a bucolic scene with trees and a river, titled *Over the Hills*. Base marks: flames mark and date. 7.5" x 4.75". *Courtesy of David Rago Auctions.*

Figure 746. Margaret Helen McDonald decorated this 1914 Vellum flaring vase with pink and brown poppies on a shaded blue ground. Base marks: flames mark, the date, shape number 1369E, the artist's initials, and a second mark X. 7.25" x 4.25". *Courtesy of David Rago Auctions.*

Figure 747. Charles J. McLaughlin painted this Vellum tapering vase in 1914 with ivory dogwood on a pink ground. Base marks: flames mark, the date, and the artist's initials. 7.25" h. *Courtesy of David Rago Auctions.*

Figure 748. In 1916, Elizabeth McDermott decorated this impressionistic Scenic Vellum vase with a stand of birch trees, rising from a lush, green field, against a nicely shaded sky. Other trees encircle the vase. Base marks: flames mark, the date, shape number 604 E, a V for Vellum glaze, and the artist's monogram. 6.5" h. *Courtesy of Mark Mussio, Cincinnati Art Galleries, LLC.*

Figure 749. Arthur Conant decorated this covered jar with a floral motif in 1921. Base marks: flames mark, the date, shape number 478, and the artist's incised mark. 5.25" h. *Courtesy of Bob Shores and Dale Jones.*

Figure 750. Elizabeth Lincoln decorated this tall, tapering Decorated Mat vase with deep red cyclamen flowers and green stems and leaves on a dark maroon ground in 1921. Base marks: flames mark, the date, shape number 807, and the artist's incised signature. 13.25" h. *Courtesy of Mark Mussio, Cincinnati Art Galleries, LLC.*

Figure 751. Charles S. Todd decorated this ovoid vase with an incised flower and foliage design glazed in Later Tiger Eye (aventurine) in 1921. This glaze is a gold Chartreuse and Empire Green combination. Empire Green ceased as World War II began, since the uranium used in the glaze was needed for atomic research. Base marks: flames mark, the date, shape number 2102, and the artist's incised initials. 6.75" h. *Courtesy of Bob Shores and Dale Jones.*

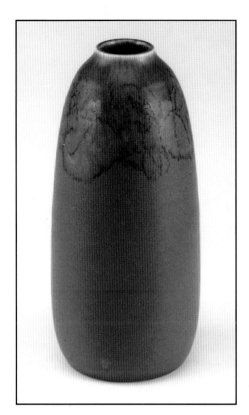

Figure 752. In 1923, Katherine Jones decorated this Wax Mat bullet-shaped vase with pansies in polychrome on an indigo ground. Base marks: flames mark, the date, and the artist's initials. 7.5" x 3.25". *Courtesy of David Rago Auctions.*

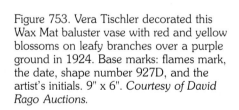

Figure 753. Vera Tischler decorated this Wax Mat baluster vase with red and yellow blossoms on leafy branches over a purple ground in 1924. Base marks: flames mark, the date, shape number 927D, and the artist's initials. 9" x 6". *Courtesy of David Rago Auctions.*

Figure 754. In 1924, John Dee Wareham decorated this rare Decorated Porcelain vase with grape decoration using glazes rarely seen at Rookwood. A metallic effect is present in some of the colors and the interior is lined in an iridescent blue-black that drips slightly from the upper rim. Cincinnati Art Galleries reports, "This vase was made into a lamp at the factory so there is a drill hole through some of Wareham's monogram. This vase was never sold, passing into the family of one of Rookwood's last owners where it has remained for over 40 years." Base marks: flames mark, the date, shape number 2819, and the artist's monogram in black slip. 17.5" h. *Courtesy of Mark Mussio, Cincinnati Art Galleries, LLC.*

Figure 755. Harriet Wilcox decorated this flaring Black Opal vase in 1924 with white roses, buds, leaves, and branches, coated with a bluish hued glaze, particularly noticeable with the roses. The interior is lined with a deep butterscotch highlighted with blue. Base marks: flames mark, the date, shape number 2789, and the artist's painted signature. 11" h. *Courtesy of Mark Mussio, Cincinnati Art Galleries, LLC.*

Figure 756. Catherine Covalenco decorated this tall Decorated Mat vase with cherries and leaves in 1925. Base marks: flames mark, the date, shape number 614 B, and the artist's monogram in blue slip. 14.5" h. *Courtesy of Mark Mussio, Cincinnati Art Galleries, LLC.*

Figure 757. Edward Diers decorated this Vellum glaze vase with blue clematis in 1925. Base marks: flames mark, the date, shape number 950 D, an incised V for Vellum glaze, and the artist's incised monogram. 9.25" h. *Courtesy of Mark Mussio, Cincinnati Art Galleries, LLC.*

Figure 759. Completing the review of artists and their works is Jens Jensen, who flamboyantly adorned this Decorated Porcelain vase with three active nudes and their long, flowing tresses in 1931. The vase's interior is lined with Rookwood's Anniversary Glaze, introduced in 1930. Base marks: flames mark, the date, shape number 915 C, a fan-shaped esoteric mark, and the artist's monogram in black slip. 7.75" h. *Courtesy of Mark Mussio, Cincinnati Art Galleries, LLC.*

Figure 758. John Wesley Pullman adorned this Mat glaze vase with pansies accented with stippling in 1929. Base marks: flames mark, the date, shape number 915 D, and the artist's initials in black slip. 7" h. *Courtesy of Mark Mussio, Cincinnati Art Galleries, LLC.*

Bibliography

Books

Barber, Edwin Atlee. *The Pottery and Porcelain of the U.S.: An Historical Review of American Ceramic Art from the Earliest Time to the Present Day*. New York & London, 1893.

Ellis, Anita J. *Rookwood Pottery. The Glaze Lines*. Atglen, Pennsylvania: Schiffer Publishing, 1995.

_____. *Rookwood Pottery. The Glorious Gamble*. New York: Rizzoli International Publications, Inc., 1992.

Gilchrist, Brenda (ed.). *The Smithsonian Illustrated Library of Antiques. Pottery*. Washington, D.C.: Smithsonian Institution, 1981.

Hay, Jane. *Christie's Collectibles. Art Deco Ceramics. The Connoisseur's Guide*. Boston, Massachusetts: Little, Brown and Company, 1996.

Henzke, Lucile. *Art Pottery of America*. 3rd edition. Atglen, Pennsylvania: Schiffer Publishing, 1999. [Original printing 1982]

Levin, Elaine. *The History of American Ceramics, 1607 to the Present. From Pipkins and Bean Pots to Contemporary Forms*. New York: Harry N. Abrams, Inc., 1988.

Nicholson, Nick & Marilyn. *Rookwood Pottery. Identification and Value Guide*. Paducah, Kentucky: Collector Books, 2000.

Owens, Nancy E. *Rookwood and the Industry of Art. Women, Culture, and Commerce, 1880-1913*. Athens, Ohio: Ohio University Press, 1992.

Piña, Leslie. *Pottery. Modern Wares. 1920-1960*. Atglen, Pennsylvania: Schiffer Publishing, 1994.

Savage, George, and Harold Newman. *An Illustrated Dictionary of Ceramics*. London: Thames and Hudson, Ltd., 1974.

Snyder, Jeffrey B. *Antique Majolica Around the House*. Atglen, Pennsylvania: Schiffer Publishing, 2005.

_____. *Depression Pottery*. Atglen, Pennsylvania: Schiffer Publishing, 1999.

_____. *Weller Pottery*. Atglen, Pennsylvania: Schiffer Publishing, 2005.

Trapp, Kenneth R. "Rookwood Pottery. The Glorious Gamble." In Ellis, Anita J. *Rookwood Pottery. The Glorious Gamble*. New York: Rizzoli International Publications, Inc., 1992.

Articles

"American Art Pottery." Christian Brothers University <http://www.cbu.edu/library/gallery/exhibit.php?n=American_pottery&t=1>

"Antiques Speak. Art Nouveau." "Antiques Roadshow." <http://www.pbs.org/wgbh/pages/roadshow/speak/nouveau.html>

"Antiques Speak. Glaze." "Antiques Roadshow." <http://www.pbs.org/wgbh/pages/roadshow/speak/glaze.html>

"Arts & Crafts Movement." <http://www.morsemuseum.org/artscrafts.html>

"The Arts and Crafts Movement in Victoria, British Columbia." <http://www.maltwood.uvic.ca/~malt wood/arts-crafts/home.html>

Barber, Edwin AtLee. "The Pioneer of China Painting in America." *The New England Magazine* 19(1), September 1895, pp. 33-49.

Bergey, Sharin. "Rago Realizes $1.6 M at Craftsman/Lambertville Auction." *NY-PA Collector*. January 1, 2001.

Bortka, Paula Miner. "Legacy of Rookwood Pottery: Rookwood Has a Distinguished Past." <http:nhcs.k12.in.us/staff/pbortka/Rookwood/LegacyofRookwood.html>

"Centennial Exhibition." *The Manufacturer and Builder*, November 1876, pp. 244-245.

Cowan, Wes. "Before Rookwood…" *The Enquirer*, March 27, 2004.

Crafton, Luke. "Aesthetic Movement: A Break with the Past." Antiques Roadshow, Oklahoma City, Oklahoma 2004. <http://www.pbs.org/wgbh/pages/roadshow/series/highlights/2004/oklahomacity/fts_hour1_…>

Cromley, Elizabeth C. "Reader's Companion to U.S. Women's History: Decorative Arts." *Houghton Mifflin College Division*. n.d.

Druesedow, Jean L., Curator. "Uncommon Clay: Ohio Art Pottery from the Paige Palmer Collection." Kent State University. Broadbent Gallery. October 25, 2000 to October 28, 2001.

Duke University. Rookwood Advertisement from J. Walter Thompson Company Archives. Rare Book, Manuscript, and Special Collections Library, Duke University.

"Elegant Innovations: American Rookwood Pottery, 1880-1960: The Gerald and Virginia Gordon Collection." Philadelphia Museum of Art Exhibition. November 15, 2003 – March 21, 2004. <http://www.philamuseum.org/exhibitions/exhibits/Rookwood.html>

Fryatt, F. E. "Pottery in the United States." *Harper's New Monthly Magazine* 62 (369), February 1881, pp. 357-370.

Hluch, Kevin A. "Crafts: A Deconstructionist View." *Critical Ceramics*, 29 January 2003.

Kamerling, Bruce. "Anna and Albert Valentien: The Arts and Crafts Movement in San Diego." *The Journal of San Diego History* 24(3), Summer 1978. <http://www.sandiegohistory.org/journal/78summer/valentine.html>

Kenefick, Kari. "Ohio Art Pottery – To Have & to Hold." *WPA Press* 16, Spring 2003.

Kennett, Linda. "Rookwood quality stands out." *Greensburg Daily News* 2004.

Levy, Marlene. "Looking at Rookwood: American pottery at the PMA." *Center City's Weekly Press*, November 2003.

Lilienfeld, Bonnie. "An Honor As Well As A Business Advantage. American Art Potters And The Smithsonian, 1885-1913." *Style: 1900's*, Spring 2001. <http://www.findarticles.com/cf_dls/m0JQN/2_14/75833122/print.jhtml>

"Mint Museum Acquires Rare Rookwood, Kataro Shirayamadani's *Dragon Vase*." <http://www.tfaoi.com/aa/2aa523.html>

"Newcomb Pottery and the Arts and Crafts Movement in Louisiana." <http://lsm.crt.state.la.us/newcomb/newcomb1.html>

"The Noble Craftsmen We Promote: The Arts and Crafts Movement in the American Midwest. Arts and Crafts in the Decorative Arts." An Exhibit at the Ward M. Canaday Center for Special Collections, Carlson Library, The University of Toledo. March 26th-June 30th, 1999.

Perry, Aaron F., Mrs. "Decorative Pottery of Cincinnati." *Harper's New Monthly Magazine* 62(372), May 1881.

Personal Communication. Rachel V. Markowitz of the Philadelphia Museum of Art, May 26, 2004.

"Progress of the Pottery Industries." *Manufacturer and Builder* 12(4), April 1880.

Raabe, Emily. "Museum Presents Comprehensive Exhibition of Rookwood Pottery from the Collection of Gerald and Virginia Gordon." Press Release. Marketing and Public Relations Department of the Philadelphia Museum of Art, Philadelphia, Pennsylvania, October 24, 2003.

Rhead, Frederick Hürten. "More About Color." *Crockery and Glass Journal*, vol. 120, 1937.

Stein, Jerry. "Decorative arts shone." *The Cincinnati Post*, May 6, 2003.

_____. "The Cincinnati Wing opens. Galleries show best local art." *The Cincinnati Post*, May 16, 2003.

Tile Heritage Foundation. "Rookwood Pottery. Cincinnati, Ohio." <http://www.tileheritage.org/THF-TileoftheMonth-Dec-03.html>

Underwood, Lynn. "Feats of Clay. American art pottery is a collectible for everyone." *Minneapolis Star Tribune*, October 31, 2001.

Veblen, Thorstein. "Arts and Crafts." *The Journal of Political Economy* 11(1), December 1902, pp. 108-111.

Vogdes, Walt. "Steins by Rookwood Pottery of Cincinnati, Ohio." <http://www.beerstein.net/articles/Rookwood.html>

"Where Do I Find? Visiting Washington, D.C. Rookwood Pottery." <http://www.si.edu/resource/faq/where/Rookwood.html>

"Women Leaders in the Art Pottery Industry: Ohio and Beyond." March 19, 2000. Art Libraries Society of North America 28th Annual Conference, Pittsburgh, Pennsylvania.

Index